THE EFFECTIVE TEACHER SERIES

Education and Cultural Diversity

EDWARD HULMES

U.M.C.
New Cross

LONGMAN
London and New York

Longman Group UK Limited,
Longman House, Burnt Mill, Harlow,
Essex CM20 2JE, England
and Associated Companies throughout the world.

*Published in the United States of America
by Longman Inc., New York*

First published 1989

British Library Cataloguing in Publication Data
Hulmes, Edward
    Education and cultural diversity. – (The
    Effective teacher series).
    1. Great Britain. Education. Sociocultural
    aspects
    I. Title II. Series
    370.19′34′0941

    ISBN 0-582-49514-8

Library of Congress Cataloging in Publication Data
Hulmes, Edward.
    Education and cultural diversity.

    (The Effective teacher series)
    Bibliography: p.
    Includes index.
    1. Education – Great Britain – Aims and objectives.
    2. Minorities – Great Britain – Attitudes. I. Title.
    II. Series.
    LA632.H78 1989   370′.941   87-35267
    ISBN 0-582-49514-8

Set in Linotron 202 10/11 pt Times

Produced by Longman Group (FE) Limited
Printed in Hong Kong

CONTENTS

EDITOR'S PREFACE

This new series was inspired by my book on the practice of teaching (*Effective Teaching: a practical guide to improving your teaching*, Longman, 1982), written for teacher training students as well as for in-service teachers wishing to improve their teaching skills. The books in this series have been written with the same readership in mind. However, the busy classroom teacher will also find that the books serve their needs as changes in the nature and pattern of education make the re-training of experienced teachers more essential than in the past.

The rationale behind the series is that professional courses for teachers require the coverage of a wide variety of subjects in a relatively short time. The aim of the series is the production of 'easy to read', practical guides to provide the necessary subject background, supported by references to encourage and guide further reading together with questions and/or exercises devised to assist application and evaluation.

As specialists in their selected fields, the authors have been chosen for their ability to relate their subjects closely to the needs of teachers and to stimulate discussion of contemporary issues in education.

The series covers subjects ranging from *The Theory of Education* to *The Teaching of Mathematics* and from *The Psychology of Learning* to *Health Education*. It will look at aspects of education as diverse as *Education and Cultural Diversity* and *Assessment in Education: The Teaching of English* and *The History of Education*. Although some titles such as *The Administration of Education* are specific to England and Wales, the majority of titles, such as *Comparative Education, The Teaching of Modern Languages, The Use of Computers in Teaching* and *Pupil Welfare and Counselling* will be international in scope.

In a period when education is a subject of general debate and is operating against a background of major change, there is little doubt that the books, although of primary interest to teachers, will also find a wider readership.

Elizabeth Perrott

A U T H O R' S   P R E F A C E

For many teachers in Britain today the real question comes down to this. How is an adequate educational service for the community to be maintained at a time when social and economic pressures threaten to damage what has been achieved in education during the past hundred years and more? When survival is at stake theoretical issues tend to be pushed even further into the background. Better (it might be argued) to concentrate on the provision of sufficient resources for present educational needs than to offer theoretical advice about how teachers, already working in difficult circumstances, can set about making their teaching more *effective*. But the crisis in education is not primarily social or economic. From the reception class in an infants' school to the seminar room in a university there is a crisis of ideas as well as of resources.

Many factors have contributed to the present state of society in this country. The impact of events beyond the shores of Britain is beginning to be felt more keenly as the world shrinks to the size of a global city. Every shift in the economic fortunes of the developed (or the under-developed) countries adds to the prevailing uncertainty about the future of education, as of other aspects of civilized life. This uncertainty is echoed in the questions of many of today's students. Is education worth the time and effort? What is the point of helping those who are educationally disadvantaged, only to find that there are no jobs for them to do when they leave school? Teachers are obliged to find answers to such questions almost every day, and it is not easy to sustain interest in the value of education for its own sake in the wake of economic and industrial decline, the consequent increase in long-term unemployment, scepticism about the continuing value of inherited religious and political traditions, the rise of secularism, and the threat of nuclear disaster. All these factors have affected the ways in which people think about education. But there is another factor which cannot be overlooked.

For centuries Britain has been a pluralist society, at least in the sense that over the years people from different parts of the world, and from different cultural backgrounds, have gradually been able to fashion for themselves a relatively congenial way of life here. Within the population there have been distinctive groups, each cherishing a set of beliefs, and each seeking to preserve the way of life associated with those beliefs. More recently, there have been considerable changes in the ethnic constitution of society as a result of immigration from the new commonwealth and elsewhere. New elements have been added to the cultural mix. These new elements also seek independence and autonomy in the larger community, as far as is possible. Only loss of identity, they feel, would be the result of failing to preserve their traditional ways of life in an alien environment. The problem is that their values do not always coincide with those of the wider community. Does an increase in the number of distinctive cultural elements mean that society is more pluralist *in fact*? Of all the questions which present themselves in an avowedly pluralist and democratic society few are more difficult to answer than this.

There are differences in the ways in which the constituent groups in British society see the role of education as serving their special needs. At the centre of the argument for and against what has intentionally been called in this book 'education and cultural diversity', rather than 'multi-culture education', there is a problem, however. If every child in this country is to be educated according to the special requirements of culturally diverse interests, the result might well be the gradual disintegration of society, for want of common educational goals. At the same time it has to be noted that the principles of liberal education, which have long influenced the ways in which children are taught in this country, are being increasingly questioned – not least by the representatives of more recent immigrant groups.

If the educational requirements of culturally diverse groups are not to be met in ways which satisfy those different interests, then what has been called 'multi-culture education' itself becomes an imposition, and assumes an ideological character of its own. Is it not enough that individual rights are respected, and that no child is placed at a disadvantage because of differences of class, race or creed? How are teachers to be effective in the face of such culturally diverse aspirations and such economic need?

All of these factors have been disconcerting to a greater or lesser extent, and all have left a mark on education. In the widest sense the questions examined in this book are educational questions, but this does not (or should not) mean that they are only of interest and concern to teachers in schools. Teachers may be the ones most intimately involved with the practical problems of trying to answer these questions in the earliest stages, but the responsibility does not rest on the shoulders of professional teachers alone. Many other people in the community at large have an educational role to play in society. Without their co-operation schools cannot work for the necessary changes in attitudes. The existing educational system is part of the problem as well as part of the opportunity.

If these questions are not to become unanswerable for want of careful attention and timely consideration, or if they are not to remain the preoccupation of a small number of dedicated campaigners, there will need to be widespread recognition of the educational opportunities and the social needs which are emerging in Britain today. This book is concerned with a severely practical issue for teachers which requires investigation whatever the state of the economy may be. What is at issue is the *kind* of society in which people of different persuasions can live together with a minimum amount of misunderstanding, mutual prejudice, social disruption, conflict and even violence. If society is to survive the *conflicting* interests of cultural diversity as well as what most people hope will be the short-term consequences of economic decline, this has to be far from a merely Utopian dream. On the contrary, it becomes a practical priority in which education has a prominent part to play.

Edward Hulmes

ACKNOWLEDGEMENTS

To the many friends and critics who have been kind enough to discuss with me the issues raised in this book I want to express my thanks. At various stages in the preparation of the chapters that follow I was able to call on their experience, and to enjoy their hospitality, in several interesting, and sometimes remote, parts of the world. I cannot mention here by name all those who have helped me, but I feel an obligation to note that they include Christians, Jews, Muslims and Hindus, who have taught me that differences of religion and culture need not stand in the way of lasting friendships, or prevent cooperation in the pursuit of common educational interests.

There are two names, however, that I mention with special gratitude. For the constant encouragement given me during the months I spent at Princeton in the United States writing most of this book I would like to thank Dr James McCord. And for her perceptive criticisms over a period of almost twenty years now, first at Manchester and later at Oxford, I would like to thank my former colleague Dr Brenda Watson. My final thanks, expressed as inadequately as ever, go to my wife, who understands better than anyone else what the writing of this book has meant to us both.

We are grateful to the following for permission to reproduce copyright material:

Associated Book Publishers (UK) Ltd for an extract from *Third Class Ticket* by Heather Wood (pub Routledge & Kegan Paul plc); Edita S A for a prayer by Rabindranath Tagore from *Eternal India* by Nou and Gandhi; Faber and Faber Ltd and Harcourt Brace Jovanovich Inc for extracts from *Notes Towards The Definition of Culture* by T S Eliot, copyright 1949 by T S Eliot, renewed 1977 by Esme Valerie Eliot; the author, Professor Kenneth Kirkwood for an extract from his letter in *The Times* 25/11/81; the National Council of the Churches of Christ in the USA for extracts from the *Revised Standard Version Bible* Copyright 1946, 1952, 1971 by the Division of Christian Education of the National Council of the Churches of Christ in the USA; SPCK for a poem by Abraham Isaac Kook from *The*

The exploration of pluralism and cultural diversity in education

We have to admit, in comparing one civilization with another, and in comparing the different stages of our own, that no one society and no one age of it realizes all the values of civilization. Not all of these values may be compatible with each other: what is at least as certain is that in realizing some we lose the appreciation of others.[1]

We are very good at training new generations not only to function with what we have discovered but to become discoverers themselves. That's the good news. The bad news is the university has become godless. We must confront so many value issues, from euthanasia to genetic engineering, to weapons that can destroy the world, and we no longer have the strong religious rallying point that we had in the 19th century. We have to develop a new value system.[2]

PURPOSE AND SCOPE OF THE BOOK

The purpose of the book can be stated quite briefly. It is to help those who are directly or indirectly working as teachers to understand the *educational* implications of pluralism and cultural diversity, to detect instances of cultural provincialism in education, and to identify some of the common human problems, anxieties, hopes and aspirations which are to be found behind cultural differences.

The book is a contribution to a series which is intended to stimulate discussion about important contemporary issues in education. The subject for scrutiny in this case is *education and cultural diversity*. It is a subject of considerable importance today, because it raises fundamental questions about the kind of society we now have in Britain, about the kind of society which is likely to evolve in this country, and about how education is to serve common needs at a time of increasing social complexity. The book deals with several aspects of this complexity, and considers a number of attempts to remove the racial and other tensions which have arisen in consequence of the accelerated cultural diversity in this country since the end of the Second World War. The principles and practice of what has come to be known (during the last few decades especially) as *multi-culture education* are examined as part of a wider analysis of the educational opportunities offered in a society which is as culturally diverse as that in Britain.

In this process of change, growth and development there is always a danger that sectional interests will emerge to endanger the common interest. Can racial and cultural diversity be understood sufficiently well to prevent these potentially damaging differences from reaching the point of open conflict? In a more positive vein, how can education contribute to the development of unity and social cohesion?

No one can afford to be complacent about the prospects for integration. At the present time there is no good reason to suppose that the differences between individuals and groups from different social, racial and cultural backgrounds can be resolved without a determined and protracted effort to inform, to understand and to remove misunderstandings and prejudice. There is a sense of immediacy, not to say urgency, in the work that teachers have to do. For them to be *effective* there needs to be a constant reappraisal of what education is for in such a rapidly developing society.

Educational aims and objectives have to be reviewed in response to changing social needs, employment patterns and leisure opportunities. It is to be expected that curriculum development and teaching methods will be influenced by technological innovation and refinement. Groups of people, isolated from one another until now by geography and culture, are increasingly being brought together. What will be the result of this? What service can education provide to reduce the possibilities of conflict?

This book is an attempt to consider what happens when groups from different cultural backgrounds find themselves living together in close proximity. In any such situation of cultural and racial mix it is clear that the maintenance of cultural identity will be a high priority for those concerned. At the same time it is clear that the maintenance of several different cultural identities within a society, without the evolution of mutually accepted values, will tend towards divisiveness and separateness, not towards unity. Apartheid is divisive in any of its possible manifestations.

Cultural autonomy, without a shared way of *thinking* about common problems and aspirations, leads at best to a wary kind of federation, not to unity. Integration depends upon a mutual recognition of cultural diversity and of common objectives. Assimilation amounts to the obliteration of cultural distinctions. These issues can be considered in several ways. This book looks specifically at what the phrase 'a shared way of thinking' may mean to different groups of people. Is education geared to the task of incorporating different cultures within a more comprehensive culture, without destroying their distinctive qualities? Are the values of religion the key to social cohesion, or the principal obstacles to it?

It is clear that a common way of life involves a common view of life, common standards of behaviour and common standards of value, and consequently a culture is a spiritual community which owes its unity to common beliefs and common ways of thought far more than to any uniformity of physical type. Now it is easy for a modern man living in a highly secularized society to conceive this common view of life as a purely secular thing which has no necessary connection with religious beliefs. But in the past, it was not so. From the beginning man has always regarded his life and the life of society as intimately dependent on forces that lie outside his own control – on superhuman powers which rule both the world and the life of man. . . .Throughout the greater part of mankind's history, in all ages and states of society, religion has been the great central unifying force in culture. It has been the guardian of tradition, the preserver of the moral law, the educator, and the teacher of wisdom.[3]

PLAN OF THE BOOK

Despite the limitations of space it has been possible to include a good deal of information and comment which it is hoped will engage the reader's interest at both a theoretical and a practical level. The book attempts throughout to combine a presentation of information with suggestions about how the ideas may be used by anyone interested in what Elizabeth Perrott has called 'effective teaching'.[4]

The practical suggestions are not treated separately from the developing argument of the book. That would make for an artificial arrangement. It seems better to rely on the reader's ability to take up a particular point of interest in context, and then to note the author's suggestions which, it is hoped, are not too obtrusive. Those most likely to be interested in the book will bring to it their own knowledge, experience and questioning, all of which should make them resistant to unsolicited advice, yet receptive to ideas different from their own. It has already been said, but it is worth repeating, that it is unreasonable to expect that a book dealing with this subject will avoid controversial issues and opinions, but controversy for its own sake is no part of the plan.

What has been done is to divide the book into seven chapters, allowing for the subject to be treated from various distinctive points of view, and using (wherever practicable) original source material for illustration, analysis and comment. It is felt that this method provides a useful framework for a preliminary study of this kind. There has not been sufficient space to include sections

on the origins, development, beliefs and practices of *all* the religious traditions to which reference might be made.

The first chapter focuses attention on the word *pluralism*, and
proceeds to examine both the concept of a *multi-culture society*
and the notion of *multi-culture education*. Chapters 2 and 3
consider the function of education in society as it is understood
among Muslims and Jews respectively. Chapter 4 is concerned
with the implications of Christian approaches to education in a
pluralist society. In recognition of the increasing importance in
Britain of citizens with an African (or Afro-Caribbean) cultural
background, Chapter 5 is devoted to a consideration of African
attitudes to education. This allows for a discussion of the role of
education as the social mechanism by which individuals are
inducted into membership of the traditional African adult
community. In Chapter 6 the subject of education is approached
from Indian – specifically, Hindu – perspectives. The final
chapter suggests some of the ways in which the richness of
cultural diversity might be directly linked to the education of
commitment in a pluralist society.

In each of the approaches to education discussed below there
are differences to be respected, if ethnic and religious minorities
in Britain are to play a full part in the life of the wider
community. Despite the differences of approach there are shared
aspirations. Behind apparently different positions lie common
interests.

Two appendices complete the book. The first provides information about sources of teaching material concerning the topics
considered in the various chapters. The second is a reading list
for those interested in further study.

PRELIMINARY ISSUES

Cultural diversity and cultural enrichment

It is often remarked that the influx of ethnic minorities provides
opportunities for cultural enrichment. This is true, but there are
always special factors to be taken into account before deciding
on the issue. Given the focus of this book, it is legitimate to note
that without a recognition of some very different approaches to
education, the possible sphere of cultural enrichment at the
deepest levels is significantly reduced. These different approaches
are often neglected in discussions about the extent to which
education does (or should) reflect the degree of cultural diversity
and pluralism which exists in Britain.

Reference has already been made to the fundamental questions
that are raised by the subject of cultural diversity in an avowedly

pluralist society. Some of these questions can be mentioned without further comment at this early stage, to give the reader an idea of what is to follow in the rest of the book. The most obvious question to raise at the beginning is this. What is meant by saying that Britain is a *pluralist* and *culturally diverse* society? This question soon leads to others. How pluralist can *any* society become without losing its organic unity? Is cultural diversity an enriching asset which is likely to contribute to the harmonious evolution of society, or is it a potential threat to social stability? How do teachers assist their pupils to find fulfilment in a society which is culturally diverse? How successfully do present arrangements in education enable individuals to identify, and to resolve, the conflicts which threaten the community in which they live?

Questions like these eventually lead to the two questions which provide the link between all the sections of this book. The first is this. How far *in practice* (whatever subject is being taught in the curriculum) can it be acknowledged that cultural diversity also means different approaches to knowledge, and to the acquisition of knowledge? It may not be desirable or reasonable to compromise the established methods of critical inquiry in education out of deference to minority views, but teachers should know what the cultural bases of these minority views are. The second question is more practical and direct. What guidance can be offered to teachers, parents and others interested in education, which will help them to cope sensitively and sensibly with the educational needs of individuals from different cultural backgrounds?

These are issues which it will be useful to reconsider. There is no doubt that further questions (and different answers) will occur to those who follow the book through to the end. The theme may be familiar, but the approach will be less so. The theme is the role and function of education in a pluralist society. The approach discusses the different ways in which educational theory and practice are understood within some of the constituent cultural traditions in British society today. Not all of these different approaches can be considered in a book such as this, and none of them can be considered as fully, or as systematically, as the author would like.

Knowledge and its assessment in a pluralist society

Examinations discriminate in several ways. It is their business to discriminate between good answers and the less good, between what is accurate and what is inaccurate, between those who know and those who do not, between the levels of understanding shown by different candidates. Examinations place candidates in an order of precedence. In spite of their admitted shortcomings these assessments are useful for many of the selection processes which follow in life. This is not intended as a criticism of the examination system. The system works this way. It has been refined over a period of many years, and it is not easy to replace.

There is, however, another aspect to this which illustrates how a genuine discussion of pluralism might bring into the open a different kind of conflict, a conflict of attitudes to knowledge itself. There are significant numbers of people in this country for whom there is a prior question to be answered, which is not *How is a student's knowledge to be assessed?*, but *What, in a pluralist society, is to be allowed to count as knowledge, understanding and acceptable comment?* Consider for a moment a point of view which will be taken further in other parts of the book, especially in Chapter 2.

The author has had many discussions with Muslim friends about the problems which face their children in British schools. For the Muslim all knowledge (in whatever subject, from the natural sciences to the humanities, and beyond, to whatever may become known) is part of the revelation which Allāh (God) makes available to his human creatures. What is the place of critical inquiry (as understood in the non-Muslim world) in a Muslim's education? A good memory for what has been revealed, and for Islamic tradition, is of more service to the Muslim scholar than critical acumen and a capacity to speculate – a point of view which Muslims reasonably expect to influence attitudes to knowledge and to its acquisition.

One way or another, education is concerned at every stage with *assessment*. In most cases the assessment is not made at the level of public written examinations. Continuous assessment, for all its disadvantages, has the merit (some would argue) of eliminating the fear of the written examination, as well as its arbitrariness. It favours those who are less confident, and less literate. It is, they would say, a fairer test of a student's ability and knowledge over a longer period of time. But who is to make the assessment? What provision in the assessment can be made for alternative theories of knowledge? Could such a provision be made in any case? If it cannot, then what specific limitations to the concepts of pluralism and multi-culture education have to be recognized?

Quite early in their formal education children can expect to be caught up in activities which are competitive and divisive. Education is one of these activities, and unquestionably one of the most influential. Education may sharpen competitive instincts. It may bring out into the open differences between individuals which have less to do with intellectual gifts than with racial and cultural distinctions. Education may also temper the socially divisive effects of these differences, and so help to remove conflict between individuals and groups. It can be argued that pluralism does bring the conflicts of society into the open, and that it is good that it does so. Only thus can the divisions, inequalities and injustices of society be detected, and dealt with effectively. But is pluralism divisive? To answer the question we need to know what the word *pluralism* means to different groups of people in Britain from different cultural backgrounds.

A pressing social problem

This section is concerned with two main issues. The first is the problem of social injustice and educational deprivation faced in so many cases by members of ethnic minorities in Britain, as a consequence of their racial and cultural differences from the majority. This is a problem which teachers are among the best placed to know about from their particular kind of work. Furthermore, teachers are among the comparatively few in society who are expected to use their professional skills to remove the injustice experienced by the under-privileged, or at least to alleviate its worst effects. This is a problem which it is difficult to over-state, not just because of the sense of despair and frustration felt by large numbers of alienated individuals, but because of the potential threat to the harmony of society in Britain which this alienation poses.

The second issue is the question of definition. It is clear that certain words and phrases such as *multi-cultural, multi-racial, multi-ethnic* are often used indiscriminately. For anyone who has a feeling for nuance, and for precision in the use of language, words and their meanings are to be treated with care. Words and phrases can be invested with an agreed meaning, and then used in a technical sense as part of the jargon of a trade or profession, but they cannot be abandoned to arbitrary use without adding to the very problem of communication which they are intended to solve. Confusion arises where the meaning of a word or phrase is left unclear. This is not pedantry; it is especially important to be clear about the use of words (and this implies teaching to that end when necessary), wherever – as in Britain – the English language is a second language, or where groups of people are unfamiliar with English usages and idioms.

It is necessary to be clear here that the depth of despair which is the bitter fruit of discrimination is being slowly acknowledged by those in Britain who have the will and the influence to do something about it. There are likely to be emotional calls for immediate changes which may be locally effective for a time. In the longer term, attempts will have to be made to bring about changes in education which are designed to *include* individuals from different racial, religious and cultural backgrounds. This work has already begun, and has already met with a measure of success. Any criticism here of what is being done should not be taken as a denial of the importance of this work, or as a rejection of the achievements of others. The author's intention is to be constructive and to foster harmony in society.

The reader will find no detailed analysis of social discrimination against individuals and groups. This does not mean that the author has neglected the difficulties of those who feel the oppressive weight of discrimination. The book assumes that there is a high level of social (and even physical) discrimination in society, and that this level must be reduced. Without wishing to overlook any of this the book concentrates on what might best be described as 'intellectual discrimination', suggesting how it can be identified, and how it may be understood, if not eliminated. Discrimination takes several forms, some more subtle and more difficult to eradicate than others. Intellectual discrimination, predicated on an unquestioned assumption of the supremacy of western analytical thought, may be one of the more difficult kinds of discrimination with which teachers have to cope in the long term.

The wider setting

Although the special interests, concerns and needs of teachers in schools provide the focus for this work, the wider sphere of teaching activity has also to be acknowledged in a book on this subject, for at least two reasons, which are confirmed by the author's own teaching experience. The first is that it is easy for teachers, preoccupied as they are with immediate professional concerns at whatever level they teach, to overlook the *continuing and sequential* nature of the educational process, and thus fail to understand what other teachers are doing. Primary school teachers may have little idea of what their colleagues in secondary education are trying to do, and vice versa. Neither primary nor secondary school teachers may have much idea about the problems of teaching in a college or university, or even have any sympathy with their colleagues in higher education. The second reason is that, despite all the differences between the primary school and the university, teachers at all levels of education face similar problems in the modern world. The future of education is uncertain, and it is vital that all teachers are aware of the wider issues if their teaching is to be effective.

Any discussion of effective teaching must take some account of the wider issues which affect education, and not only in Britain. It is appropriate to note here that economic policy and political ideology often override strictly educational concerns, and make teaching far less effective than it might be. It lies beyond the scope of this book to discuss the impact of these wider issues on education, but the concepts of society, or community, central to what is to be discussed in the following chapters, have inescapable political and economic implications which it would be foolish to ignore. There can be no useful discussion of a pluralistic or multi-cultural society until it is clear what is meant by *society*.

Is Britain a pluralist and multi-cultural society? In spite of racial and cultural differences is there agreement about common social and educational aims? Is the school a pluralist society? These are questions which do raise wider political and economic issues which it is easy for teachers to overlook because there is little they can do as individuals to change the situation. There are countries in the world, notably the United States, which already have a considerable experience of the problems of pluralism. From that wealth of experience it is possible to identify some of the specific problems of the *educational society*, or *community* – that is to say, the school or the university – which are likely to crop up in Britain in the near future. What is it that holds a society together? Is a university a pluralist society? Recent experience in America suggests that the answer to this question depends on the size of the institution concerned.[5] In the mid-1960s Columbia University in New York City had three vice-presidents and a budget of $134.6 million. In the mid-1980s there are twelve vice-presidents, and the budget amounts to $618.6 million. These are economic and managerial concerns, primarily, but a more basic question is raised. What is the optimum size for an organic community or society? In trying to keep pace with the increasing demands of a managerial nature academics are being diverted from their proper function as researchers and teachers. It is difficult to see how this makes for effective teaching or effective research. Schools also are beginning to suffer from the same misuse of human resources and skills, as more teachers are diverted to what are, essentially, managerial tasks for which they are not trained.

More damaging, perhaps, is the control exercised by those who provide the funds for education. As a government changes the amount of public funding for education, there is recourse to private funding. Academic institutions, financially pressed because public funding is being decreased, now realize that there is a price to be paid for private patronage from business, industry and other sources. Schools in Britain have already felt the effects of reduced investment from central government sources. It is not yet clear whether they will ever be allowed to solicit financial support from private agencies. But whether the money comes from the state or from private benefactions, teachers will always have to face the pressures of political and ideological constraints.

Common responsibilities and aims

This book has been written with different kinds of readers in mind. In the first place it has been written for teachers, but not only for specialist teachers of religious and moral education. Pluralism and cultural diversity are subjects which, by definition, require to be investigated from many points of view. It would be a disadvantage if these subjects were to be associated exclusively in the minds of teachers with *specialist* areas of the curriculum such as religious or moral education. The responsibility for making pluralism and cultural diversity a central issue in education extends further than that. It involves many more teachers in a common aim. One of the criticisms of society in Britain today is that it is still essentially monolithic, and likely to remain so, despite the presence of new cultural elements.

Teachers, whatever their own special qualifications, may be assumed to have a common interest in the best possible education for their students at each successive stage. Today there are some special factors to be taken into consideration, few of which can be more potentially destructive of complacency than those linked to the notion of pluralism, especially in those cultures where it is repeatedly affirmed that every aspect of human existence, *including education*, is to be seen as an integral part of an existing religious (or non-religious) world-view. In questions of values and beliefs, however, traditional dividing lines between subjects in the curriculum may be misleading and unhelpful. Teachers of other subjects may have (or may be encouraged to have) a less direct, but no less important, responsibility for contributing to an education for cultural diversity, suited to present needs.

This means that every teacher has a unique part to play in encouraging a continuing inquiry into the values which society seeks to protect and to transmit. Moreover, in a broader sense there are many others outside the confines of school – parents, employers, clergy and ministers – who may reasonably be described as teachers, and who may also find the book of interest. The subject of the book ought to commend itself to anyone who is interested in the difficult, but rewarding, task of exploring the diversity of religious and non-religious belief, with all that this may mean for educational opportunity and social integration in individual cases. And where the interest extends to include professional responsibilities for helping students to explore that same diversity for themselves there is another, and perhaps more important, reason for reading the book.

HOW PLURALIST IS BRITAIN?

The description of Britain as a pluralist and culturally diverse society has provoked lively discussion in many places. Responses to the discussion have led to interesting innovations in the teaching of several subjects in the curriculum, in religious education in particular. Careful attention is given to the educational needs of children from ethnic minority backgrounds. More emphasis is placed on teaching about the different religions of the world. It is now much more common than it was a generation ago for children, at appropriate stages in their development, to learn about the religious beliefs and practices of Jews, Muslims, Hindus, Sikhs and Buddhists (for example), as well as about the attitudes of Humanists (and others) whose beliefs are of a different order.

In spite of these demanding developments in new areas of study, Christianity has not been ignored, although some would argue that it is suffering from neglect in education at the present time. Christianity remains one of the most important subjects to be taught, not only because it is one of the major world religions, but also because it has been so influential in the history of this country. It is difficult to imagine how intelligible European history, literature, music and art would be to anyone who is wholly ignorant of the Christian religion. Teaching about Christianity is irreplaceable if this heritage is to be properly appreciated and understood. This is one of the reasons why many members of ethnic and religious minority groups, far from opposing such teaching, are among its most enthusiastic advocates in principle.

Britain has been a pluralist society for centuries for the British are a hybrid people. Racial purity in Britain is a fiction. Celts, Angles, Saxons, Scandinavians, Normans all found homes here, and contributed to the development of a nation. Later on came Jews, Huguenots and other refugees from Europe, Asia and Africa. More recently there have come substantial numbers of immigrants from India, Pakistan, East and West Africa, and the West Indies. As a result of this the pluralist nature of British society is more visible than ever before. This has given rise to racial hostility in many cases. The comment of Alistair Cooke about his fellow-Americans is probably no less true of sections of public opinion in Britain: 'We welcome immigrants, but recoil from the cultures they bring.'[6]

Human beings present many differences in personal appearance and cultural diversity. There are conspicuous differences of colour, speech, dress, food and music, and a wide range of religious and non-religious belief. Local environmental variety is presented by the architecture of churches, synagogues, mosques, temples, meeting houses, ashrams and gurdwaras. If it were possible to observe this variety of shapes, sounds, colours and tints in a detached way, the general impression might be very confusing. It is possible, however, to over-state the extent of the range of cultural diversity in British society and so to give a misleading picture of what is happening in Britain today, particularly in education.

The communities within society are not monolithic in character. They are neither isolated from outside pressures, nor free from internal tensions. Children and grandchildren of immigrants express different views about maintaining the cultural distinctiveness of their ancestors. The desire to participate fully in the dominant culture makes for a progressive weakening of older cultural ties. No two churches, mosques, synagogues, temples or ethical societies inhabit the *same* culture for long. And before discussion about pluralism is over it should be remembered that large numbers of people, perhaps the majority of the population, belong to no discernible community of belief. They are indifferent to the claims of religion and life-stance alike, having already adopted a life-style in which explicit religious beliefs, or explicitly secular attitudes, exercise little consciously felt influence on the course of daily life.

HOW MULTI-CULTURAL IS BRITAIN?

The claim that Britain is a multi-cultural society is more controversial, and increasingly disputed by the members of ethnic and religious minorities whose views need to be carefully considered on the point. One of the purposes of this book is to draw attention to some of these alternative views which minority groups have developed over centuries in widely dispersed communities. These views do not always coincide with the views of those who proceed from quite different assumptions. A decade ago the authors of a report prepared by a joint working party of the Community Relations Commission and the Association of Teachers in Colleges and Departments of Education were in no doubt about the fundamental change in the nature of British society.

Britain is a multi-cultural society. Our awareness of the many strands in our culture has been sharpened by recent changes in the racial composition of this society. It now includes approximately one and a half million black and brown people, over 40% of whom were born here. What happens to them in our schools is crucial to the development of a racially just society. The training of teachers and other professionals should equip them to work towards such a society.[7]

On this basis the members of the working party proceeded to consider issues such as education for a multi-cultural society, the initial training of teachers, specialist options, postgraduate

on prompt action. In the longer term, efforts must be made to ensure that 'distinctive or peculiar British ways' will be influenced by cultural insights which have become British by adoption, to the benefit of the whole community. What, in point of fact, do these peculiar British ways amount to? Would it be 'un-British' not to accept them? The capacity for compromise, and the ability to give and take are, presumably, on the list, in which case a further question arises. How useful in practice would the 'essentially British' capacity for compromise prove to be in a multi-culture society? The assumption that it will provide a solution to the problem of cultural diversity might be construed by members of minority groups as a further example of cultural provincialism. For large numbers of British citizens, compromise on matters of principle would be a betrayal of cultural identity.

HOW USEFUL IS THE ADJECTIVE 'MULTI-CULTURAL'?

It is questionable that the Britain of the mid-1970s was accurately described as a multi-cultural society, although the authors of the report *Teacher education for multi-cultural society*, from which the opening paragraph was quoted above,[11] made their recommendations on the assumption that it was. And it is doubtful that the members of minority groups most affected in Britain would be prepared to concede that the description is any more fitting today. A society which can be described as multi-racial may be far from being a multi-cultural society. A society in which the majority practise the virtue of tolerance as a matter of course is not the same as a multi-cultural society, unless the latter is somewhat arbitrarily defined in terms of the former.

The question is whether Britain (or, indeed, any society) is, or can become, multi-cultural in an *organic* way. This is not merely playing with words. If distinctions in meaning are not taken seriously, it is likely that dangerous confusions will result, even when intentions are honourable and just. It may be objected that the priority should be given to action, not to definitions, and that unqualified support should be given to those who, under whatever name, are working to eliminate injustice and inequality in society. It is difficult to disagree with the underlying sentiment of such a view, or to criticize the work which is being done in many instances to solve the problems arising from racial tension.

The objection is, none the less, unacceptable because a more accurate term could be found to describe what is to be attempted in the pursuit of racial harmony. The phrase 'multi-culture education' is ambiguous and misleading, whatever its apologists claim. This is partly because, in practice, it turns out that multi-culture education does not reflect the variety of approaches to knowledge and to the acquisition of knowledge. It continues to be an instrument of a *particular* (and, presumably, dominant) *western* culture. There is a paradox here. A situation appears to be developing in which an educational mechanism (multi-culture education), ostensibly designed to reduce prejudice, is perceived to be alien to the cultural traditions of some of the groups which it is intended to help most. It is fanciful to suppose that the cultural life of a society can be enriched by social planning, by educational fiat, by a process of cultural permeation or social osmosis. Muslims, for example, complain with good reason that their understanding of the theory and practice of education is ignored in public education.[12] They may be mistaken to think that it should not be ignored. But it is inconsistent, on the one hand, to speak warmly of the cultural enrichment which immigrant groups can bring to the wider community and, on the other hand, to ensure that this influence is carefully filtered lest it enrich anything as important as education. Minority groups are entitled to feel puzzled by the double standard. The counting of heads is not enough. Whatever the cultural make-up of British society may be, it is indisputable that the predominant philosophy of education is secular.

It is misleading to say that the presence of ethnic minorities, free to practise their own distinctive ways of life in an 'open society', shows how pluralist *British culture* is, or is now becoming. The word *culture* is one of those words (like *religion*) which it is difficult to define. It is used in several different senses. The attempt to set bounds to the meaning of a word like *culture* (and hence, to limit its use) may add to the difficulty when different *cultures* meet. Analysis and definition, of the kind to which teachers in Britain have become accustomed, are critical tools which are characteristic of a *particular* intellectual tradition.

The *Oxford English Dictionary* includes the following definitions of the word *culture*. Culture is 'the cultivating or development (of the mind, faculties, manners, etc.); improvement or refinement by education and training'. It is 'the training, development, and refinement of mind, tastes, and manners; the condition of being thus trained and refined; the intellectual side of civilization'. These are familiar definitions for familiar usages, giving primacy of place to the needs of an individual rather than to a group, and tending to separate *culture*, as a rather rare thing in itself, from the rest of *civilization*. The poet and critic T. S. Eliot took a more practical view:

The term *culture* has different associations according to whether we have in mind the development of an *individual*, of a *group*, or of a *whole. society*. It is part of my thesis that the culture of the individual is dependent upon the culture of a group or class, and that the culture of the group or class is dependent upon the culture of the whole society to which that group or class belongs. Therefore it is the culture of the society that is fundamental.[13]

The African scholar mentioned earlier, E. Bolaji Idowu, makes a similar point about the fundamental importance of the culture of a society, but he sees it from a different perspective, emphasizing the primacy of the spiritual. He notes the confusion throughout Africa today about the meaning of 'African culture', and about the search for an African identity. Can the continent of Africa ever become an organic pluralist, multi-culture society on the basis of an African personality? It is one thing for very different groups to unite for the purpose of throwing off European colonial and cultural domination, but when that task has been largely achieved the basis for unity is less apparent.

What then is culture? [asks Idowu] Culture we define as a people's or a nation's total way of life (what someone has described as 'ways and wisdom') which shows itself by various means in actions and expressions. Culture is therefore primarily metaphysical or spiritual – because it is closely inherent with being – the corporate being or corporate personality of a people, thus making for a *bona fide* distinctiveness and peculiarity. Because it is grounded in the being of the corporate personality, it becomes the source from which emanate the issues as well as the distinctive complexion of identity.[14]

Do the cultural norms of our society encourage the hope that with the passage of time such *cultural* diversity as is said to exist in Britain will gradually disappear? The culture of society, to which Eliot refers, is always being influenced by change. Education is a major influence in the processes of change, development and renewal.

If it is answered that students are 'not up to that sort of thing', or that the practical constraints of teaching in schools make the achievement of such an ideal impossible, then two things seem clear. The first is that those who *are* interested (or those whose interest can be kindled) and those who are naturally curious will learn to educate themselves with some guidance here and there along the way from teachers. For the rest, and they are the vast majority, it is time to abandon the rhetoric about encouraging empathy, about education for personal choice, and to acknowledge what an American observer has already noted, namely, that schools in some areas (and for understandable reasons) have become places where the diversion, and even the amusement, of students has replaced any serious attempts to educate them.[15]

In a chapter on 'Children and Youth', Abraham Heschel makes a similar criticism of what he sees as the superficiality of public education. His criticism is that teachers are not prepared to ask the right questions of their pupils. The curriculum is not geared to real need. Children, he concludes, are being protected from reality rather than helped to cope with it; they are being *diverted* rather than *educated*. And this despite the fact that increasing numbers of them come to school with experience of deprivation in one form or another which their teachers may suspect, but which they can do little to remedy in practice.

We have denied our young people the knowledge of the dark side of life. They see a picture of ease, play, and fun. That life includes hardships, illness, grief, even agony; that any hearts are sick with bitterness, resentfulness, envy – are facts of which young people have hardly an awareness. They do not feel morally challenged, they do not feel called upon.[16]

CONFESSIONAL AND NON-CONFESSIONAL APPROACHES TO EDUCATION

Education is a means to an end. The question is not *should* education be instrumental. It *is* instrumental, and always has been, in both the public and the private domain, because it inevitably reflects the consensus view about society. From time to time it may be instrumental in bringing about radical change as the consensus shifts, but it is principally an agent of conservation. It strengthens the civilization it serves, and nurtures the dominant culture of which it is a part. This remains true even when the society in question elects to substitute what is taken to be a non-confessional for a confessional approach to education. In this sense, new approaches to religious education (for example) are not so different from the old. It usually turns out that the non-confessional approach has an ideological, confessional character of its own.

The goals of 'non-confessional' education, in so far as they influence the discussion of pluralism and cultural diversity, may include the assimilation and integration of disparate cultural groups within a unified society. The foundation for this is the principle of mutual tolerance. But if this is the case then these goals cannot be reached without accepting that the inculcation of tolerance is a major aim in education. In which case an ideological, 'confessional', thrust is imparted to an apparently 'non-confessional' approach. Children in schools are to be prepared for – to be trained for – adult life in a society where certain attitudes and responses are expected of them. The transformation of society may take several generations, or it may never be achieved, but any deliberate decision to make education serve a new social objective marks a fresh departure from non-confessionalism.

THE ADVANTAGES OF A MULTI-CULTURAL APPROACH TO THE CURRICULUM

Having registered some scepticism about the ways in which the phrase 'multi-culture education' is being used, the observer is obliged to recognize, however, that at the present time the approach to across-the-curriculum teaching that it stands for is enjoying steady growth in various parts of the country. Some of the advantages to be gained from multi-culture education are said to be *the undermining of myths, stereotypes and prejudices; the incorporation of the experience of minority cultures into the curriculum*; and *the promotion of intercultural understanding*.

In a general sense one can understand why prejudices should be 'undermined'. There is nothing objectionable about this in principle. Unacceptable prejudices need to be identified before they can be removed, however. In particular cases it would be helpful to know precisely what these prejudices are, and on what grounds they are considered to be unacceptable. In addition, it would be helpful for teachers to know precisely what the word *undermining* means in this context.

Most people have a vague idea about what is meant by prejudice, but there is room for confusion here, when different cultural values come into conflict. Teachers may find themselves subverting principles which are interpreted in different ways in different traditions. The principle of tolerance provides a good case in point. If prejudices are defined as attitudes which, in the widest sense, militate against tolerance, then cultures which are established upon an exclusive revelation are already on trial in a pluralist society. In these cultures (minority cultures so far as the present constitution of society in Britain is concerned), it may be the principle of *pluralism* itself which is unacceptable.

Stereotypes are more difficult to deal with, partly because they are not so comprehensively uncongenial to the modern temper as prejudices. The real objection to the stereotype is that it reduces a human being, with all his or her individual qualities and idiosyncrasies, to a two-dimensional figure. But what about myths? In popular usage myths are untrue. They are unhelpful fabrications that are better forgotten. It is not so easy to forget fanciful stories, however. They tend to be vivid and memorable. And so they have to be 'undermined' in the transition from ignorance to knowledge. The task of undermining falls to education. There is a much more important sense in which the word *myth* is to be understood. It stands for a category of story in which the element of truth does not depend upon the historicity or factual accuracy of the narrative. Myths (for there are many such stories in different cultures) are intimately associated with the origins of the culture in which they are to be found. They are of the greatest significance.

To load the word *myth* with negative associations is to be insensitive to its educative usefulness. It is to be unaware of its power to express common experiences and aspirations. Myth is not necessarily culture-bound. In the hands of imaginative teachers myth can help to remove cultural barriers. It can show teachers and pupils from very different cultural backgrounds how their ancestors, widely separated in time and place, found ways to express a universal kind of knowledge which was (and which is) otherwise inexpressible. Social instability awaits a society which lacks myths to express a usable past, however diverse.

The other two advantages said to flow from a multi-culture approach to the curriculum are less easy describe in detail. The incorporation of the experience of minority cultures into the curriculum, and the promotion of intercultural understanding would both be distinctly advantageous. It is difficult to quarrel with either as reasonable and prudent intentions given the problems which face society today. How these indisputable advantages are to be realized is not clear. The word *incorporation* provides a clue. It suggests much more than the word *inclusion*. It implies that changes to the curriculum are to be *organic* rather than merely incremental. But if the incorporation is to be effective it will also require a thorough reassessment of curriculum content, of teaching methods and of the dominant philosophy of education.

A VARIETY OF AIMS IN EDUCATION

It is precisely over this point – namely, the aims of education in a pluralistic society – that disagreements are likely to occur. The twentieth-century American philosopher/theologian Paul Tillich distinguishes three educational aims, naming them as technical education, humanistic education and inducting education. For the purposes of analysis they can be so distinguished from one another, but they are not mutually exclusive. Ultimately education, however defined and conducted, reflects an understanding of what skills are useful to society, an understanding of human achievement and aspiration, and an understanding of how individuals are to be inducted into the adult community.

Broadly speaking, Tillich associates *technical education* with the acquisition of knowledge and skill in the use of tools. Discipline, perseverance, continued practice and the willingness to accept criticism are all necessary for progress and success. Every society requires the services of well-trained technicians and skilled craftsmen for a multiplicity of services. One aim of education is to produce them in sufficient numbers. This kind of education is concerned in one way or another with the acquisition of skills, some of them quite basic, others much more sophisticated. Among the former are the use of tools for a variety of manual tasks. The skills of reading, writing and elementary figuring are also included here, because they are general skills without which individuals are at a great disadvantage in comparison with their more skilled neighbours. Each generation adds to the list of necessary skills in response to the demands of developing technology. Compared with the knowledge now being acquired by quite young children about the use and the workings of computers, the knowledge of many parents is minimal, if not non-existent. Such adults are dependent on a generation more knowledgeable than themselves about something essential for human progress and survival. It is common to hear the phrase 'the acquisition of skills' used in association with other knowledge, and the ability to use it.

Thus, for example, the ability to decide for oneself about accepting (or rejecting) a particular set of beliefs or attitudes to life has been identified as a skill to be acquired. This is something which has a special bearing on the role of teachers in a pluralist society. Are they to encourage pupils to think for themselves, to weigh the evidence, and then to decide on the basis of the evidence? What is to be admitted as evidence? How is such a skill to be tested? Are exceptions to be made to the otherwise general educational objective of developing a critical faculty in every child capable of responding, whenever there are complaints that the school is undermining the influence of an ethnic minority culture? Education is not limited to the school. The home is a major influence, and there it inevitably assumes the nature of an induction to a set of values which may find no approval in the school or in society at large.

Tillich notes that *humanistic education* goes far beyond technical education, however widely the acquisition of skill in the use of tools is understood. It is concerned with individual human and social potential, as understood in Europe since the Renaissance. It adds another dimension to technical education by providing less parochial opportunities for self-fulfilment:

Every human being . . . is a microcosm, a small universe, in whom the large universe is mirrored. As a mirror of the universe and its divine ground, the individual is unique, incomparable, infinitely significant, able to develop in freedom his given endowment. Education is supposed to actualize his potentialities, generally and individually. The aim of the educational process is the humanistic personality in whom as many potentialities as possible are developed, among them being technical skills and the religious function.[17]

The implication of Tillich's argument is that a human being whose potential for religious experience is not nurtured in the education he or she receives will not function nearly so well, either as an individual or as a member of society, as one to whom opportunities for developing this faculty are given. To be fully human is to recognize that religion is a biological necessity, and so to make provision for the satisfaction of this need, particularly for the young in their formative years.[18] It would be as improper to leave this human faculty to develop itself as to neglect the nourishment of a child's bone structure. In either case, growth and development would be stunted.

Even in less technologically sophisticated times than the present the acquisition of socially useful skills was more than a matter of practical necessity and prudence. It was linked to the transmission of other values which gave coherence to the society as a whole. The training given, whether in the home, at school or at a place of work, helped to transmit the values of society, to inculcate certain attitudes to the community and to the discipline required for the mastering of specific skills. It was a continuing educational activity, by means of which succeeding generations were inducted into the responsibilities of adult life.

Tillich's third educational aim, that of *inductive education*, is contrasted with the aim of humanistic education, but the distinction does not carry conviction. Inductive education has always been associated with indoctrination and the suppression of critical thought, with programmes of directed learning; with compliance and obedience on the part of the student, and with scrupulous adherence to the inherited tradition on the part of the teacher.

The induction of children into their families, with the tradition, symbols, and demands of the family, is the basic form of inducting education. Its aim is not development of the potentialities of the individual, but induction into the actuality of a group, the life and spirit of community, family, tribe, town, nation, church. Such an induction happens spontaneously through the participation of the individual in the life of the group. But it can also be made a matter of intellectual guidance.[19]

The truth of it seems to be that these three aims of education, technical, humanistic and inductive, are closely interdependent. In the final analysis, all education is inductive in the sense that it helps to introduce individuals into what, for them, are new aspects of the mystery of human existence.

SOCIETY AND COMMUNITY

The words *society* and *community* suggest a group in which the members share and transmit a particular set of values. They suggest associations, relationships and links which are based upon an identity of interest and concerns. Such relationships are regulated by law and custom. Relationships within a society may be friendly, even intimate. They can also lead to disagreement and conflict, but whatever character they assume, either of harmony or of conflict, an underlying organic unity is assumed. Not to subscribe to that convention of unity is, effectively, to be outside the society in question. The acceptance of certain quite specific values is essential for the health of an *organic* society or community. This seems to be especially true of religious communities.

On the problems faced in Britain by immigrants from different cultures, and with different religious beliefs, Professor John McIntyre, has written:

What I think must be clear by now is that the values and concepts of the culture, deriving as they do from religious sources, cannot be extracted and replaced by a totally different set, with a different religious inspiration. If you change what might be called the nucleus of the culture, you change the cultural expressions derivable from it. In fact, you change the culture.[20]

A little further in the same essay he writes:

The advent of these numbers [i.e. immigrants to Britain] does not lead to the creation overnight, of a multi-culture society, in the sense that we now have independent, co-existent and alternative cultures. The strictures imposed by a new social setting, economic conditions, legal and even political unfamiliarities, all conspire to reduce to a minimum that range of expressions in art and literature, architecture and ballet, etc., which give the culture visible and discernible reality.[21]

Education is one of the principal means by which society is transformed, and by which citizens are prepared to take their place in it. This is clearly recognized in the summary of the Swann report published in 1985. At the end of the first chapter of the summary which deals with the nature of society in Britain, the following paragraph appears:

What is looked for is not the assimilation of the minority communities within an unchanged dominant way of life, but the 'assimilation' of *all* groups within a redefined concept of what it means to live in British society today. What is sought is not to fit ethnic minorities into a mould originally cast for a society relatively homogeneous in language, religion and culture, nor to break this mould completely and replace it with one which is in all senses 'foreign' to our established way of life. Instead, the mould should be recast in a form which retains the fundamental principles of the original but with a broader pluralist conspectus – diversity within unity.[22]

Precisely what this recasting of the mould is taken to mean by the members of the Swann committee is explained in the rest of their published report, especially in the section called *Education for all: a new approach*. The issue for the members of this committee was the education of ethnic minority children, without isolation from the majority.[23]

It would be difficult, and probably not helpful, to describe comprehensively the extent of the racial and cultural origins of people in Britain. The range is astonishing, and includes members of major groups like Christians, Jews, Muslims, Sikhs and others, who from time to time consider themselves as minorities in an inconsiderate world. One thing is clear: in the absence of consensus about fundamental beliefs, attempts must continue to be made to provide the kind of education which contributes to the stability of society. Some radical proposals have already been made for solving the inequality which exists. Of these, the rehabilitation of inner city areas would require considerable public expenditure, and positive discrimination in education and employment for the disadvantaged might lead to additional tensions in society. Nevertheless, action of a decisive kind needs to be taken: 'Unless major efforts are made to reconcile the concerns and aspirations of both the majority and minority communities along more genuinely pluralist lines, there is a real risk of the fragmentation of our society along ethnic lines which would seriously threaten the stability and cohesion of society as a whole.'[24]

This statement contains a warning about the penalty for inaction. It also recognizes something which can be overlooked: namely, that no solution which isolates the minorities from the majority in the long term can hope to succeed. In a genuinely pluralist society there must be a fair amount of give and take. No single community can expect to remain untouched. If there is to be cultural enrichment as a result of the close proximity of distinct cultural groups it needs to be mutual. For if the majority has to learn how to be hospitable, the minorities cannot expect to remain unchanged: 'To seek to represent "being British" as something long established and immutable fails to acknowledge that the concept is in fact dynamic and ever changing, adapting and absorbing new ideas and influences.'[25] The present situation is not entirely satisfactory. Society is becoming increasingly complex, but not only in consequence of technological change. This complexity needs to be acknowledged in education, neither merely described, nor indirectly noted. Helping individuals to cope with the opportunities (as well as the tensions) which arise out of religious, ethical, political and technological diversity, may be a task to which all teachers are finally obliged to make a conscious and planned contribution. This task can scarcely be undertaken without a lively interest in the practical implications of pluralism.

There are good reasons, therefore, for looking at the prospects of *education for cultural diversity*, to see how far different approaches to education can be reconciled without destructive compromise in the framework of commonly accepted values designed to promote tolerance. How reasonable will it turn out to be that Jews, Christians, Muslims, Hindus, Sikhs, Humanists and others are prepared to compromise on matters of cherished convictions in the common interest? Or will each community insist on going its separate way, so that 'society' is more akin to a federation, united by what might both literally and metaphorically be called its foreign policy?

Some of the evidence for this will be found throughout this book. A consideration of different cultural traditions reveals relationships between belief and action which influence both the content and the methods of education, but which tend to be overlooked in standard practice. Here in Britain there are several culturally distinct, and possibly conflicting, ideas about education (and thus about society). Wherever there is racial tension in the wake of cultural diversity it is reasonable and just to work for harmony and mutual respect between individuals and groups. But if education is held to be an important instrument for reducing the adverse effects of misunderstandings in society which may arise between groups from different cultural backgrounds it will inevitably assume an ideological role which itself may become the subject of controversy and disagreement.

NOTES AND REFERENCES

1. Eliot T S 1949 *Christianity and Culture*, part 2 in *Notes Towards the Definition of Culture*. Harcourt, Brace & Co., New York, p 91. See also the appendix on 'The unity of European culture', in the same book, pp 187–202
2. Muller Dr Steven 1986 President of Johns Hopkins University, Baltimore, quoted by Fiske Edward B. in *The New York Times*, 7 Sept.
3. Dawson Christopher 1948 *Religion and Culture* (Gifford Lectures given in the University of Edinburgh in 1947). Sheed & Ward, pp 48–50
4. Perrott Elizabeth 1982 *Effective Teaching: a practical guide to improving your teaching*. Longman
5. The author was able to discuss some of these issues with American colleagues during the course of several visits to the United States between 1981 and 1986. Emotions are easily roused in a pluralist society by public statements about what is stated to be the relative educational aptitude and performance of students from different cultural backgrounds. The tension which is thus created may involve national governments as well as local communities. An example of this was noted by the author in a visit to New Jersey, Pennsylvania and New York, from July to December 1986. It makes an interesting

contemporary case study, and it deserves to be quoted at length. On Friday, 26 September 1986 *The New York Times* carried a piece by Susan Chira, with the dateline Tokyo, 25 September. The Japanese Prime Minister was reported to have made some derogatory comments about the educational achievement of some minority groups in the United States, and to have compared the situation there unfavourably with the situation in Japan. Several prominent black and other minority group leaders in the USA, including spokesmen for Japanese-Americans, took instant exception to these comments and called on their government to press for a full apology

6. Cooke Alistair 1986 *Letter from America*. BBC Radio 4, 6 July
7. *Teacher Education for a Multi-cultural Society* 1974 The Community Relations Commission and the Association of Teachers in Colleges and Departments of Education. London, June p 5
8. Idowu E Bolaji 1975 'Religion and cultural renewal' in *Orita*. Journal of the Department of Religious Studies in the University of Ibadan, Nigeria, vol ix, no 2, Dec. pp 77–78. The Yoruba word *orita* means 'where the ways meet'
9. Hutchinson John 1981 in a letter to *The Times*, 21 Nov.
10. Kirkwood Kenneth 1981 in a letter to *The Times*, 25 Nov. The italics have been added
11. See note 7 above
12. This point is considered in Chapter 2
13. Eliot T S 1949 *Christianity and Culture*. Harcourt, Brace & Co., New York, p 93
14. Idowu 'Religion and cultural renewal', p 78
15. Postman Neil 1986 *Are We Entertaining Ourselves to Death*? New York University
16. Heschel A J 1966 *The Insecurity of Freedom*. Farrar, Straus & Giroux, p 43, OUP, 1969, pp 24–25
17. Tillich Paul 1959 'A theology of education', in *Theology of Culture*. Oxford University Press New York, p 147
18. This point is developed in a stimulating and controversial way by Hardy Alister C in *The Divine Flame* 1966 (Gifford Lectures, University of Aberdeen 1964–65), Collins and in *The Biology of God: a scientist's study of man the religious animal*, Jonathan Cape, 1975
19. Tillich 'A theology of education', p 147
20. McIntyre John 1978 *Multi-culture and Multi-faith Societies: some examinable assumptions*. Farmington Occasional Papers (ed. Hulmes Edward), no 3, Oxford, p 2
21. Ibid.
22. *'Education for All': A Summary of the Swann Report on the Education of Ethnic Minority Children* 1985 The Runnymede Trust
23. Ibid. The report has useful things to say about the nature of society, the theory and practice of racism, the question of achievement and under-achievement of children in schools, English as a second language and the provision for the use of ethnic languages. There are sections on religious education and the 'separate' schools issue, teacher education and the employment of ethnic minority teachers, and useful notes on the educational needs of black children in Liverpool, of the children of travellers, and of children of Chinese,

Cypriot, Italian, Ukrainian and Vietnamese origin. The report has already been considered by Muslims in Britain. See *Swann Committee's Report: A Muslim Response* 1987 National Muslim Education Council of UK, London

24. Ibid., p 1
25. Ibid., p 2

CHAPTER 2

Muslim perspectives: 'O my Lord, increase me in knowledge'

Let parents refrain from sending their children to foreign schools that tend to change their habits and religious faith, until God ordains that religious instruction be excluded from all schools throughout the world, that it be given in special institutions only, and that the schools be restricted to teaching subjects other than religion – an impossible development in our lands.[1]

It is for education to *mould* the character of the child into the Islamic pattern.[2]

For those who wish to follow some wishy-washy culture, based on something roughly British, the state system is fine. But for the real thing, there is a need for the voluntary aided system. We ask no more than that which is already established for Jewish and Catholic children.[3]

The purpose of this chapter is to identify some of the characteristic features of Islamic education. In pursuing this objective it is not necessary to consider either the original contributions which Islamic scholars have made down the centuries to the common store of human knowledge, or the achievements of Muslims in helping to transmit the treasury of classical learning to Europe. The question to be asked here is one that has often been put to the author. It has two parts. What is Islamic education, and what can teachers who are not Muslims learn from it in order to help in furthering education for cultural diversity? A start can be made in answering this question by raising some practical issues which affect the lives of Muslims living in Britain today.

EDUCATIONAL THEORY AND PRACTICE IN ISLAM: ISSUES FACING MUSLIMS IN BRITISH SCHOOLS

It can be argued that the major issue faced by Muslims in British schools today is that their approach to knowledge, and to the acquisition of knowledge, is simply disregarded in the educational system of this country. *Islamic* education, in short, although a vital aspect of Islamic culture, is effectively denied to those who need it most – namely, the children of Muslim parents – except by private arrangement after normal school is over. As for non-Muslims, they have no opportunity to find out for themselves

what it might mean to be educated in the light of Islamic principles. The inclusion in the curriculum of courses *about* Islam is,
from a Muslim's point of view, no substitute for an education in
which the whole curriculum is set to reflect Islamic beliefs. It is
for this reason that Muslims face an almost insoluble problem in
education in a western, non-islamic society.

Muslims face other difficulties with which it is easier to deal.
Compromise or what they consider to be matters of principle is
not easy, especially when it appears to betray the cultural tradition. It is true that efforts are being made to ensure that Muslim
opinion about issues such as single-sex schools, the segregation
of the sexes after a certain age, the preparation of acceptable
food, regulations for dress in school, the recognition of the
demands made upon Muslims by fasting during the month of
Ramaḍān, the celebration of feasts such as *ʿīd al-fiṭr* (breaking
of the fast at the end of *Ramadān*) and *ʿīd al-aḍhā* (feast of
sacrifice during the pilgrimage to Mecca), is understood and
respected as far as possible. Important as these issues are, they
remain secondary. The primary issue is about the nature of
education itself. What, from the Islamic perspective, is education
for? What are its aims and objectives? What constitutes knowledge, and what is the manner of its acquisition? These are the
questions which are considered in this chapter.

The third of the statements quoted at the head of this chapter
expresses a point of view commonly held by Muslims in this
country. Not all of them, however, would agree that the imper-
fections of state education in Britain would be removed if
Muslims were only granted the right (enjoyed, as they see it, by
other religious groups) to send their children to voluntary aided
schools where education would be conducted according to Islamic
principles. In the case of a recent proposal for the setting up of
a separate school for Muslims, there was both support and
opposition from within the local Muslim community.

We are very grateful [to Yusuf Islam]. He spends his own money and
he knows more about Islam than me, who was born a Muslim. He gives
up show business, and no one can now believe that he was what he was.[4]

We salute Mr Yusuf, but we cannot support him. I come from a Muslim
family. I haven't changed my religion like Mr Yusuf. But I must concern
myself with 10,000 poor Muslim kids in the state schools, and with
ratepayers who are not Muslims.[5]

The problems which educational theory and practice present
to members of the Islamic community in Britain can be illustrated
from many other sources. In 1983 a Religious Education competition for students in the secondary schools of Birmingham was
organized by the Selly Oak Colleges. The organizers invited
students to submit essays, poems or drawings in one of the

following classes: Hinduism, Judaism, Christianity, Islam, Sikhism or another religion. Entries were divided into three age groups. Prizes for the winning entries were provided by the Spalding Trust. Despite the fact that the competition was held in May, when most of the older students in schools were preparing for public examinations, 350 entries were submitted. Most of the students wrote about their own religion. In many cases this was Islam. Commenting on the difficulties which face Muslims in British schools, and discussing the quality of entries in the competition, the Muslim educationist Ghulam Nabi Saqeb subsequently wrote as follows:

Muslims claim to be the largest religious minority community today in the United Kingdom, and yet they feel they have not been able to secure, anywhere in the country a sound type of education for the moral and spiritual development of their children. Their major worry is that the county and denominational schools which their children mostly attend fail to provide them with an adequate understanding and knowledge of their religion and culture. The only committed Islamic education which their children receive is given at the supplementary evening and week-end mosque schools where the Imams who are employed by the [Islamic] community to lead prayers also improvise in the teaching of fundamentals of Islam. As these Imams are not trained to teach, they follow archaic and rule of thumb methods, and thus teach Islam in a lifeless and stereotyped fashion.

Consequently the Muslim child fails to discover a sense of meaning in life in the Islamic vision, and remains restricted to the external descriptions of the rituals and liturgies which he, his parents, and the community perform at home and at the mosque. An ideologically sound and consistent grounding in Islam is given to a few children only by those parents who are themselves educated, and – realizing the importance of the faith as a system of morality and as a source of spiritual guidance – make extra efforts to educate their children through well-written books and by taking them to lectures, seminars, and similar other programmes organized by the Islamic centres. *Formal education that the Muslim children receive at schools remains inadequate and superficial so far as Islam is concerned.*[6] [Italics have been added to the last sentence.]

Many who are not Muslims will readily understand the criticism of education in contemporary Britain which is made here from a Muslim point of view. The author of the paragraphs quoted is well informed about education in Britain, and knows that vigorous attempts have been made in recent years to include teaching about different world religions, especially Islam, in the curriculum. Nowhere in Britain has this policy been implemented more sensitively than in Birmingham, where this competition was held. Despite this, a Muslim commentator observes that the formal education received in British schools is both inadequate and superficial so far as Islam is concerned. The external, descriptive approach to the ritual and liturgy of Islam belongs to an *un-Islamic* phenomenology. For Muslims such an approach is inescapably reductionist and inadequate.

At the conclusion of his comments on the competition and on the implications of its results for education in Birmingham and elsewhere in the United Kingdom, Ghulam Nabi Saqeb has this to say:

Of course the best results in religious education of the Muslim children could only be achieved in schools where an Islamic environment is created just like in the voluntary-aided Catholic, Anglican, and Jewish schools. But as things stand there seems little likelihood of Local Education Authorities agreeing to allow Muslims to set up such schools. Nor do the Muslims, on their own, have the finances, the trained teachers, and organized religious bodies to help them. Muslim communities in Britain must organize themselves and make sacrifices to secure better education for their children. They cannot go on blaming and expecting the LEAs to prepare good Muslims in the county/state schools. This is primarily the duty of the Muslims themselves. By organizing themselves at the national level and involving themselves at the local levels in the political processes of the country Muslims, being the largest minority community, can secure the rights of their children in education and other spheres.[7]

THE SIGNIFICANCE OF THE WORD ISLĀM

What are the factors to be considered for an understanding of Islamic perspectives on education, pluralism and cultural diversity?[8] The first thing to be noted is that the word *Islām* is not only the name of a religion. It is certainly that, and the religion concerned is both vigorous and world-wide. Islam also promotes a coherent way of life by means of submission to God. Islam expresses a specific disposition of the mind, will and intellect. Its root meaning is 'submission', or 'surrender'. It describes a voluntary act, constantly repeated through life, of submitting individual wishes and desires to the revealed will of God.[9]

Conformity to the revealed will of God is, thus, both an obligation and a privilege for Muslims. It is by way of submission that human creatures find wholeness, integrity, inner harmony and peace. In consequence, Islam means both 'submission' (to God) and 'peace', with the associated suggestions of harmony, security and safety. From the same consonantal root in Arabic the word *Muslim* means one who, through submission to God, enters into peace. There is no part of human existence which can remain unaffected by Islam. It is an irony of history that Jerusalem, the city of peace, a city which is a holy place for Muslims as well as Jews and Christians, should have become a focal point of conflict. Education plays its part in the coherent plan which has been revealed for the benefit of all human beings. One of the fruits of obedience to God is knowledge. From the Islamic point of view education is instrumental in bringing succeeding generations to a knowledge of the sovereignty of God, of their own creatureliness, and of their total dependence upon the creator.

Submission to God liberates human beings everywhere to serve him as he requires. Muslims do not accept that their religion is merely one of many. Islam is not just a local religion. It makes universal demands on the allegiance of God's creatures. For this reason the word *Islām* suggests several things which non-Muslims may find instantly uncongenial. Islam appears to make exclusive claims to be the one true religion for all. It appears to brook no rivals and tolerates no other systems of belief, except in a subordinate way. In requiring obedience and submission it appears to limit speculation and critical inquiry. At first sight it would seem that in a secular society dedicated to principles of pluralism Islam can scarcely fail to be a challenging influence.

THE ISLAMIC COMMUNITY

The notion of the Islamic community is conveyed by the Arabic word *ummah*. The word carries with it comprehensive associations of unity and brotherhood which are fundamental to Islamic belief and practice. Membership of the Islamic community confers duties as well as rights. The health of the body politic depends upon the fulfilment of social duties as well as the exercise of individual rights. The *ummah* is an organized community, to which loyalty is always due. A clear line of division exists between those who are members of the community and those who are not. But this exclusiveness is not necessarily permanent. No one is excluded from the Islamic community on grounds of race or colour. Individuals exclude themselves by not accepting the claims of Islam.

In Islamic belief the world is divided into the *dār al-islām*, and the *dār al-ḥarb*. The former is, literally, 'the house(hold) of Islam'. In this phrase, the word *Islām* bears the meanings already considered above. The *dār al-islām* consists of those parts of the world where the principles of Islam are practised. The *dār al-ḥarb*, literally, 'the house of war', consists of those parts of the world where Islamic principles do not prevail. The most important practical consequence of this division into spheres of influence is that it requires Muslims to work to strengthen the *dār al-islām* where it exists, and strive to establish it where it does not. The work of helping in the world-wide expansion of Islam devolves to some extent upon every Muslim. There are Muslims who are specially trained to bring the teachings of Islam to parts of Europe and the United States, for example, but it is the patient witnessing of countless ordinary Muslims down the centuries which has brought about the greatest advances in the conversion of the *dār al-harb* in Africa and elsewhere in the world.

For a Muslim to acknowledge the concept of religious freedom, as understood in a non-Islamic society, and then to work for the building up of a new kind of society, based upon principles of pluralism, is to invite the criticism of fellow-Muslims. The preservation of the health and integrity of the *ummah* depends upon the success which Muslims have in protecting the community from the danger of alien elements. This should occasion no surprise among non-Muslims; from their point of view Muslims are acting in a perfectly responsible manner. No Muslim would willingly allow the unity and health of the *ummah* to be threatened by alien elements.

The responsibilities of Muslim parents

On the other hand Muslims see no inconsistency in pursuing the best interests of Islam outside as well as inside the Islamic community. They claim the right to spread the teachings of Islam as the true religion anywhere in the world, while refusing access to would-be missionaries from other religions to the heartlands of Islam. Furthermore, Muslims seek to extend the right they have in an Islamic country to live according to the provisions of the *sharīᶜa* (Islamic law) to Muslims who live in non-Islamic societies. If more considerate attention than hitherto is given by non-Muslims to Islam in education as a religion which is a wholly integrated way of life, Muslims may welcome it cautiously in the short term. In the longer term they will try to find ways of educating their children so that the distinctive claims of Islam are fully recognized. Successful or not, Muslims are attempting to counter what they take to be the corrosive influences of western secular education. The following example comes from a manual written for the guidance of Muslim parents in the United States:

As Muslims, our aim in bringing up our children should be to train their personalities in such a way that their best qualities will be developed and that they will be conscious of their responsibility to Allah, serving him with all the talents and resources He has given them. We are living in a society which, either directly or indirectly, is completely opposed to such a goal, and we have to realize that the task is not an easy one.

In American society, oriented as it is toward man, materialism and machines, the very idea that there is an All-Controlling Power, to Whom man owes unswerving devotion and responsibility, is out of place and out of context except in religious circles. In attempting to train our children, therefore, we should not underestimate the extent to which the forces of this society are working against us, and we should think and plan carefully how we can best achieve our goal under these conditions. This goal will (if God wills) be achieved in part by working to build in them Islamic attitudes and Islamic personalities through an Islamically oriented family life.[10]

ISLAMIC ATTITUDES TO KNOWLEDGE AND TO EDUCATION

The most important thing to be noted about the Islamic theory of knowledge (whatever differences there may be about points of emphasis and interpretation between Muslims) is that all knowledge is *of* God, in every sense. 'O my Lord, increase me in knowledge' is a Qur°ānic petition.[11] It is for knowledge of God that the Muslim prays. Such knowledge (°ilm) is to be sought in every way that is consistent with the principles of Islam.

The theory and practice of multi-culture education are based upon other principles. The inclusion of Islam as one of several different religions to be studied in various aspects across the curriculum is no substitute for Islamic education. Muslims are suspicious of what passes for cultural pluralism in the west as potentially inimical to the *ummah*. No part of life, no thought, *no way of thinking*, can be considered rightful if it presumes to be independent of the Islamic revelation. For Muslims, education is the means of initiating the young and immature into their *full* cultural heritage as Muslims. Education begins and ends with the revealed will of God. Muslim education is normative in quite specific ways. Education is ideologically oriented, a means to an end, not an end in itself. The point to note for anyone interested in developing multi-culture education is that this orientation is quite different from, and incompatible with, the ideology of a secular and pluralist state. The contemporary Muslim scholar Khurshid Ahmad makes it clear why this is so.

The importance of education hardly needs any emphasis. It is the 'knowledge of things' as such which distinguishes man from the rest of creation and which, according to the Qur°an, establishes his superiority over all others. °ilm (knowledge) is an essential quality for leadership and is one of those factors of prime importance which lead to the rise and growth of civilization. That is why the Holy Prophet (peace be upon him) said: 'the acquisition of knowledge is incumbent on every Muslim', and 'acquire knowledge, for he who acquireth it in the way of Allah performeth an act of piety; he who speaketh of it, praiseth the Lord, he who seeketh after it, adoreth God; he who dispenseth instruction in it, bestoweth alms, and he who imparteth it to others, performeth an act of devotion to Allah. . . .

Through education a people communicate their culture and intellectual heritage to the future generations and inspire them with their ideals of life. Education is a mental, physical and moral training and its objective is to produce highly cultured men and women fit to discharge their duties as good human beings and as worthy citizens of a state.[12]

From time to time in the Islamic world attempts are made to clarify this central educational issue. Scientific and technological expertise has an international currency which is acceptable anywhere in the world. Newly developing countries are eager to have it. The dissemination of this knowledge has another influence which is less acceptable: can the western world's scientific and technological knowledge be imported without the secularism which is so closely associated with it? It is secularism which is eyed as a threat to Islamic cultural identity. A policy which is designed to exclude unacceptable western ideas is justified from the Muslim point of view because it is judged to be necessary for cultural survival.

The elementary laws of economics require that the exchange of goods between nations be mutual; this means that no nation can act as buyer only while another nation is always seller in the long run, each of them must play both parts simultaneously, giving to, and taking from, each other, be it directly or through the medium of other actors in the play of economic forces. But in the cultural field this iron rule of exchange is not a necessity, at least not always a visible one, that is to say, the transfer of ideas and cultural influences is not necessarily based on the principle of give-and-take.[13]

The author of this passage, himself a European who has converted to Islam, conveyed a word of warning on behalf of many fellow-Muslims when he said to Europeans who were just beginning to recover from the ravages of the First World War:

We believe that Islam, unlike other religions, is not only a spiritual attitude of mind, adjustable to different cultural settings, but a self-sufficing orbit of culture and a social system of clearly defined features. When, as is the case today, a foreign civilization extends its radiations into our midst and causes certain changes in our own cultural organism, we are bound to make it clear to ourselves whether that foreign influence runs in the direction of our own cultural possibilities or against them; whether it acts as an invigorating serum in the body of Islamic culture, or as a poison.[14]

The Muslim concludes that it is prudent to protect the Islamic community from the poisonous effects of western, non-Islamic values, because western culture is based upon non-religious, materialistic values, which are in direct conflict with the teachings of Islam. There is, therefore, a point at which it has to be recognized that it is improper and dangerous to participate in multi-culture education. The Islamic way of thinking cannot be adapted to the cultural values of the non-Islamic world. Nevertheless, this incompatibility

should in no way preclude the possibility of Muslims receiving from the West certain impulses in the domain of exact and applied sciences; but their cultural relations should begin and end at that point. To go further and to imitate Western civilization in its spirit, its mode of life and its social organization is impossible without dealing a fatal blow to the very existence of Islam as a theocratic polity and a practical religion.[15]

THE INFLUENCE OF NON-ISLAMIC ATTITUDES

The history of events in the Islamic world during the past five decades has shown that it is not possible for Muslims to put a fence around their community, nor to select the influences which they are prepared to accept from the West. It has not been possible for Muslims to benefit from the fruits of western technology without importing what they consider to be less wholesome fruit at the same time. The figures often quoted in support of the growth of Islam in various parts of the world are impressive; they show that Islam is still a vigorous missionary faith. What these figures tend to conceal is the rise of a purely nominal profession of Islam among the educated elites of countries which are parts of the heartland of Islam. Indifference and scepticism with regard to religious beliefs have already penetrated the protective curtain:

Western education of Muslim youth is bound to undermine their will to believe in the message of the Prophet, their will to regard themselves as representatives of the peculiar theocratic civilization of Islam. There can be no doubt whatever that religious belief is rapidly losing ground among the 'intelligentsia' educated on Western lines. This, of course, does not imply that Islam has preserved its integrity as a practical religion among the non-educated classes. But there, anyhow, we generally find a far greater sentimental response to the call of Islam – in the primitive way they understand it – than among the Westernized 'intelligentsia'. The explanation of this estrangement is not that the Western science with which they have been fed has furnished any reasonable argument against the truth of our religious teachings, but that the intellectual atmosphere of modern Western civilization is so intensely anti-religious that it imposes itself as a dead weight upon the religious potentialities of the young Muslim generation.[16]

In this paragraph western attitudes are criticized, not only regarding Islam but regarding revealed religion in general. It is a criticism which is often echoed by Muslims today. It may be asked if the pre-suppositions of western education place Christians, Jews and others, as well as Muslims, at a disadvantage in schools dedicated to the pursuit of pluralist ideals. If Marx was correct in insisting that environment determines consciousness, it is clear that children raised in an educational environment in which cultural values are outwardly valued but implicitly ignored will find it difficult to accept for themselves the cultural values and beliefs of their parents. The values of the school and the values of the home will be in conflict, but not in a constructive educational way which might ensure that differences of opinion are carefully examined.

In the remote parts of the Islamic world these alien, and alienating, cultural influences from the West will hardly be felt, but the centres of Islamic authority and enterprise have not been left untouched by modernist tendencies. It is not easy to follow Islam even in a society which reflects Islamic values; in the case of Muslim minorities living in the western world it is more difficult still. This makes for increasing tension between the attraction of prevalent social values and the commands of Allāh. This tension is particularly troublesome with regard to education, but it is often overlooked or disregarded, even by teachers who are genuinely trying to understand what it is like to be a Muslim in Britain today. To understand this tension it might be better to change the more general question from 'What problems are faced by Muslims in a non-Islamic society?' to the specific question, 'What would it be like to be educated according to Islamic principles?'

The contemporary Muslim sees the basic assumptions of modern Western civilization, nearly all of which are the very antithesis of the Islamic principles he cherishes. He sees philosophies based either on man considered as a creature in rebellion against Heaven, or on the human collectivity seen as an ant-heap in which man has no dignity worthy of his real nature. He sees the Universe reduced to a single level of reality – the spacio-temporal complex of matter and energy – and all the higher levels of reality relegated to the category of old wives' tales or – at best – images drawn from the collective unconscious. He sees the power of man as ruler upon the earth emphasized at the expense of his servanthood, so that he is considered to be not [the viceregent of God], but as the [viceregent] of his own ego, or of some worldly power or collectivity.[17]

This point may be taken further. On the one hand, there are the traditional interpreters and transmitters of Islamic values, the parents and grandparents, whose responsibility for inculcating the principles of Islam begins with the birth of each new infant. This is an obligation which they share with the rest of the Islamic community. But for the parents and the immediate family this is both a special duty and a great privilege. On the other hand, other educational forces are at work. The western media of mass communication are influential, conveying the attitudes and mores of a different society with an immediacy which sweeps past national boundaries. Despite the skill of translation and dubbing, these attitudes are conveyed in a language which usurps the primacy of Arabic as the key to Islamic culture. The ideas, ideals and fruits of western expertise are, intentionally or not, the instruments of cultural imperialism in various subtle ways. And all are potentially subversive of Islamic values.

The impact of alien cultural values is an important factor in evaluating the revolutionary situation in Iran which led to the establishment of an Islamic republic in place of what was described as an alien infidel regime. The fall of the Shah in 1978 to the supporters of the Ayatollah Khomeini marked not only the repudiation of western secularism in Iran and the rejection, for example, of western educational and medical standards, but also a determination to root out internal corruption, to resist modernism and to put an end to all forms of foreign domination, in the name of fundamental and unchangeable Islamic values. 'We live', said the revolutionaries, 'by different rules.'

Islamic fundamentalism continues to pose a threat to the stability of other Islamic countries, where it is felt by the fundamentalists that the existing regimes have betrayed the true ideals of Islam. This threat is felt even in the heartland of Islam, in Saudi Arabia on the other side of the Gulf from Iran. Islamic fundamentalism has been used to justify a series of violent attacks in the name of *jihād*[18] on persons and property outside the Muslim world which have done little to commend the cause of Islam among non-Muslims. Resistance to cultural infection from outside is also to be seen in other Islamic countries. In recent years leading Muslims have sought to protect their brothers and sisters in non-Islamic countries from what they think of as the baleful influence of western secularism. Consider the implications of the following paragraph, from the report of an Islamic conference on education held in Jedda, Saudi Arabia, in 1978, for the prospects of a genuinely multi-cultural education in Britain:

The primary aim of this conference is not merely to re-define the goal of education as the training of human sensibility so that a human being becomes aware of his destiny as the vice-regent of God, but also to find ways of translating this aim into action. [This will come] through revised courses, a re-classification of knowledge from the Islamic point of view, and the construction of a curriculum on the basis of this re-classification. [By this means] the secularizing process which is going on in Muslim countries because of their adoption of the western system of education will be stopped.[19]

This paragraph raises an important question. How far is education to be used as an instrument of social change? It would be misleading to suggest that 'the training of human sensibility' for a specified purpose, or 'the re-classification of knowledge' from the point of view of a particular ideology are unknown outside Islamic education. All educational systems tend towards authoritarianism with the passage of time. The charge of indoctrination is normally reserved for those cases where, as in the example just cited, individuals are trained according to specific religious principles to take their place in the community of believers. In what are often prematurely described as non-directive systems of education in the non-Islamic world the degree of direction given to the curriculum needs to be constantly reviewed lest its 'openness' be unjustifiably assumed.[20]

THE IMPORTANCE OF THE QUR'ĀN, THE HOME AND THE MOSQUE IN EDUCATION

In education, as in every other aspect of life, the Muslim looks to the Qur'ān for authoritative guidance. The Qur'ān is the source book for belief and action, and it remains the pre-eminent guide as the Word of God. It is in every sense the textbook of Islam. It is inconceivable to a Muslim that God should have provided a final revelation of his will and purpose for all mankind in the Qur'ān and not have established principles for guiding succeeding generations to a knowledge of that revelation. Education without religion, or independent of religion, is a contradiction in terms for a Muslim. The chief aim of Islamic education is to obtain knowledge *of God*, through the medium of the religion which God revealed in its final form to Muhammad. Anything beyond this is unnecessary. Traditionally, Muslims have resisted secular knowledge as being dangerous to faith, although it has always been urged that it is not knowledge itself, but the *attitude to knowledge*, which is the critical factor.[21]

Long before children are able to understand the meaning of the words, their mothers whisper to them the basic creed of a Muslim, 'There is no god but Allāh (God), and Muhammad is the Messenger of God.' This parental influence is a prelude to the influence of the Qur'ānic school (*maktab*), the Islamic school (*kuttāb*), the traditional centre of higher education (*madrasah*). In Britain, for example, it is still common to find that Muslim children who attend a local education authority school are obliged to spend one or two evenings each week attending a local Qur'ānic school, where the curriculum and the teaching methods are very different. The Qur'ānic school is normally to be found in the precincts of the mosque. The importance of the mosque as a place of Islamic education, as well as a place for prayer (especially on Fridays) is not to be under-estimated.[22]

Throughout the Islamic world the mosque serves the community in a variety of ways. It is the most important religious institution. In cities and towns the mosques are quite often large, with ample space for private meditation, as well as public prayer.

The mosque and its surrounding courtyards are places for relaxation and social activity. In smaller and more remote areas mosques serve to bring together individuals and groups for the same purpose, but in humbler surroundings. The classical elegance of stone and decorated tile to be seen in the mosques of the great cities gives place to the simplicity of mud huts and thatched roofs. But every mosque, whether in Cairo, in a remote part of northern Nigeria, or a converted room or church in an English town, is also a centre of Islamic education.

It is usually an imam,[23] or some other official of the mosque, who teaches in the *maktab*, or Qurᵓānic school. In the larger city mosques, the study of the Qurᵓān and the traditions of Islam is taken further in the *madrasah* (literally, 'place of study'). The curriculum is carefully chosen. Discipline is strict, and special attention is given to memory work, particularly memorizing the whole or parts of the Qurᵓān. Many of these old ways have changed, but they still exercise an influence on the practice of education in the Qur'ānic school. To understand this legacy the western student can still make use of the work of nineteenth-century scholars who described a situation which their twentieth-century successors would recognize today in parts of the Islamic world:

In connection with all mosques of importance, in all parts of Islam . . . , there are small schools, either for the education of children, or for the training of students of divinity. The child who attends these seminaries is first taught his alphabet, which he learns from a small board, on which the letters are written by the teacher. He then becomes acquainted with the numerical value of each letter. After this he learns to write down the ninety-nine names of God,[24] and other simple words taken from the Qurᵓan. When he has mastered the spelling of words, he proceeds to learn the first chapter of the Qurᵓan, then the last chapter, and gradually reads through the whole Qurᵓan in Arabic, which he usually does without understanding a word of it. Having finished the Qurᵓan, which is considered an incumbent religious duty, the pupil is instructed in the elements of grammar, and perhaps a few simple rules of arithmetic.[25]

There have been great changes in education in the Islamic world since those words were written a hundred or so years ago. In the Near East, and in other parts of the Islamic world, there have been considerable strides in education, in the provision of modern buildings and resources, and in the training of teachers. But from the perspective of some Islamic purists, many of the recent innovations are evidence of the influence of western attitudes and techniques. This is even more notable in the field of higher education. There is no shortage of modern universities in the Islamic world, and they are thronged with students. It is in the universities that the impact of the natural sciences, the social sciences and the behavioural sciences, to say nothing of the critical approach to the humanities, is most keenly felt as a potential threat to the values of traditional Islamic higher education.

It has to be remembered that from the time of the Prophet Muhammad there have been at least two distinct systems of education in the Islamic world, and a consequent tension between the demands of both. In its simplest terms this is the tension between what is Islamic and what is not. The legacy of Rome and Byzantium preserved the values of Latin and Greek culture in education in those areas which were incorporated into the Islamic empire. It is a matter of history that Arab scholars were instrumental in helping to preserve those values against the day when they were re-examined by Europeans at the time of the Renaissance. The other system of education was based upon Islamic principles. To some extent this distinction still remains today in the Islamic world, with modern universities patterned on western models on the one hand, and a traditional institution of higher education such as al-Azhar in Cairo on the other.[26] Some idea of what that meant (and in many places still means) in the Islamic world can be gained from the following description – again from the pen of the observer already quoted, who wrote a century ago.

The ordinary schoolmaster is generally a man of little learning, the [learned man] usually devoting himself to the study of divinity, and not to the education of the young. Amongst students of divinity . . . , the usual course of study is as follows: grammatical inflection; syntax; logic; arithmetic; algebra; rhetoric and versification; jurisprudence; scholastic theology; commentaries on the Qur⁾an; treatises on exegesis, and the principles and rules of interpretation of the laws of Islam; the traditions and commentaries thereon. These are usually regarded as different branches of learning, and it is not often that a [learned man] attains to the knowledge of each section.[27]

In the modern world education plays a vital role in countries which are moving from colonial dependency to self-determination and independent nationhood. In many parts of the Islamic world this has been the case during the course of the present century. A contemporary opinion of the problems which face those who want to press as speedily as possible towards political, economic and *cultural* independence, without surrendering the classical values of Islam, is given by A. L. Tibawi. The passage is notable for its criticism of the invocation of traditional cultural values in a vague way in support of a desirable aim, whether it be political, social or educational. Since Islam does not recognize any distinctions which appear to make certain kinds of human endeavour inaccessible to divine commands, it would be better, Tibawi affirms, to make the Islamic values explicit. The implication for Islamic education is clear enough, when:

Science or learning for its own sake would place on the state responsibilities that are beyond its present capacity, We must therefore seek
science for the benefit of society . . . leaving our participation in the
universal quest for learning for its own sake to a later stage. But 'science
for society' must not be interpreted narrowly to mean simply 'the loaf
of bread'. . . . Let us always remember that the spiritual energies which
nations derive from the ideals of their divine faiths, or from their cultural
heritages, are capable of performing miracles.

Every educational system is caught between conflicting pressures, such
as respect for tradition and the necessity for change. Partly on this
account and partly because of the complexity of the process of
education, every system is liable to fall short of its objectives. The above
quotation indicates a desire to link the present with the Islamic past or
at least to assert the Islamic values. Yet it does not mention Islam. The
circumlocution signifies the climax of the gradual secularization of the
state and education. In the Arab world the process was dictated largely
by the necessity of enlisting the active participation of the Christian Arab
minorities, first in the struggle together with the Muslim Arab majority
against foreign control and then in the national life after independence.[28]

EFFECTIVE TEACHING FOR MUSLIMS: THE REVIVIFICATION OF ISLAMIC EDUCATION

From the Muslim point of view it is Allāh (God) who is the
source of all knowledge that is beneficial to his creatures, God
is *one*. Beside him there is no other. Centuries before the nineteenth-century impact of European colonial expansion on the
world of Islam, Muslims had built and developed their approach
to education from that conviction. After looking to the Qurʾān
Muslims look to Islamic traditions for guidance, showing a willingness to imitate[29] the example of those who have gone before.
The supreme example to be followed is that of the Prophet
Muhammad, whose actions, beliefs and counsel on a multiplicity
of topics are contained in the various collections of traditions
(*ḥadīth*, plural *aḥādīth*) compiled after his death.[30]

Muslims living in Britain and in other parts of Europe are of
course concerned about the Islamic culture of their children.
Most Muslims would tacitly agree that the old-fashioned teaching
methods of the Qurʾānic school are inadequate and ineffective
today. At the same time they would insist that education should
be instrumental in bringing the young to a fuller understanding
of Islam, and to a deeper awareness of their distinctive cultural
heritage. The question is whether or not the core of the Islamic
curriculum can be revitalized to attract and hold the interest of
young students who have increasing access to western ideas.
Attempts have been made from time to time by groups of
concerned Muslims in Europe to recognize this problem, and to
revivify an approach to education which has become somewhat

ossified. One of these recent initiatives produced a handbook of suggestions which (whatever its eventual success) shows evidence of an attempt in Britain to revitalize education for Muslims on classical Islamic principles.

This handbook is entitled *Guidelines and syllabus on Islamic education.*[31] Both the first part (Guidelines) and the second part (Syllabus) are designed to provide religious education for Muslim children in Great Britain. The guidelines make suggestions about the meaning of religious education, implying – as has already been noted – that for Muslims religious education is not just one subject among many. The handbook contains sections on suitable material for different age groups in school, with some comments which may surprise those unfamiliar with this approach. On the teaching of children in the first stages of school there is this paragraph:

> As children are too small to understand any abstract concept, the only form of religious teaching that can be imparted is by making them imitate the parents and teachers and by conditioning their minds. They should learn by heart the *Arabic* version of the *kalimah*[32] and through the question–answer method know that they are Muslims, their religion is Islam, their prophet is Muhammad, peace and blessings of Allah the Almighty be on him, and that Allah the Almighty and his Prophet love us and we should love and respect them and obey them.[33]

Among the guidelines suggested for the teaching of children at the secondary school stage the authors comment:

> This is by far the most crucial period in the mental development of children. It is a period of idealism as well as questioning, doubts, rebellion, and frustrations. In modern times when the atmosphere of the society in the west is charged with anti-religious sentiments and attitudes, it is becoming increasingly difficult for our children to accept dogma and orthodoxy unquestioningly and to obey authority with reverence. Only by making children see religion as a historical and spiritual reality, by showing that the basis of our culture is in absolute values, that religion alone enunciates and provides, and by presenting Islam as a natural and psychologically acceptable reality, that we may build up within children the force that will resist evil powers and strengthen the forces of the good. [Children] should be made to realize that if they choose relativism in place of absolute values, they will become morally, spiritually, and intellectually thoroughly confused.[34]

The recommendations for theological and cultural studies include study of the *Qurᵓān* and the *Ḥadīth*. With regard to other world religions the authors of the handbook are explicit.

> As students at this stage are going to be confronted with the problem of realizing in what way Islam is superior to all other religions and ideologies, in what way it is the most liberal as well as the most comprehensive way of life, how it is the most orthodox and at the same time the most advanced form of ideal, they should be allowed to compare

Islam with other forms of religion and all new ideologies, especially the humanistic ideology of Humanism and Marxism.[35]

The pre-suppositions of the authors of these guidelines are nowhere more apparent in their section on the cultural aspects of Islamic education:

The last two years of the secondary stage should be devoted to [the development of a] full appreciation of Muslim culture, and of the Muslim contribution to modern civilization. This contribution has to be assessed from two points of view: the point of view of the historian who looks at past contributions and finds out how modern western civilization and its culture are indebted fundamentally to the growth and spread of Islam; and the point of view of the modern Muslim thinker who wants to find how Muslim Culture, based on the Islamic concept of values, can resist the onslaught of technological dehumanization, and establish man's position as the vice-regent of Allah the Almighty on earth.[36]

There is much more in this handbook which teachers will find of interest. The extracts quoted here are by no means untypical of the general approach to education of many influential Muslims. The point to be noted is that these recommendations are for Muslims who are already British citizens. If the suggestions genuinely reflect the educational wishes and aspirations of Muslim parents for their children in British schools, it is clear that the declared aims of pluralism and of multi-culture education are contrary to Muslim expectations.

No system of education can be protected from the stultifying effects of student apathy and teacher indifference. Islamic education is no exception, but from time to time during the history of Islam there have been great teachers who have revived its traditions and given them renewed significance. In doing so, they have given encouragement to teachers far beyond their own time and outside their own community of faith. Two of the most famous exponents of a revitalized Islamic education were al-Ghazālī and Ibn Khaldūn. Al-Ghazālī, one of the greatest theologians and mystics in the history of Islam, lived from AD 1058 to 1111.[37] Ibn Khaldūn, known primarily for his philosophy of history, lived from AD 1332 to 1406. Both men influenced their contemporaries profoundly, and both left a legacy of guidance for teachers on the principles of education which can be studied with profit today whether one is a Muslim or not. Both demonstrate that Islamic education may proceed in conformity with orthodox religious beliefs without degenerating into sterile indoctrination.

According to al-Ghazālī and Ibn Khaldūn the key to effective teaching is the right relationship between the teacher and the pupil. On the subject of knowledge as a Muslim would understand it, al-Ghazālī wrote:

This knowledge is not attained by means of the various special branches of knowledge to which most people devote their attention. As a result, most people's knowledge only makes them bolder in disobeying God most high. Genuine knowledge, however, increases a man's reverence and fear and hope; and these come between him and sins (in the strict sense) as distinct from the unintentional faults which are inseparable from man in his times of weakness.[38]

Al-Ghazālī's achievement was to show how Islam, properly understood, is perfectly compatible with modernity in any age. As a scholar and a teacher he was able to demonstrate this in education, in *Islamic* education, and to show that Islam is a dynamic faith which is capable of great flexibility, and well able to meet contemporary needs as they arise. The authentic tradition of reform within Islam, as of Islamic education by which it is transmitted from one generation to the next, is rooted in orthodoxy. Reform which is not consistent with the inherited tradition is innovation of an unacceptable kind. The past cannot be jettisoned to make Islam acceptable to the modern temper.

On the subject of educational practice al-Ghazālī has a good deal to say. Education begins in the environment of the home long before the start of formal education in school. The child is a trust placed by God in the hands of his parents, and his innocent heart is a precious element capable of taking impressions.[39] If a child's teachers (including his parents) bring the child up according to the principles of Islam, they will be rewarded by God, and the child will live happily in this world and the next. If the teachers fail in this responsibility, they will be judged for their neglect, and the child will be unhappy in both this world and the next.

Anyone who instructs the young 'must be as tender to his pupils as if they were his own children'. He must correct moral lapses through hinting rather than direct prohibition, gentle advice rather than reproof. Above all, he himself must set an example so that his actions accord with his precepts. The pupil's own diligence responds to divine inspiration under the guidance of the teacher. 'Knowledge exists potentially in the human soul like a seed in the soil; by learning the potential becomes actual.' This does not deny the importance of human reason, but it places reason lower than divine grace.

Ibn Khaldūn followed some two hundred years after the death of al-Ghazālī, and shared the latter's views on the limits of human reason, especially in higher education, with which he was chiefly concerned. He urges all students in difficulties with their studies to seek the guidance of God 'which illuminated the way of learners before you and taught them that which they knew not'. Young children are to be treated with compassion in education. Teachers are not to expect that students from different cultural backgrounds will necessarily attain comparable standards in their achievement.

The people of the east are on the whole more steeped in the craft of teaching as well as in other crafts, so much so that those who travel from the west to the east in quest of learning presume that the people of the east are naturally endowed with better minds, and that the difference between them is one of a difference between two species of human beings, whereas it is simply the result of an increased intelligence through civilization.[40]

The influence of al-Ghazālī and Ibn Khaldun was decisive for several centuries, and still has a powerful hold on many Muslim minds. In the nineteenth and twentieth centuries the tradition of internal reform, in education as in every other aspect of life, based on the conviction that Islam is compatible with modernity, was developed in more radical ways by men like Muhammad Abduh, Rashīd Riḍa, and Tāhā Husayn.[41] In the continuing attempts to revitalize Islamic education teachers are reminded that generations of their predecessors have faced sharp criticism because of their failure to live up to the Islamic ideal. Nevertheless, in spite of human failings the ideal remains to present a challenge to all teachers today.

The essence of Muslim education is stated in the divine revelation in the Qurʾan, and is re-stated in greater detail in the traditions of the prophet Muhammad. It took more than two centuries of practice for still more detailed exposition of theory to be formulated . . . . During this long period of practice that preceded the detailed formulation of theory there developed in the public mind an unfavourable image of the teacher who taught for material reward. In anecdotes, proverbs, and poetry he is depicted as a person of little intelligence and less judgement, an object of caustic and pitiless ridicule, very much like the pedagogue in Greek history.

'Know, O brother, that your teacher is the begetter of your soul, just as your father is the begetter of your body. Your father gave you a physical form, but your teacher gives you a spiritual one. Your teacher nourishes your soul with learning and wisdom, and guides it to attain everlasting bliss. Your father brought you up and trained you to make a living in this transient world.'[42]

A CONTINUING DILEMMA

This chapter began with a recognition of the fact that Islamic education is not provided in state schools, and that as far as can be reasonably foreseen, there is little likelihood that it will ever replace existing practice. It would, however, be unrealistic to pretend that even among Muslims in this country there is much support for radical change. The attraction of western methods is almost irresistible, despite the vigorous protests of Islamic teachers. It is not so easy in a secular society to preserve the inviolability of Islamic principles. But even in Islamic societies the dilemma remains. The Muslim scholar, the 'religious' graduate, the $^c\bar{a}lim$ – defined earlier as one who is learned in the knowledge which God reveals, as a result of his study of the classical religious sciences

is liable to find himself a less esteemed, less significant, member of the community; the 'scientific' graduate enjoys a more lucrative and estimable rôle. It is, in part, this recession in social status that underlies the assertive temper aiming to arrest it, though aggressive conservatism of mind can also be found among students in scientific disciplines determined to resist their secular temptations.

The sensitive observer will recognize the human emotions these tensions entail, for – in human terms – there is nothing about them unique to Islam. . . . Islam is not static. For many the old allegiance loses its sacrosanct authority. Religion may then be a cultural expression, rather than a sure conviction.[43]

The Islamic world is divided by internal conflicts and dissension. This is not only the legacy of ancient divisions between *Sunnī* Muslims and *Shīʿī* Muslims, once again brought into focus by drawn-out struggles such as the war between Iran and Iraq.[44] The tension between the old and the new is nowhere more evident than in the intellectual life of Muslims, and in their attitudes to education. Despite intensive local efforts, the incidence of illiteracy in Islamic countries is still high. What kind of education will best serve the needs of those who have to live and work in the modern world? Will it be the modern 'western' type of education which Muslims affect to despise, but which many of them pursue for the benefits it undoubtedly brings to their developing economies? Or will it be the traditional kind of Islamic education, rooted in the past, and founded on the Qurʾān, the *sunna* of the Prophet Muhammad, the *ḥadīth*, and the *sharīʿa*? In a pluralist society like Britain many younger Muslims have already effectively chosen the former.

There are other things to be considered if these different emphases are to influence the development of education in Britain. Earlier in the book[45] reference was made to the responsibilities which all teachers have to share if education for cultural diversity is to be anything more than a sectional interest. Here is a case in point: the ability of Islam to meet the needs of human beings living in a world that owes so much to the principles of the Enlightenment is being questioned inside, as well as outside, the Islamic world, although internal criticism has been made more costly recently, as Fouad Ajami has recently pointed out.

On the present situation under the Ayatollah Ruhollah Khomeini in Iran he wrote:

At every turning point, when the dust settled, the battle [i.e. between 'un-Islamic' privilege on the one side and indiscriminate wrath based on 'Islamic' principles on the other] was won by men – soldiers, dynasts, and lately mullahs – who harboured no illusions about the ground on which they stood, who were not 'burdened' with enlightenment ideas, or consumed with petitioning the West, who did not have their heads crammed with foreign books and doctrines. The outcome has been the same in Sunni societies – Egypt, Syria, Pakistan – and in Iran, the sole Shī^ca state in the realm of Islam.[46]

This criticism, from one who knows the Arab and the Islamic worlds well, is not so easy to answer at a time when the impact of violence in the name of Islamic *jihād* is being felt in several parts of Europe as well as in the Near East. It may be that from the point of view of western educational theory a more damaging criticism is made of the approach of a man who has already been acknowledged above as one from whom educators, whether Muslim or non-Muslim, still have much to learn. Speaking of al-Ghazālī, S. L. Jaki, one of the most articulate interpreters of the history of science,[47] made the following comment:

A thousand years ago the great Muslim mystic al Ghazzali denounced natural laws, the very objectives of science, as a blasphemous constraint upon the free will of Allah. Today, the impossibility of making ends meet without science forces the Muslim world to reconsider its notion of Allah. It is an agonizing process, which, in spite of bloodshed, may, in the long run, bring a more rational mentality to troubled parts of the world.[48]

Are these views to be summarily dismissed as hostile to Islam, and to the Islamic approach to education, merely because they do not reflect the orthodox views which many Muslims (for understandable reasons) wish to see prevail universally? Is any attempt at critical evaluation to be instantly identified as further evidence that the West can only misunderstand Islam? At some point education about Islam, even in schools, has to go beyond the Five Pillars i.e. the religious duties of a Muslim, important as these are. Or are teachers *in a pluralist society* to make exceptions when it comes to critical inquiry? These are educational questions, and we need the help of Muslims who are prepared not only to interpret their own cultural pre-suppositions and to defend their own beliefs, but also to show that they are aware of the real difficulties presented to the western mind by Islamic theory of knowledge. Teachers of science who are also Muslims have a unique opportunity to respond to this real need.

NOTES AND REFERENCES

1. The words are those of the nineteenth-century Muslim reformer, Muhammad Abduh, quoted in Tibawi A L 1972 *Islamic Education: its Traditions and Modernization into the Arab National Systems.* Luzac, p 71
2. Ahmad Khurshid 1968 *Principles of Islamic Education.* Lahore, p 24
3. Yusuf Islam, the former pop-singer Cat Stevens, who converted to Islam in 1977, commenting in 1986 on his efforts to establish the Islamiya Primary School in Brondesbury Park, London. A report by Edward Vulliamy about the attitudes of Muslims in London towards this project, the first attempt in Britain to set up an Islamic voluntary aided school, appeared in the *Guardian*, 2 April 1986, p 3. Yusuf Islam's song 'Morning has broken' has become widely popular in state schools and elsewhere
4. Ibid., giving the views of Raja Riaz, secretary of the local Pakistani Workers' Association
5. Ibid., quoting the opinion of Mohammed Rashid, leader of the local Pakistani Social and Cultural Association. Although still a lively issue, the question of single-sex education, and the alleged inequality of educational opportunity as between men and women in the Islamic world, is a less pressing practical problem in Britain. It is duly acknowledged here, but not treated further for reasons of space. The subject is dealt with by Yvonne Haddad in *Contemporary Islam and the Challenge of History*. State University of New York, Albany, 1982, pp 57ff.
6. Saqeb Ghulam Nabi 1983 'Comments from the Islamic point of view', in *Muslim Children Present their Faith*, Research Papers, Muslims in Europe, no 19, Nielsen Jørgen S (ed), Centre for the Study of Islam and Christian–Muslim Relations, Selly Oak Colleges, Birmingham, Sept. p 28. A further comment from this report is mentioned in Chapter 7 below, p 146
7. Ibid., p 35
8. As was made clear in the Introduction, there is insufficient space to include general information about the origins and development of all the religions and life-stances referred to in this book. Each chapter will include references to useful introductory books on the broader subject of beliefs and practices, and the reading list at the end contains additional titles for further reading
9. The Koran (*al-Qurʾān*) is the holy book of Islam, which contains in its 114 chapters (*sūrahs*) what God (Allāh) revealed to the Prophet Muhammad during the period AD 610–632. The first of these dates marks the call of Muhammad to be the Messenger of God. The second is the year of Muhammad's death. The Qurʾān is, supremely, a book for public lection. Muslims are taught to respect it as the Word of God, to read it privately, and to learn as much of as they can it by heart, but this Word of God is, above all, to be *heard*. The word *Qurʾān* means 'that which is recited' or 'read aloud', and its public reading is regarded as a great responsibility which may call for years of study and practice.
   The Qurʾān is still of decisive importance for Muslims today. They

believe that it is untranslatable. Indeed, the literary excellence of the original Arabic is such that it is held to be evidence of its divine origin. It is the *Arabic* Qurʾān which remains at the heart of Islamic worship and devotion, even where Arabic is not the language of ordinary conversation. Vernacular *versions* are permitted, but they can never displace the original, or come close to its grandeur.

English versions of the Arabic text include: Pickthall M M 1960 *The Meaning of the Glorious Koran*, New York, Mentor Books; and Arberry A J 1964 *The Koran Interpreted*, World's Classics, republished in paperback as *The Koran*, 1984 (Oxford University Press). For a study of Islamic interpretation of the Qurʾān, see Ali A. Yusuf 1976 *The Holy Qurʾ-an*, Lahore. This large volume contains both the Arabic text and an English version side by side. It also has extensive explanatory notes in English

10. *The Parents' Manual* 1972 Muslim Students' Association. Crescent Publications. Takoma Park, Maryland, p 3
11. Qurʾān 20: 114
12. Ahmad Khurshid *Principles of Islamic Education.* p 1
13. Asad Muhammad 1969 *Islam at the Crossroads*, republished in Lahore, p 8 (first published 1934). Muhammad Asad was the Islamic name taken by Leopold Weiss in 1926 when he converted to Islam. Weiss was born in Poland in 1900. He was the grandson of an Orthodox rabbi and the son of a lawyer. He declined to train as a rabbi himself, and became a journalist instead, with special interests in the Arab world. He was a sensitive interpreter of Islamic culture to Europeans. His book *The Road to Mecca* (see Recommended Reading, p 168) is a classic interpretation of the attraction of Islam for one brought up in the European tradition
14. Asad Muhammad *Islam at the Crossroads*, pp 9–10
15. Ibid., p 61
16. Ibid., p 84
17. Nasr S H 1975 *Islam and the Plight of Modern Man.* Longman, p 19
18. The root meaning of the word *jihād* for a Muslim is 'striving to one's uttermost', especially to fulfil the commands of God. Not without reason, the word *jihād* has assumed a rather sinister meaning in the western world, calling up visions of terrible acts committed in a 'holy war'. The word merits closer scrutiny. There are many different ways of striving on behalf of God, ways which use the word *warfare* in a figurative sense. Those Muslims who engage in *jihād*, i.e. *mujāhidīn* (another word with sinister overtones in the western media) may not all be freedom fighters or terrorists, depending on which side of the war one is fighting. Students and teachers are also engaged in a form of *jihād* in education. Striving for the sake of God involves a level of continuing effort worthy of being called *ijtihād*
19. Extract from the report of the first World Conference on Muslim Education held in Jedda, Saudi Arabia, 31 March to 8 April 1978. See my article, 'Contemporary Muslim attitudes to the relationship between religious faith and education', in *Spectrum*, vol. 10 no 2, Jan. 1978, pp 29–30
20. The tendency of non-directive education to assume a distinctly directive character has been examined in my book, *Commitment and*

Neutrality in Religious Education. Geoffrey Chapman, 1979 (see especially pp 39–53)
21. The Qurʾān encourages the pursuit of knowledge by all Muslims who are *ṭullāb*, or seekers after knowledge (of God). Several examples could be given, but teachers who are interested would gain a great deal from reading the book through for themselves in one or other of the English versions mentioned in note 9 above. The Qurʾān is not a long book. It is less than two-thirds of the length of the New Testament. Knowledge of God is wisdom, but it is not gained merely through human striving. One quotation will demonstrate the point: '[God] giveth wisdom to whom he will, and he to whom wisdom is given hath had much good given him' (Qurʾān 2: 27)
22. The word *mosque* is derived from the Arabic word *masjid*, i.e. 'place of prostration', and hence, a place where public prayer (notably public congregational prayer) takes place in the community. But the mosque is an important meeting place for other reasons, as the paragraph in the text makes clear
23. Muslims do not think of the imam as a priest, or minister, in the European sense. He is the leader of the local community, and frequently a teacher and an arbiter in matters of dispute. His title, which derives from an Arabic preposition, indicates that he stands *before*, or *in front of*, the community which he leads in public prayer. In every sense he is an exemplary figure
24. 'The Beautiful Names of God' number ninety-nine, and each of them reminds a Muslim of some aspect of the nature of God's dealings with his human creatures. The names are taken from the Qur'ān, and include the following, 'the Merciful', 'the Compassionate', 'the King', 'the Holy', 'the Protector', 'the Creator', 'the Forgiving', 'the Truth', 'the Destroyer', 'the One', 'the First', 'the Last', 'the Light' and 'the Incomparable'. This litany of names is often committed to memory by Muslims, and recited as an act of devotion with the aid of a rosary which consists of thirty-three beads, told three times over. This practice is not universally accepted in Islam, however
25. Hughes T P 1885 *A Dictionary of Islam*. Scribner Welford & Co., p 106
26. The success of modern institutions modelled on western standards tends to obscure the issue which many Muslims are eager to raise about Islamic education. This is one of the reasons why, even in Britain in recent years, there has been talk about the establishment of an Islamic university in this country
27. Hughes *A Dictionary of Islam*, p 106
28. Tibawi *Islamic Education*, pp 223–24
29. The word *imitate* has been used here deliberately. The Arabic word *taqlīd* bears several meanings, one of which is of interest in the context of educational theory and practice. *Taqlīd* may stand for tradition which is inaccessible to criticism, a tradition which encourages students to emulate their teachers in fidelity to Islamic teachings and principles. The authority of the tradition (and the authority of the teacher who is transmitting it to the student) give a different

quality to Islamic education, where a good memory takes precedence over the development of critical acumen. Applied to education, the principle of *taqlīd*, though respectful of tradition, may be considered by non-Muslims to encourage learning by rote, and to discourage free and critical inquiry. Muslims do not accept that this is necessarily so. What emerges from discussions on the point with Muslims is the fear that the authority of Islamic beliefs and traditions might be diluted if their children are encouraged to question it in an un-Islamic way

30. The literature on *hadīth* is extensive. There are some interesting collections in English which provide a good introduction to the subject, and which are a rich source of teaching material. See, for example, *Gardens of the Righteous, Riyadh as-Salihin*, 1975, by Imam Nawawi, translated from the Arabic by Zafrulla Khan, Curzon Press, London. Recapitulation of the life of the Prophet Muhammad (AD 570–632) is beyond the scope of this book. The *hijra*, or 'decisive move' from Mecca, the city of his birth, to Medina, where he established the first Islamic community (*ummah*), took place in 622. This date marks the beginning of the Islamic era, hence AD 622 becomes AH 1 in the Islamic calendar (i.e. the first year after the *hijra*) For simplicity in this book conventional European dating has been used throughout, with exceptions where necessary. Useful information is to be found in Philip Hitti's *History of the Arabs*, Macmillan, 1973. Important topics in Islam such as *shahāda* (bearing witness), *salāt* (public worship and prayer), *zakāt* (the giving of alms), *sawm* (fasting during the month of Ramadān) and *hajj* (the pilgrimage to Mecca) are treated fully in the *Encyclopaedia of Islam*, which is a mine of information for students

31. The handbook was published in London in 1976 by the Union of Muslim Organizations of the United Kingdom and Eire (UMO)

32. The Arabic word *kalimah* means, literally, 'word'. In this case it is the basic creed of Islam which is 'There is no god but Allāh [God], and Muhammad is the Messenger of God'

33. UMO *Guidelines and Syllabus on Islamic Education*, p 8. On the question of imitating parents and teachers, see note 29 above

34. *Guidelines and Syllabus on Islamic Education*, p 10

35. Ibid., p 12

36. Ibid., p 13

37. Al-Ghazālī's dates, according to the Islamic calendar, are AH 450–505 i.e. 450–505 years after the *hijra*

38. Watt W. Montgomery (tr) 1953 *The Faith and Practice of Al-Ghazali*, Allen & Unwin, pp 84–85. The passage quoted comes from the closing parts of *al-Munqidh min al-Dalāl*, literally, 'that which delivers from error'

39. This necessarily brief section is based on a reading of *The Deliverance from Error* and *The Beginning of Guidance*, in W. Montgomery Watt's *The Faith and Practice of al-Ghazali* and A L Tibawi's *Islamic Education*, pp 35–44

40. Tibawi *Islamic Education*, pp 43–44

41. The work of these three influential Muslims cannot be discussed here, but readers who are interested can consult A Hourani 1962

Arabic Thought in the Liberal Age, 1798–1939. Oxford University Press, pp 130–92, 222–44, 324–40

42. Tibawi *Islamic Education*, pp 35, 39
43. Cragg Kenneth 1986 *The Call of the Minaret*. 2nd edn, rev and enlarged, Collins, p 21
44. See Momen Moojan 1985 *An Introduction to Shiʿi Islam: the History and Doctrines of Twelver Shiʿism*, Yale University Press
45. See section in text, *Common responsibilities and aims*, Chapter 1, p. 10
46. Ajami Fouad 1986 'The impossible life of Moslem liberalism: the doctrines of Ali Shariati and their defeat', in *The New Republic*, 2 June, p 26
47. Jaki Stanley L 1966 *The Relevance of Physics*. University of Chicago Press. The chapters on 'Physics and Ethics', 'Physics and Theology', pp 371–457, and 'The Place of Physics in Human Culture', pp 501–33, do not set out to draw attention to any difference between 'western' science and 'Islamic' science, but for a 'western' scientist (and theologian) like Jaki the difference is clear. His book is not lacking in controversy, but its ideas might well be used – at suitable levels – by teachers with qualifications in science, to probe some of the issues of cultural diversity from a different perspective
48. Jaki S L 1985 'On whose side is history?', in *National Review*, 23 Aug. p 46

CHAPTER 3

Jewish perspectives: 'You shall teach them diligently to your children'

In contrast with the tendency of Western education to break up the content of a social heritage into different kinds of subject matter, the traditional type of Jewish education retained the Jewish social heritage in the undifferentiated form in which it was lived. When the youngster studied Torah, he studied simultaneously everything that had to do with making him a worthy member of the Jewish community.[1]

In a discussion between two scholars of the fourth century, one asked, 'Is it possible to find any Jew without an elementary education?' He was answered, 'Yes, it is possible – a child taken captive by non-Jews.'[2]

During the last twenty-five years or so the number of Jews in Britain has declined. It might be more accurate to say that the number of *practising* Jews has declined. A reason for this is the tendency for young Jews to lose something of their distinctive identity by marrying out of their own community. The latest figures show that there are still some 350,000 Jews in this country. While expressing disappointment at the loss of any member of their communities, Jewish leaders have claimed that the *quality* of Jewish life among those who remain has improved. If this is so, education has played its part, for at every level, from the primary school to the *yeshivah*,[3] in the home and in the synagogue, Jews are encouraged to work out the implications of *Torah* and *Talmud* for life in the modern world.[4]

It is well known that Jews have made outstanding contributions to learning in many fields of study in the secular world, but here is not the place to consider this formidable achievement. What is being sought in this chapter is an understanding of the basic principles of Jewish education as they have been expressed in the scriptural title-deeds of Judaism, and in the reinterpretation of those principles by Jewish teachers. Here, as in other chapters of the book, the question is, 'What can be learned from *this* tradition which might be of service in promoting education for cultural diversity?' Before this can be attempted, however, another question must be raised. What *is* Jewish education?

Although this is a vast subject, with an extensive literature, some useful pointers can be given. To begin with, attention may be drawn to the Jewish understanding of the *creative* work of God, and of the *Covenant* relationship between God and his chosen people. Then there is the Jewish experience of God's power to deliver them from both physical and spiritual bondage. Knowledge and understanding of these aspects of divine activity are an essential part of the Jewish religious experience. The transmission of this knowledge to succeeding generations of students, and the development of an understanding in them of what it means to be a Jew is an essential part of Jewish education. And among the distinctive beliefs and values which influence the course and content of Jewish education are the following.

A belief in the unity of God, interpreted in a qualitative way; that is, a belief not only that God is one, but that *in his being* he is *uniquely* one. *The value of community*. Judaism, while protecting the rights and freedoms of the individual, is not a solitary religion. Jews are urged not to separate themselves from the community. *The right to choose*. Jews resist the imposition of external authority, without denying the importance of their ancient traditions. But respect for the past does not prevent them from subjecting it to critical scrutiny. The choice to observe the ordinances is a personal one. It is made, not because it is commanded, but because it is seen to bring peace and harmony. *The unique value of every individual*. Life is precious. Each person has a contribution to make to the health of society. Every life can make a difference in the 'fixing', or the changing of the world (*tikun olam*, 'repair of the world'). And without denying the possibility of life after death Jews prefer to give their attention to this life. *The value of charity*. Deeds rather than words help to mitigate the suffering and need in the world. Each individual has a responsibility for others. *The value of celebration*. Despite the existence of evil and suffering there is much in the world to affirm and to celebrate. Religious liberty and human freedom are to be affirmed, defended and celebrated.

There is an important point to be noted about the relationship between the teacher and the pupil in traditional Jewish education. Ideally, it is a one-to-one relationship, involving master and pupil in a common pursuit of knowledge. The former is more than a purveyor of knowledge. He is an exemplary figure who exemplifies what he teaches. The pupil seeks to emulate the teacher in every aspect of Jewish life, and in the company of a fellow-student seeks to learn more by reflecting on what is being taught. This approach is very different from that which is to be found in schools today, where over-sized classes, specialist subject teachers and a broad curriculum make individual tuition over lengthy periods almost impossible.

REVELATION AND RESPONSE

The dealings of God with his chosen people, the Jews, are documented and, to some extent interpreted, in the Bible.[5] The Bible is the record of God's *educative* activity. For this reason it is to be taken as the primary source-book for understanding Jewish education. The interpretation of that experience, in the light of all that has happened to the Jews, individually and collectively, remains a vital part of Jewish education. In the widest sense, the revelation of God's purposes for his creation, expressed not only in divinely instituted Teaching (*Torah*) but also in the history of a particular people, continues to provide the principal focus for Jewish education. For present purposes it will be helpful to identify some of the issues in Jewish education, and to note in particular the importance of the Bible in establishing the principles by which Jewish education proceeds.

WHO IS A JEW?

Judaism presents no simple picture of uniformity to an outside observer. Like other living religions, Judaism is reinterpreted by its adherents in each succeeding generation. Controversy and disagreements are not unknown among Jews, but all Jews recognize their dependence on a shared background of religious history and ethical teaching. Underlying the differences of opinion and interpretation there is a sense of community. One of the most distinguished Jewish teachers of the twentieth century maintained that there was only one way to define the essence of Judaism, despite all the differences of opinion and interpretation:

It is the awareness of God's interest in man, the awareness of a covenant, of a responsibility that lies on Him as well as on us. . . . God is in need of man for the attainment of His ends, and religion, as Jewish tradition understands it, is a way of serving these ends, of which we are in need, even though we may not be aware of them; ends which we must learn to feel the need of.[6]

Many Jews would sympathize with this attempt at definition, and might agree that it provides a basis for a systematic approach to Jewish education. An awareness of what Heschel describes as 'God's interest in man', of a covenant relationship between God and his human creatures which imposes responsibilities on both parties, and of the purposes of God, is to be *acquired*. Education serves to promote this awareness. The fruit of education is knowledge, and the wisdom to use it. This knowledge cannot be acquired without instruction, discipline and correction. God is the ultimate source of knowledge and wisdom, and it is in response to what is taken to be a divine command that Jewish

education begins. This instruction to teach includes a reference
to the content of the teaching, 'You shall teach *them* [i.e. the
details of the instruction, or teaching, which God revealed to
Moses on Mount Sinai] diligently to your children.'[7] Who, then,
is a Jew? An ancient tradition gives the answer: 'Whoever
proclaims the *Shema* is termed a Jew.'

Hear, O Israel: the Lord our God is one Lord; and you shall love the
Lord your God with all your heart, and with all your soul, and with all
your might. And these words which I command you this day shall be
upon your heart; *and you shall teach them diligently to your children*,
and shall talk of them when you sit in your house, and when you walk
the way, and when you lie down, and when you rise. And you shall bind
them as a sign upon your hand, and they shall be as frontlets between
your eyes. And you shall write them on the doorposts of your house and
on your gates.[8]

To be a Jew is to be saved from isolation by being identified
with a community. Others might add, especially in more recent
times, that it is to be saved from *placelessness* by being identified
with a *particular* land, the Land of Israel. In the modern world
Jews aspire to be released from the bondage of oppression so that
they may be free to pursue their vocation as Jews. Throughout
their history the Jewish people have been sustained in their
individual and collective suffering by recalling the Covenant
relationship. No event in that history has tested the nature of the
relationship between God and his people more than the Holocaust when, between 1939 and 1945, six million Jews were
systematically destroyed in Nazi concentration camps. Many
millions more who were not Jews also suffered a similar fate, but
for Jews this fearful slaughter of their own people, amounting to
genocide, retains a special significance.[9] Writing of this terrible
period in terms which call readers not only to a remembrance,
but also to a re-living, of the past, the winner of the Nobel Peace
Prize for 1986, Elie Wiesel, wrote:

By its uniqueness, the Holocaust defies literature. We think we are
describing an event, we transmit only its reflection. No-one has the right
to speak for the dead, no-one has the power to make them speak. No
image, is sufficiently demented, no cry sufficiently blasphemous to il-
luminate the plight of a single victim, resigned or rebellious, walking
silently towards death, beyond anger, beyond regret.
   Therein lies the dilemma of the story-teller who sees himself essentially as a witness, the drama of the messenger unable to deliver his
message. . . . Still, the story had to be told. In spite of all risks, all possible misunderstandings. It needed to be told for the sake of our children.
So they will know where they come from, and what their heritage is.[10]

Freed from the threat of vulnerability Jews seek to build up
a community based upon justice, peace and love, in obedience
to what God has revealed. This is the ideal to be realized in the

state of Israel. The word *Jew* is indivisible from that Land. The re-creation of the Jewish state of Israel re-established and re-focused Jewish identity for many Jews. Failure to re-establish their homeland in Palestine prior to 1948 resulted from their power-lessness, not from lack of desire or interest. No other place outside the Land could be the goal for Messianic-oriented Jews. That particular geographical setting alone meets the needs of the Messianic vision. This follows from the Jewish understanding of Covenant promises, and the continuity of peoplehood, all of which derive from the unique relationship which Jews believe to exist between God and his chosen people. The Hebrew language, synagogue services, holy days, Jewish education and the insti-tution of Sabbath, all connect the participants directly with the Covenant and with the Land. Yet none of these distinct features of Jewish culture is prized by Jews because it invests them with a superiority over other people. On the contrary, they are living signs of a faith which, even in the darkest recesses of oppression and suffering, carries a note of optimism for everyone in the world. By being faithful to their tradition, Jews feel that they can best serve the interests of others as well as themselves.

The unique quality of Judaism's optimism is that despite the prevalence of wickedness in this world, it does not succumb to mere indifference to, or resignation in, this world. Its ideal is not that of the sage of antiquity who, satisfied with his own wisdom and peace of mind, is no longer moved by the struggles of man. In this respect, Judaism differs radically from the thought of Greece and India. It faces the world with the will to change it and with the commandment to realize the good in it. The sage of antiquity knows only the satisfaction of his own content-ment. Judaism never abandons the goal of the world since it has no doubt in the God who has bid men to march to that goal. Its optimism is the strength of the mortal will; its call is 'Prepare the way!'[11]

Jews today consider themselves to be descendants of the Jewish people of antiquity, and heirs to the Covenant, even though the majority of modern Jewry may no longer be motiv-ated by traditional religious concerns, such as keeping the detailed religious laws and statutes (*mitzvoth*). For religious Jews the fulfilment of the Messianic kingdom will come in the last days. The Messiah will be of Jewish lineage, of the House of David. Signs of *shalom* (an almost untranslatable word, but meaning 'peace' in the most profound sense) accompany the coming of the Messiah. Before this can happen comes the return of the Jews to their own Land. This return brings hope not merely for Jews, but also for all those who have experienced alienation. For Jews there will be an in-gathering of the diaspora Jews outside the Land of Israel. The light of deliverance will dawn for all the world. For the present, however, the *Torah*, the div-inely revealed teaching of God, remains the agent of salvation.

THE JEWISH EXPERIENCE OF DELIVERANCE: EDUCATION AND FREEDOM

The belief that 'in the beginning God created the heavens and the earth'[12] is decisive for Jewish education. The creation stories and the other myths in the first eleven chapters of the book of Genesis describe in vivid language the origins of a unique relationship between God and his human creatures. The Bible insists that the initiative for the relationship is God's. It is for human creatures to respond, and they can choose to do so in a variety of ways. They can choose to be obedient to his revealed will, or they can choose to disobey. The crucial turning point for a people who claim the rights of inheritance to *eretz Israel* [13] (the Land of Israel), because of a promise made by God to their ancestor Abraham,[14] was the Exodus. Under the leadership of Moses, God delivered them from slavery. This deliverance has never been forgotten by Jews.

[The Egyptians] set taskmasters over them to afflict them with heavy burdens; and they built for Pharaoh store-cities, Pithom and Ramses. But the more [the people of Israel] were oppressed, the more they multiplied and the more they spread abroad. And the Egyptians were in dread of the people of Israel. So they made the people of Israel serve with rigour, and made their lives bitter with hard service, in mortar and brick, and in all kinds of work in the field.[15]

In the course of time God 'heard the groaning of the people of Israel whom the Egyptians hold in bondage',[16] and brought about their deliverance, guiding them under the leadership of Moses to safety through the waters of the Red Sea (most probably the narrow north-western part of it known as *Yam Suf*, or 'Sea of Reeds').

Then the Lord said to Moses, 'Stretch out your hand over the sea, that the water may come back upon the Egyptians, upon their chariots, and upon their horsemen'. So Moses stretched forth his hand over the sea, and the sea returned to its wonted flow when the morning appeared; and the Egyptians fled into it, and the Lord routed the Egyptians in the midst of the sea. The waters returned and covered the chariots and the horsemen and all the host of Pharaoh that had followed them into the sea; not so much as one of them remained. But the people of Israel walked on dry ground through the sea, the waters being a wall to them on their right hand and on their left. Thus the Lord saved Israel that day from the hand of the Egyptians; and Israel saw the Egyptians dead upon the seashore. And Israel saw the great work which the Lord did against the Egyptians, and the people feared the Lord; and they believed in the Lord and in his servant Moses.[17]

The deliverance from slavery was a unique mark of divine favour for the people of Israel, whose descendants believe that the promise God made at that time still stands: 'The Lord said to Moses, "Depart, go up hence, you and the people you have brought up out of the land of Egypt, to the land of which I swore to Abraham, Isaac, and Jacob, saying, To your descendants I will give it. . . . Go up to a land flowing with milk and honey."[18]

THE BIBLE AS A SOURCE-BOOK FOR UNDERSTANDING JEWISH EDUCATION

The Bible provides Jews with guidance about the regulation of personal and community life. The Bible is the primary source for an understanding of the principles on which Jewish education is based. It is not a handbook of educational theory and practice. It contains many instructions (but few tips) for would-be teachers, no detailed curriculum suggestions and no developed philosophy of education. Nevertheless, the importance of education is assumed throughout. There are many passages which have educational implications. It is these which make the reader aware of the seriousness with which teaching and learning continue to be regarded by Jews. What emerges from a reading of the Bible is an impression of the basic principles upon which Jewish education has been built and developed.

The source of knowledge and instruction for Jews is God. God has provided divine instruction (*Torah*) which it is the purpose of Jewish education to disseminate. But this fact has not affected either the confidence or the vigour with which Jews express their differences of opinion about the nature and content of education. This demonstrates the freedom they enjoy to interpret and to reinterpret their tradition. It is a freedom which Jews claim to be the consequence of obedience to a divinely revealed Law. Despite the differences there is an underlying unity which is derived from the Bible.

The religious and ethical principles which Jews seek to pass on to their children are to be found in the Bible. These principles are taught by religious Jews in obedience to the divine command noted above, 'you shall teach them diligently to your children'. For the religious Jew certain characteristic educational aims and objectives follow from the belief that God created the universe, that he sustains it, and that he continues to reveal his will and purpose. Education provides for the systematic transmission of the tradition from one generation to another, in an environment which is conducive to inherited Jewish cultural values. Education encourages a critical exploration of the tradition, and encourages individuals to appropriate for themselves the values in which they are being nurtured. Through education knowledge is disseminated, and the search for new knowledge promoted. In addition, education both transmits and refines the professional and technical skills which society needs for survival and growth. In the state of Israel since 14 May 1948, no less than in earlier times under the kings of Israel and Judah, skills of a different order are also required, in order to defend the community from external military threat.

The Biblical view pre-supposes that everything serves, or should serve, to glorify the creator. Everything which does not serve this end misses the mark. Education, in its turn, should serve to foster an understanding of God's purpose in the created order. In this sense the word *religious* as applied to education can be misleading, in that it distracts attention from the central truth that all knowledge is from God. The essence of *all* knowledge ('the beginning of wisdom', as the Wisdom literature makes clear) is 'the fear of the Lord'.[19] The aim of Jewish education, in which all the parts contribute in an organic way to the whole, is implicit in Biblical passages such as the following, where God is recorded as saying to Moses,

You have seen what I did to the Egyptians, and how I bore you on eagles' wings and brought you to myself. Now, therefore, if you will obey my voice and keep my covenant, you shall be my own possession among all peoples; for all the earth is mine, and you shall be to me a kingdom of priests and a holy nation.[20]

The Biblical record covers the events of many centuries, from the early days of nomadic existence[21] to the disturbances of the Maccabean period. Throughout this long period of time the Biblical writers stress the need for obedience to divine Law, individual responsibility and community action. With the establishment of monarchy in Israel a thousand years before the birth of Jesus, and all the administrative infrastructure which that entailed, it was necessary to make more formal arrangements for the regulation of the life of the community. Training was required to develop all the skills upon which the community depended. The source of unity amid all the diversity was the Law, which all were obliged to keep.

TORAH: DIVINE INSTRUCTION

From the beginning of their history Jews have held that moral and religious training from childhood is of the greatest importance. The responsibilities of parents to transmit to their children a knowledge and an understanding of the 'Way of the Lord' are emphasized as early as the time of Abraham'. '[The Lord said] I have chosen him, that he may charge his children and his household after him to keep the way of the Lord by doing righteousness and justice; so that the Lord may bring to Abraham what he has promised him.'[22]

Just before the Israelites crossed the Jordan to enter the Promised Land, their leader Moses said to them:

Lay to heart all the words which I enjoin upon you this day, that you may commend them to your children, that they may be careful to do all the words of this law. For it is no trifle for you, but it is your life, and thereby you shall live long in the land which you are going over the Jordan to possess.[23]

Torah, the divine instruction, or written law, revealed to Moses was the subject of public instruction. On the day when the Israelites successfully completed their crossing of the Jordan before the settlement of Canaan, Moses gave instructions for the Law to be written 'very plainly' on large stones so that the people could read it.[24] This suggests that in time sufficient numbers of the people were able to read the Law for themselves, and make the spread of literacy a matter of educational priority. Every leader was to 'write for himself' a copy of the Law, and 'meditate on it day and night'.[25] Every seventh year, at the end of the festival of Sukkoth,[26] all the people were to assemble to hear the Law read and to learn its contents. In ancient Israel the priests and Levites, as keepers and teachers of the Law, instructed the people.[27]

The teaching of *Torah* to their children has always been of the greatest importance to Jews. In its narrower sense *Torah* is the Hebrew name for the Pentateuch, the first five books of the Bible – namely, Genesis, Exodus, Leviticus, Numbers and Deuteronomy. These books are traditionally associated with Moses. Orthodox Jews believe that they were given to Moses by God on Mount Sinai. Moses then handed on to his people the teaching which he received. For Jews, *Torah* contains the Laws of God with regard to religious, moral and social conduct. It begins with accounts of creation and ends with the story of the death of Moses just before the children of Israel moved into Canaan, the Promised Land. In its wider sense *Torah* refers to the teachings of Judaism, including all that is in the Bible and the *Talmud*.

A study of the Bible discloses the range of the educative activity of God in dealing with his people. It is he who provides the measure of knowledge. Wisdom and guidance come from him. To know and to understand the will of God is to be obedient to his commands. In essence these instructions were revealed to Moses, and thence through him to the people of Israel, on Mount Sinai. The Decalogue, or the Ten Commandments, contains the principles by which God's people were to live. The Commandments are concerned with man's duties to God and to neighbour. They continue to command attention far beyond the Jewish community for whom they were first intended. They express an ethical consensus that has been interpreted and reinterpreted in the spirit, as well as according to the strict letter, of the Law.

Yet they are not so well known in detail outside Judaism as they were once. This reflects a shift in attitude in Britain from a concentration on what used to be called 'memory work' to the use of informal discussion, in which the inability to recall information accurately is more easily concealed. No doubt there have been gains as a result of the change, but there have been losses as well. For some years this reaction to intelligent rote-learning has been allowed to flourish in schools, largely unchecked. Without the accurate factual knowledge which the power of recall can provide, many discussions are merely uninformed and pointless. With such knowledge many more discussions are unnecessary. It may not be long before the training of memory is to some extent reinstated in popular educational theory and practice, thus acknowledging the continuing value of an educational insight long known to Jewish and Muslim teachers.

In this light it may be useful to quote the appropriate Biblical passage here. Apart from their obvious importance as the title-deeds of Jewish faith and practice, the Commandments provide a basis for Jewish education.

And God spoke all these words, saying,
[1] 'I am the Lord your God, who brought you out of the land of Egypt, out of the house of bondage. You shall have no other gods before me.
[2] 'You shall not make for yourself a graven image, or any likeness of anything that is in heaven above, or that is in the earth beneath, or that is in the water under the earth; you shall not bow down to them or serve them; for I the Lord your God am a jealous God, visiting the iniquity of the fathers upon the children to the third and the fourth generation of those who hate me, but showing steadfast love to thousands of those who love me and keep my commandments.
[3] 'You shall not take the name of the Lord your God in vain; for the Lord will not hold him guiltless who takes his name in vain.
[4] 'Remember the sabbath day, to keep it holy. Six days you shall labour, and do all your work; but the seventh day is a sabbath to the Lord your God; in it you shall not do any work, you, or your son, or your daughter, your manservant, or your maidservant, or your cattle, or the sojourner who is within your gates; for in six days the Lord made heaven and earth, the sea, and all that is in them, and rested the seventh day; therefore the Lord blessed the sabbath day and hallowed it.
[5] 'Honour your father and your mother, that your days may be long in the land which the Lord your God gives you.
[6] 'You shall not kill.
[7] 'You shall not commit adultery.
[8] 'You shall not steal.
[9] 'You shall not bear false witness against your neighbour.

[10] 'You shall not covet your neighbour's house; you shall not covet your neighbour's wife, or his manservant, or his maidservant, or his ox, or his ass, or anything that is your neighbour's.'[28]

This is the summary of the Law which Moses is said to have received from God on Mount Sinai. In Christianity and Islam, as well as in Judaism, the Law is honoured first and foremost because of its divine origin. Christian attitudes to the Law are influenced by what Jesus said about his own Jewish heritage:

Think not that I have come to abolish the law and the prophets; I have come not to abolish them but to fulfil them. For truly, I say to you, till heaven and earth pass away, not an iota, not a dot, will pass from the law until all is accomplished. Whoever then relaxes one of the least of these commandments and teaches men so, shall be called least in the kingdom of heaven; but he who does them and teaches them shall be called great in the kingdom of heaven.[29]

It is interesting to note that Muslim attitudes to the Law which God gave to Moses on Mount Sinai are influenced by passages in the Qur'ān such as the following. Having been told of the Ten Commandments by Moses,[30] the 'children of Israel' persisted in their disobedience to the Law of God. In the Qur'ān God is recorded as saying to the children of Israel:

And remember We appointed
Forty nights for Moses,
And in his absence ye took
The calf (for worship),
And ye did grievous wrong.

Even then We did forgive you;
There was a chance for you
To be grateful.

And remember We gave
Moses the Scripture and the Criterion[31]
(Between right and wrong): there was
A chance for you to be guided aright.[32]

The respect which Jews, Christians and Muslims continue to have for the monotheistic emphasis of the Law given to Moses, for its clear guidance about primary duties to God, and for its unambiguous ethical requirements, derives from their belief in the God who revealed it. For adherents of each of these three religions these duties and requirements were revealed at a particular point in human history. The responsibility for preserving the revelation, and for transmitting it to the next generation, is one which devolves upon the community of believers, but which is delegated in a special way to teachers, among whom parents have a special educational role to play. Knowledge of the Law and its requirements calls for disciplined instruction and for correction, first of all in the home. In the course of centuries the synagogue became a focal point for Jewish education. The synagogue was a house of prayer, but it also became a place where adults were encouraged to study. Respect for learning, and for the man or woman of learning, has long been a feature of Jewish life.

Later still, during the first century BCE,[33] Simeon ben Shetah, an influential Pharisaic teacher who served as President of the Sanhedrin (the Jewish religio-legal court in Jerusalem), is said to have established schools in Palestine. Within a century universal elementary Jewish education was introduced by the High Priest Joshua ben Gamala, who obliged every Jewish community to provide elementary schooling. Shortly after this, in 70 CE, the Jewish Temple at Jerusalem was captured and destroyed by fire by invading Roman soldiers under Titus, son of the Emperor Vespasian. Ever since that date the Temple ruins have been a symbol of the dispersion of the Jewish people throughout the world.

The Diaspora marked the end of independent national life for the Jewish people until the re-establishment of the state of Israel in the middle of the twentieth century. But in the countries in which they were permitted to pick up their lives they set up their own places of learning. As a place of assembly for worship the synagogue goes back to Temple times, but it gained in importance as a centre for preserving the teachings and values of Judaism after the destruction of the first Temple, and the Babylonian exile. The Temple fell in 586 BCE, and the exile lasted for some forty years from that date. In the Middle Ages, in particular, the synagogue was the focal point for the religious, intellectual and social life of Jews. It became a centre for teaching and learning. Two Biblical passages have featured prominently in synagogue worship from the earliest times. Both remind fathers of their duty to teach their children. The first, the *Shema*, 'Hear, O Israel', has already been quoted above. The second is as follows:

And if you will obey my commandments which I command you this day, to love the Lord your God, and to serve him with all your heart and with all your soul, he will give the rain for your land in its season, the early rain and the later rain, that you may gather in your grain and your wine and your oil. And he will give grass in your fields for your cattle, and you shall eat and be full. Take heed lest your heart be deceived and you turn aside and serve other gods and worship them, and the anger of the Lord be kindled against you, and he shut up the heavens, so that there be no rain, and the land yield no fruit, and you perish quickly off the good land which the Lord gives you.[34]

Educational institutions provided an inner strength and sense of tradition despite exile and local persecution. By the middle of the fourth century BCE, under the leadership of Ezra, the Jewish community in Jerusalem was revitalized after the years of exile in Babylon. The Temple was rebuilt. The Mosaic Law was codified for the regulation of the life of the re-established community. A kind of elementary school, *Bet ha-Sefer* ('the House of the Book'), and the higher 'place of study' (*Bet ha-Midrash*), became 'houses' where knowledge of the *Talmud* was disseminated. The *Ḥeder* (another kind of elementary school) and the *Yeshivah* (for higher levels of Talmudic studies) have been maintained by Jews in different parts of the world. Few Jewish children can have escaped some form of elementary education in prayers and the Hebrew Bible. Many more will have had the benefit of a fuller education in the Hebrew language, prayers, the Bible, Jewish history and Jewish culture.

THE HOME AS A CENTRE OF JEWISH EDUCATION

To the present day the Bible speaks to Jews in terms of divine instruction, *Torah*, which includes both discipline and correction. Education based on this divine instruction begins in the home and continues throughout life.

The centre of Judaism is in the home. In contrast to other religions, it is at home where the essential celebrations and acts of observance take place – rather than in the synagogue or temple. . . . The synagogue is an auxiliary. . . . A Jewish home is where Judaism is at home, where Jewish learning, commitment, sensitivity to values, are cultivated and cherished.[35]

In the Jewish home children are taught to understand what membership of a unique community entails. Their elders learn to discharge their responsibilities in conformity with the Law of God. The inherited wisdom of a distinctive people is passed in a variety of ways from one generation to the next, in the light of centuries of experience and reinterpretation. The family has never lost its importance as a centre of Jewish education, from earliest Biblical times to the present day. It is the Jewish home, rather than the Jewish (or any other) school, which is the centre of Jewish) education.

We, the adults, have delegated our moral responsibility to the schools, the social agencies, or the community funds. . . . Significantly, the Biblical injunction does not say that we are to appoint a teacher to train our children. The Biblical injunction is that the parent be the teacher. School education is a supplement. The problem is not only the scarcity of teachers; the problem is the absence of parents. Education is not only a business of professionals. It is the vocation of all men at all times.[36]

It is in the family that the individual is nurtured. The relationship between parents and children is to be based on mutual love and respect. Parents have a duty to their children. This is made clear in several key passages. Children have a duty to their parents: 'Every one of you shall revere his mother and father.'[37] The commandment to 'honour your father and mother' has already been mentioned above. From their earliest days children were to be educated in the Law of Moses, and in the traditions of their forebears. The Wisdom literature in the Bible contains many rules for the guidance of teachers, of whom parents are among the most important. Parents are the child's natural instructors: 'Hear, my son, your father's instruction, and reject not your mother's teaching; for they are a fair garland for your head, and pendants for your neck.'[38]

In one of the books of the Apocrypha there is an interesting passage which shows how the education of children, especially boys, involved correction (and even corporal punishment for disobedience and sloth) as well as instruction. 'He who disciplines his son will profit by him, and will boast of him among acquaintances. He who teaches his son will make his enemies envious, and he will glory in him in the presence of friends.'[39]

There are other revealing passages in similar vein. 'He who spares the rod hates his son, but he who loves him is diligent to discipline him',[40] although one who is intelligent will benefit more from reproof than from a beating.[41] In any case, the most important consideration is to begin the training early in childhood.[42] It is sons, not daughters, who are singled out for special mention in these texts. In those days daughters seem to have received at home the training deemed necessary for their future roles in the community. In the modern period the gradual emancipation of women has provided them with many of the educational advantages previously reserved for men.

THE IMPORTANCE OF CELEBRATION AND QUESTIONING IN JEWISH EDUCATION

Jewish celebrations and feasts provide children with specific religious and moral lessons, with reminders of their history and instruction in their obligations. 'And when your children say to you, "What do you mean by this service?" you shall say, "It is the sacrifice of the Lord's passover, for he passed over the houses of the people of Israel in Egypt, when he slew the Egyptians but spared our houses."'[43]

The repetition of words and signs impresses the mind with the fundamentals of the faith:

When your son asks you in time to come, 'What is the meaning of the testimonies and the statutes and the ordinances which the Lord our God has commanded you?' you shall say to your son, 'We were Pharaoh's slaves in Egypt; and the Lord brought us out of Egypt with a mighty hand. . . . And the Lord commanded us to do all these statutes, to fear the Lord our God, for our good always, that he may preserve us alive, as at this day.'[44]

Jewish education bears witness to the fact that the recognition of God's authority does not quench the critical spirit. There is a place in the Bible for questioning the acts of God. The suffering of Job drives him to complain bitterly about the treatment he has received at the hands of God:

I will speak in the anguish of my spirit; I will complain in the bitterness of my soul. . . .
I loathe my life; I would not live for ever: let me alone, for my days are a breath.[45]

But there are limits to what may be gained from critical inquiry, and limits to the extent of human knowledge. The truth is that finally the Law of God is decisive in human affairs, and that no creature can change the smallest part of it. The Bible does not encourage anyone to suppose that human beings can finally escape the education that God has in store for them, even if they continue to reject it. This is simply another lesson to be learnt. Job himself acknowledges this: 'Can you find out the deep things of God? Can you find out the limit of the Almighty? It is higher than heaven – what can you do? Deeper than Sheol – what can you know?'[46]

Even the familiar questions which are repeated at moments of great liturgical significance in Jewish life such as Passover, and the familiar answers which make up the response, encourage deeper questioning of the tradition. In this way both the tradition, expressing as it does the accumulated wisdom of the community over many centuries, and the personal freedom to reinterpret its significance are safeguarded.

As part of the *Seder* ritual makes clear, even within the Jewish community there are different attitudes to knowledge and different motives for seeking to acquire it. In the Homily of the Four Children the wise child wants to know all there is to be known, and asks, 'What are the statutes, the laws and the ordinances which Adonai our God has commanded us?'[47] The wicked child asks, 'What does this [Passover] ritual mean to *you*?' The question expresses an attitude of mind which seeks to objectify knowledge; the questioner seeks to protect himself from any personal involvement. The simple child asks, 'What is this [ritual] all about?' His question reflects an unsophisticated willingness to be told. Finally, there is the child who does not know how to ask. What is to be done with him? 'You should open the discussion for him, as it is written, And you shall explain to your child on

that day, It is because of what Adonai did for *me* when I went
free out of Mitzrayim.'[48] The case of the child who does not
know how to ask is more significant than might appear at first,
as the following interpretation shows: 'Highest of all [four kinds
of children] is the son who does not know how to ask,
representing that stage of worship in which the worshipper is so
overwhelmed by the divine that even the quest for knowledge
becomes an intrusion, and God is adored in a silence more
eloquent than words.'[49]

The Jewish teachers who composed this set of questions
recognized that among the children they were to teach there
would be differences of age, aptitude and maturity, which would
require differences of approach and method. The Passover
Haggadah[50] – the narration of the familiar account of the deliverance of the Hebrew people from slavery in Egypt under the
leadership of Moses – plays an important part in Jewish
education. The annual repetition of the ritual serves a number
of educational purposes. The Passover celebration begins on the
fifteenth day of Nisan, the month of spring, the first month of
the Jewish religious year. It reminds all those present of the
historical event which brought about their deliverance from
bondage. It is an act of recollection in which the past is re-lived.
The narration of the story also reminds them of the unity, the
solidarity, which binds Jews together. Every Jew is to make the
Passover feast the occasion of more than a remembrance of the
past. All are to feel that *they* have been actually in Egyptian
bondage, and redeemed from slavery. Children and parents,
young and old alike, are mutually engaged in an educational
activity which has become an inseparable part of the renewal of
Jewish life.

Mah nishtanah . . . ? Why is this night different from all other
nights? There are reasons why this night (the night of the
Passover of the Lord) is different from all other night; in the
history of the liberation of Jews it is unique. But *this particular*
night of celebration is also different from other nights of celebration. It too is unique for those present, who expect and
encourage the familiar questions to be asked. What is slavery?
What is freedom? Are we not free? And are we not still
enslaved? A good example of this is provided during the *Seder*,
the joyous festive meal[51] shared by Jews as part of the annual
ritual of the celebration of Passover. This is when they recall with
special intensity the deliverance of their ancestors from slavery
in Egypt, retelling the story of that deliverance in a highly styl-
ized and memorable form. It is the custom for the youngest child
present to ask four specific questions.

On all other nights we eat either *hametz* or *matzah*.[52]
Why, on this night, do we eat only *matzah*?

On all other nights we eat all kinds of vegetables.
Why, on this night, must we eat bitter herbs?

On all other nights we do not usually dip vegetables even once.
Why, on this night, do we dip twice?

On all other nights we eat either sitting upright or reclining.
Why, on this night, do we eat reclining?[53]

In terms of educational practice this careful ritual of regularly repeated questions and answers is interesting for the use it makes of intellectual curiosity on the part of the young, a readiness to provide (and check) the answers in the light of tradition and experience, and the exemplary encouragement provided by the adults by their attentive listening. The importance of this shared activity is shown by the following explanatory comments printed alongside the four questions just mentioned in a version of the Passover *Haggadah* recently published in the United States:

Questioning is a sign of freedom, proof that we are free to investigate, to analyse, to satisfy our intellectual curiosity.

The simplest question can have many answers, sometimes complex and contradictory ones, even as life itself is fraught with complexity and contradictions. To see everything as good or bad, *matzah* or *maror*,[54] is to be enslaved to simplicity.

The Haggadah challenges us to ask ourselves whether we are asking the right questions.

To accept the fact that not every question has an answer, that not every problem can be neatly resolved, is another stage of liberation. In the same way that questioning is a sign of freedom, acknowledging that some things are beyond our understanding is a sign of faith. Says Rabbi Wolfe of Zhitomir, 'For the believer', there is no question; for the non-believer there is no answer.'

When we find the answers for ourselves, we find ourselves experiencing and understanding the true meaning of the Exodus.[55]

By means of this exchange of questions and answers the truth of what it means to be a Jew in a world which does not appreciate Jewish values is re-established with each new generation. This is an essential part of Jewish education.[56] We ask in order to know how to live. A great deal still depends on the decision to obey, or to disobey, the Law of God. The decision to take leave of God may not compromise one's Jewishness,[57] but from the Biblical point of view it distances the unbeliever from the source of true knowledge and wisdom.

THE BIBLE AS A TEACHING RESOURCE IN A PLURALIST SOCIETY: A PRACTICAL SUGGESTION

The Bible could be used much more profitably in education today without denying the importance of the quiet revolution which has been going on in schools during the last few decades. This quiet revolution has been given some publicity from time to time, but rarely on account of its educational merits. Publicity has come more often as a result of controversy that has been stirred up outside schools by various pressure groups. With some notable exceptions in the specialist field of curriculum development, these important changes have provoked little discussion in educational circles, and less in the community at large. Several reasons might be given to account for the absence of wider professional interest, but a major factor is the general lack of esteem for the subject in which the changes have been taking place. The subject, the only one which suffers the indignity of being statutorily required to be taught in many schools (and hence, so often neglected in practice), is religious education.

The changes in question have led to the introduction of the subject of world religions into the curriculum, on a scale that could scarcely have been imagined even a few years ago. Extra burdens have been placed on the teachers most concerned, not the least of which is the charge that 'the Judaeo-Christian tradition' – a somewhat misleading phrase – is being wilfully neglected. The charge is based on a misunderstanding. Inclusion, rather than exclusion, was intended to be the guiding principle. There has been a shift in emphasis, but only to allow for other religious traditions to be accommodated in *religious* education, alongside Christianity.[58] The unique relationship between Christianity and culture in Britain need not be denied or neglected by the inclusion of other traditions in religious education.

Considerations of this sort have done little to reassure those who take the view that children in schools should not have their lives complicated by the complexities of other faiths before they are safely grounded in their own. This controversy cannot be discussed here, but a practical matter related to it can be considered, arising from difference of opinion about the use of the Bible in religious education. Critics of the inclusion of world religions in education correctly draw attention to the importance of the Bible in the evolution of British culture. Ignorance of what the Bible contains is a cultural disadvantage. But how, given present circumstances, can there be a return (as some apparently wish) to 'teaching the Bible' in a 'confessional' sense? One way might be to use the Bible as a source-book for ideas about the kind of education which the author of the following passage appears to have in mind.

We teach the children how to measure, how to weigh. We fail to teach them how to revere, how to sense wonder and awe. The sense for the sublime, the sign of the inward greatness of the human soul and something which is potentially given to all men, is now a rare gift. Yet without it, the world becomes flat and the soul a vacuum. Here is where the Biblical view of reality may serve us a a guide.[59]

A preliminary exploration of the importance of the Bible as a source-book for *Jewish* education might prepare the way for a more detailed consideration of what it has to say in answer to the question raised at the beginning of this chapter, namely, 'What can be learned from *this* tradition, which might be of service in promoting education for cultural diversity?' This would provide an alternative way of considering Biblical material in schools, without raising the spectre of 'confessionalism' associated in the minds of many with the phrase 'teaching the Bible'. There are many other important subjects in the Bible which can be treated thematically, but in this context it is the subject of *education itself* which may be most useful in the first instance.

With this thematic approach it might be possible, to some extent, to reinstate a book which has already been dismissed – prematurely, it would seem, in some cases – as a repository of obsolete rules about faith and morality. This is not to deny that the scriptures which are held to be sacred by Jews and Christians are normative for faith and action, both individually and collectively. But the practical problem is one of encouraging teachers and students for whom the Bible is a closed book to start to look at its contents. The Bible is a potentially rich teaching resource, not least on the subject of cultural diversity, yet it is in danger of being neglected. This is readily admitted by most observers, but those who simply insist that the Bible must be taught in schools have an obligation to suggest how, as well as why, this is to be done.

Jewish education is instrumental in facilitating induction into the Jewish community. Its objectives, which are to foster a deeper appreciation of Jewish experience and to strengthen commitment to Judaism, do not make it essentially indoctrinatory, in a pejorative sense, because children, no less than adults, are encouraged to question the tradition in a way which involves them directly and personally with the way of life in which they are being nurtured. It was noted earlier that 'non-directional', and 'non-confessional' education, as advocated in a secular society are not free from 'confessional' bias.[60] Opinions and values may be inflicted, though rarely imposed, on students in more subtle ways than by an approach that is explicitly 'confessional'. In a pluralist society educational practice encourages self-expression and the exercise of personal choice. Autonomy is associated with the pursuit of personal freedom, with a refusal to submit to unquestioned external authority, or to obey without question the requirements of an ancient tradition. In so far as it signals an educational objective and the will to pursue it, the word *autonomy* carries ideological nuances which are hard to distinguish from those associated with other types of 'confessional' education.

The paradox already noted in the chapter on Islamic education presents itself again in Jewish education, though in a modified form. The point is that human beings can never be truly *free* if they reject God's ordinances, or fail to be obedient to His will. Submission to God, defined as a willing acceptance of divine commands, is the way to freedom and personal fulfilment. It is the *service* of God which makes for perfect freedom. Freedom to disobey God's will is a spurious freedom. This, on the face of it, seems to place limits on what individuals can do in the pursuit of knowledge, for example, to which both Muslim and Jew might respond that nothing of lasting value is lost if the rule of God (theonomy) is acknowledged at the outset in all human affairs including education, and that human freedom is enhanced rather than degraded by such an acknowledgement.

JEWISH EDUCATION: PROBING BEYOND THE SUPERFICIAL

The authentic voice of the religious Jew in search of the highest knowledge is heard in a poem by Abraham Isaac Kook:

My soul aspires
For the mysteries,
For the hidden secrets of the universe.
It cannot be content
With much knowledge
That probes
The trivialities of life.[61]

Knowledge which 'probes the trivialities of life' comes through obedience to God who is the source of all wisdom and knowledge. It comes also through the bitter experiences which often follow disobedience. God's instructions are not obeyed by fulfilling the requirements of a merely *external* code. It is an *inner* disposition of the heart, prompting obedience to the inner spirit of the Law, which makes possible a new relationship between the divine and the human. The new relationship brings a liberation from the bondage of narrow legalism and exclusivism. It is a creative relationship, which liberates *all* human beings to acquire knowledge and wisdom. Education fosters this relationship, and in the process promotes genuine knowledge and true wisdom. The Jewish tradition teaches that learning is a religious commandment. Education is never completed. Being involved in study is an act of witness which brings a share in the wisdom which belongs to God. Jewish education inculcates a sense of reverence and awe for the grandeur and mystery of God's creation.

Behold, the days are coming, says the Lord, when I will make a new covenant with the house of Israel and the house of Judah, not like the covenant which I made with their fathers when I took them by the hand to bring them out of the land of Egypt, my covenant which they broke, though I was their husband, says the Lord. But this is the covenant which I shall make with the house of Israel after those days, says the Lord: I will put my law within them, and I will write it upon their hearts; and I will be their God, and they shall be my people. And no longer shall each man teach his neighbour and each his brother, saying, 'Know the Lord', for they shall all know me, from the least to the greatest, says the Lord; for I will forgive their iniquity, and I will remember their sin no more.[62]

Characteristic of Judaism is the prophet's ideal of the future as a time when 'the earth shall be full of the knowledge of the Lord as the waters cover the sea'.[63] At that time, all will know the Lord, 'from the least to the greatest'. In the meantime it is the vocation of Jews to bear witness to the unique vision of knowledge and wisdom which they have received, and to pass it on to their children. The final words of this chapter are from an essay on 'Children and Youth' by Abraham Joshua Heschel. In the course of this essay he points out to the teacher the danger of entertaining too low an expectation of a student, in which case education can easily fail to provide a serious challenge to intellectual and spiritual development. From his own Jewish perspective he adds some comments which are appropriate in the wider study of education for cultural diversity.

Genuine reverence for the sanctity of study is bound to invoke in the pupils the awareness that study is not an ordeal but an act of edification; that the school is *a sanctuary*, not a factory; that study is *a form of worship*. True learning is a way of relating oneself to something which is both *eternal* and *universal*. The experience of learning counteracts *tribalism* and *self-centredness*. The work of our hands is *private* property; the fruits of the intellect belong *to all men*. The ultimate meaning of knowledge is not power, but the realization of a unity that surpasses all interests and all ages. Wisdom is like the sky, belonging to no man, and true learning is the astronomy of the spirit.[64]

NOTES AND REFERENCES

1. Kaplan Mordecai M 1985 'Jewish education' in *Contemporary Jewish Thought*, edited, with introductory notes, by Noveck Simon, *The B'nai B'rith History of the Jewish People*, vol 5, Washington, DC. p 354

2. Blumenfield Samuel M 'Thou shalt teach', in *Concepts that Distinguish Judaism*, 1985 edited, with introductory notes, by Millgram Abraham Ezra, *The B'nai B'rith History of the Jewish People*, vol 3, Washington DC, pp 135–36
3. The Hebrew word *yeshivah* (plural, *yeshivoth*) may refer to a school for Talmudic studies, a seminary for the education of Orthodox Jewish rabbis, or a day school which provides secular and religious instruction. The *yeshivah* was a place where students were instructed in the *Talmud*, and has assumed a more important role in Orthodox Jewish life as a defence against the spread of secular culture – an important consideration when there is fear that the influence of *Torah* on the lives of Jews is being undermined. Originally the *yeshivoth* were for unmarried young men who wished to devote themselves to serious supervised study. In recent times other more comprehensive and all-embracing educational institutions, *kolelim*, have been established to provide for married students to devote themselves to advanced Talmudic study
4. The Talmud is the *Oral Law* of the Jews, as distinct from the *Torah* (see in the text above), which is the *Written Law*. The *Talmud* ('Learning') consists of a vast collection of rabbinical explanations and commentaries on the details of Jewish life and thought. The text of the Oral Law is known as *Mishnah*. The *Gemarah* supplements and comments on the *Mishnah*. The *Mishnah* was compiled principally by Judah ha-Nasi, who used the earlier work of scribes such as Hillel and Shammai, and the elaboration of the legal material by teachers (*Tannaim*) such as Akiba ben Joseph, to produce an authoritative work by the close of the second century CE. A later group of Jewish teachers (*Amoraim*) further interpreted the minutiae of Jewish life, and it was out of these deliberations that the *Gemarah* was compiled to complete the *Talmud*. Two compilations of the *Talmud* were completed. The Palestinian *Talmud* was completed in the fifth century CE. A considerably longer version, known as the Babylonian *Talmud*, was completed a century later. For the English reader a helpful introduction is given in Goldin J 1957 *The Living Talmud*, University of Chicago
5. Misunderstanding can easily arise over the use of the word *Bible*. The Jewish Bible consists of the scriptures which Christians know as the Old Testament. The New Testament, which completes the Bible for Christians, has no canonical status for Jews. In this chapter the word *Bible* is used in the Jewish sense, i.e. *Tanach*
6. Heschel A J 1972 *Man is Not Alone: a philosophy of religion*, Farrar, Straus and Giroux, New York, p 241
   In quoting from the Bible, both in this chapter and the next, the English text used is that of the Revised Standard Version in *The New Oxford Annotated Bible, with the Apocrypha* (expanded edn) 1977, May Herbert G and Metzger Bruce M (eds), Oxford University Press, New York
7. Deuteronomy 6: 7
8. Deuteronomy 6: 4–9. The italics have been added. Phylacteries (Hebrew: *tefillin*) are worn by Orthodox Jews as a constant reminder of the presence of God. The *tefillin* consist of two small leather

boxes, each of which contains strips of parchment on which are written verses from the scriptures, Exodus 13: 1–10, 13: 11–16; Deuteronomy 6: 4–9 and 11: 13–21. One box is fastened to the forehead, and the other to the left arm. The *mezuzah* is also used by Orthodox Jews as a reminder of the presence of God. A piece of parchment bearing the text of Deuteronomy 6: 4–9 and 11: 13–21 is rolled up and inserted in a wooden, metal or glass tube, which is then attached to the doorpost of the house in accordance with the instructions of the text

9. On the significance of the Holocaust for Jews, and for its meaning to non-Jews, see Dawidowicz Lucy S 1975 *The War against the Jews*, Holt, Rinehart & Winston, New York

10. Wiesel Elie 1971 *One Generation After*, Weidenfeld & Nicolson

11. Baeck Leo 1985 'The Optimism of Judaism', reprinted in Noveck Simon (ed), *Contemporary Jewish Thought*, B'nai B'rith Books. Washington, DC, p 182

12. Genesis 1: 1

13. The important phrase '*eretz Israel*' is the Hebrew name for the Land of Israel. It is a Biblical name which was first used of the land occupied by the Israelites (cf. 1 Samuel 13: 19). Later it referred to the northern kingdom of Israel (cf. 2 Kings 5: 2). Later still it was used by Jews to mean 'the Promised Land', and now refers to the land which makes up the modern state of Israel

14. Abraham enters history in Genesis 12 as a father in faith who was obedient to God's call, leaving his homeland in eastern Mesopotamia to take his family westwards into Canaan, the Promised Land.

And I [God] will establish my covenant between me and you and your descendants after you throughout their generations for an everlasting covenant, to be God to you and to your descendants after you. And I will give to you, and to your descendants after you, the land of your sojournings, all the land of Canaan, for an everlasting possession; and I will be their God. (Genesis 17: 7–8)

For both Jews and Christians Abraham is an exemplary figure. For Muslims, too, *Ibrāhīm* is an honoured figure who set an example to be followed:

And remember that Abraham
Was tried by his Lord
With certain Commands,
Which he fulfilled:
He said: 'I will make thee
An Imam [i.e. a model, pattern, or example] to the Nations'.
He pleaded: 'And also
[Imams] from my offspring!'
He answered: 'But My Promise
Is not within the reach
Of evil-doers'. (Qur'ān 2: 124)

Ibrāhīm was a *Muslim*, i.e. one who submitted to God and obeyed the divine call, thus being recognized as *khalīl ullāh*, 'the friend of God'.

See also the section on *Islam*, pp 31-2 above
15. Exodus 1: 11-14
16. Exodus 6: 5
17. Exodus 14: 26-31
18. Exodus 33: 1, 3
19. Psalms 111: 10; Proverbs 1: 7
20. Exodus 19: 4-6
21. The nomadic period of Israel's history is recalled whenever the following verses are repeated:

A wandering Aramean was my father; and he went down into Egypt and sojourned there, few in number; and there he became a nation, great, mighty, and populous. And the Egyptians treated us harshly, and afflicted us, and laid upon us hard bondage. Then we cried to the Lord the God of our fathers, and the Lord heard our voice, and saw our affliction, our toil, and our oppression; and the Lord brought us out of Egypt with a mighty hand and an outstretched arm, with great terror, with signs and wonders; and he brought us into this place and gave us this land, a land flowing with milk and honey. (Deuteronomy 26: 5-9)

22. Genesis 18: 19
23. Deuteronomy 32: 46-47
24. Deuteronomy 27: 1-8
25. Deuteronomy 17: 18; Joshua 1: 8
26. The feast of Tabernacles, or Booths (Hebrew *Sukkoth*), is one of the oldest and most joyous Jewish feasts. The festivities last for eight days and begin each year on the 15th of the seventh month (*Tishri*) of the Jewish calendar. This is usually in September or early October. The feast originally came at the end of the gathering-in of the harvest in ancient Palestine. It is now celebrated by constructing temporary booths in memory of the wandering in the wilderness after the Exodus from Egypt. Meals are taken in the booths during the period of the festival, at the close of which comes another holiday feast, that of *Simchat Torah*, 'rejoicing of the Law'. Services in the synagogue on this day take the form of a series of processions with the Scrolls of the *Torah*. On Jewish feasts and holy days, see Epstein Morris 1970 *All About Jewish Holidays and Customs*, rev edn. KTAV Publishing House; Goldin Hyman 1952 *A Treasury of Jewish Holidays*. Twayne Publishers, New York
27. Deuteronomy 31: 9-13
28. Exodus 20: 1-17
29. Matthew 5: 17-19
30. In Islam, Moses (Arabic, *Mūsā*) is one of the messengers of God, honoured for his exemplary obedience to the law of God, and because God entrusted to him the *Book* (see note 31 below) for the guidance of his own people (see Qurʾān 14: 4-6). Similarly, Jesus (Arabic ʿĪsā) is an Islamic prophet, honoured as an exemplary Muslim, and because God gave him the *Book* for the guidance of his own people (see Qurʾān 5: 46-50). Muhammad was the last of the messengers to be sent to his people with the Book of guidance. In his case the Book was the Qurʾān. In Islamic belief all the messengers of God, and all the Books which were sent with them, teach the religion of Islam (see Qurʾān 13: 38-43)

31. The Arabic for 'the Book' is *al-kitāb*. In Islam Jews, Christians and Muslims are called *ahl al-kitāb* – i.e. 'people of the book' – because they have each been favoured with a written book of guidance by God. It is this fact which, as Muslims see it, should make for more than a superficial unity among adherents of these three religions. In Islamic belief, the book given to Moses was *al-tawrah* (cf. *Torah*). In the case of Jesus the book was *al-injīl*, the Gospel. For Muslims the essential point is that each book, culminating in the Qurɔān, originally contained the same message of Islam. Only the Qurɔān now preserves the truth

32. Qurɔān 2: 51–53

33. The use of the abbreviations BCE (Before the Common Era) and CE (Common Era), instead of BC and AD, is favoured by many today because it is considered to give less offence to non-Christians

34. Deuteronomy 11: 13–17

35. Quoted by Goodhill Ruth Marcus in 1975 *The Wisdom of Heschel*. Farrar, Straus & Giroux, New York, p 84

36. Heschel A J 1966 *The Insecurity of Freedom*. Farrar, Straus & Giroux, New York, p 48

37. Leviticus 19: 3

38. Proverbs 1: 8; see also Proverbs 4: 1; 6: 20–1; 13: 1

39. Sirach 30: 1–3

40. Proverbs 13: 24; cf. 19: 18; 22: 15; 23: 13; 29: 15, 17

41. Proverbs 17: 10

42. Proverbs 1: 2, 7, 8; 22: 6

43. Exodus 12: 26–27

44. Deuteronomy 6: 20–24

45. Job 7: 11, 16

46. Job 11: 7–8

47. Deuteronomy 6: 20. Out of respect for the Name of God, Jews do not pronounce it when reading from their scriptures. Instead they say the word *Adonai*, which means means 'my Lord', or 'my master'

48. Exodus 13: 8. *Mitzrayim* is Egypt, but the Hebrew word now refers to more than one specific geographical location. *Mitzrayim* stands for everywhere in the modern world where there is tyranny and oppression

49. Rabinowicz Rachel Anne (ed) 1982 *Passover Haggadah: the feast of freedom*. 2nd ed, The Rabbinical Assembly, USA. p 39

50. The Passover *Haggadah*, 'telling, narrative', is a set form of blessings, narration and prayers, recited each year at the *Seder* ritual on the eve of Passover. It retells the story of the bondage in Egypt and of God's redemption of the Israelites from slavery. It is both a remembrance and a re-living of those events. It expresses thanksgiving for liberation and for the acquisition of the Land of Israel

51. The Seder is without parallel in its significance, its scope, its format and its objectives. This is a very specific ceremony, carefully choreographed, *designed to take place in the home, designed to involve every member of the household, particularly the children*, in a ritual that is in some instances thousands of years old, in rites that are rich with layer-upon-layer of meaning. The Haggadah serves as the blueprint for the Seder, and is indispensable to its proper observance.

Rabinowicz *Passover Haggadah.* p 10. The italics have been added. This edition of *Haggadah* is described by the editor as the first to reflect the ideology of Conservative Judaism
52. *Hametz* is fermented dough. It refers to leaven, and the products containing it, which are forbidden to Jews at Passover. This includes mixtures of flour and water which have been allowed to ferment for more than eighteen minutes. Bread is the best example. *Matzah* is unleavened bread. It is the cake baked in haste, without leaven, by those who were preparing for the first liberation from Egyptian slavery. This 'bread of affliction' was to be replaced by *manna*, the 'bread of redemption'
53. Rabinowicz *Passover Haggadah.* p 33, to which a note is appended, '*The forty-nine questions.* "To attain truth," says Rabbi Barukh of Medzebezh, "man must pass forty-nine gates, each opening to a new question. Finally he arrives at the last gate, the last question, beyond which he could. not live without faith".'
54. *Maror* refers to the 'bitter herbs' which symbolize the bitterness of the bondage endured by the children of Israel in Egypt. The Passover *Haggadah* contains the following passage: 'Maror. Why do we eat it? To remind ourselves that, as it is written, the Egyptians in Mitzrayim (Egypt) "embittered the lives of our ancestors with hard labour, in water and in brick, and in every manner of drudgery in the field; and worked them ruthlessly in all their labour".' (Exodus 1: 14)
55. Rabinowicz, *Passover Haggadah*, p 33
56. This is not merely questioning for its own sake. 'It is not enough for me to be able to say "I am"; I want to know *who I am*, and in relation to whom I live. It is not enough for me to ask questions. I want to know how to answer the one question that seems to encompass everything I face: What am I here for?' Heschel A J 1965 *Who is Man?*, Stanford University Press, p 52
57. See Goodman S L (ed) 1976 *The Faith of Secular Jews.* New York
58. See Smart Ninian 1971 *The Religious Experience of Mankind.* Fontana Books
59. Heschel A J 1955 *God in Search of Man: the Philosophy of Judaism.* Farrar, Straus & Giroux, New York, pp 36–37
60. See above, p 18
61. This is a translation of a poem by Kook Abraham Isaac 1978 in *The Lights of Penitence*, tr Bokser Ben Z. The Classics of Western Spirituality, Paulist Press, New York, p 371. Rabbi Kook was a Jewish mystic who was elected to the Rabbinate of Jerusalem at the end of the First World War. He served the Jewish community in Palestine under the British Mandate, until his death in 1935.
62. Jeremiah 31: 31–34
63. Isaiah 11: 9
64. Heschel A J 1966 *The Insecurity of Freedom: Essays on Human Existence.* Farrar, Straus & Giroux, New York, p 42

CHAPTER 4

Christian perspectives: 'A reason for the hope that is in you'

The Gospels are an offer, a naive and tentative offer: Would you like to live in a completely new way? . . . When the Gospels say that in the Kingdom of God there are neither Jews nor Gentiles, do they just mean that all are equal in the sight of God? I don't believe it means only that – that was known to the Greek philosophers and the Roman moralists and the Hebrew prophets. What the Gospels tell us is that in this new way of life and of communion, which is born of the heart and which is called the Kingdom of God, there are no nations, but only persons.'[1]

For it is the God who said, 'Let light shine out of darkness', who has shone in our hearts to give the light of the knowledge of the glory of God in the face of Christ.[2]

SOME KEY QUESTIONS

What are the characteristics of Christian approaches to education? How do Christian approaches to education differ from the Islamic and Jewish approaches already considered? Is 'Christian education' more than a convenient term for the contribution that Christian teachers are assumed to make to the life of society when they happen to be engaged in teaching? These are the questions with which this chapter is chiefly concerned. The position taken here is that Christian education is more than a subjective notion, or a pious aspiration, and that its principles can be identified. Do these principles have a wider application beyond the Christian communities which they help to build? If so, can they be more widely understood, and *used*, to further educational objectives in a culturally diverse society? Or is it fanciful to suppose that Christian approaches to education can ever do more than serve specifically Christian interests?

THE INFLUENCE OF CHRISTIAN BELIEFS

It is not as easy as some suppose to give an unambiguous answer to the question, 'What is *Christian* education?' It is indisputable that Christianity, and Christian teachers, have exercised a lasting influence on the development of education in this country at every level. Anyone who sets out to find answers to these questions is immediately confronted with the failure of Christians to agree among themselves about the objectives, the content and the methods, of education that may reasonably be said to be founded upon Christian beliefs. Christianity is no more monolithic a system of religious belief and practice than either Islam or Judaism. Given the wide-ranging differences of belief and worship to be found among Christians, it is inevitable that Christian approaches to education should reflect a measure of diversity.

Christian approaches to education are influenced by beliefs which – so Christians affirm – are founded upon the historic events through which God continues to reveal himself. Beginning with the initial act of creation itself, the activity of revelation proceeds in many different ways, notably in God's dealings with his chosen people, the Jews. In the life, death and resurrection of Jesus of Nazareth Christians claim to see unique evidence of God's intervention in history. The Christian doctrine of the Incarnation expresses the belief that in the figure of Jesus the human and divine were united. God, in fact, took human form and lived among those whom he had created. Among the most important of these beliefs for the development of Christian approaches to education are those concerned with *creation, contingency* and *the freedom of the individual.*

Of fundamental importance for Christian education is the work of God in creation, re-creation and redemption. It follows that the universe which God has chosen to create is contingent. The universe is dependent upon God not only for its creation, but for its continuing existence. The universe could have been ordered differently had God decided on another course. In Christian belief God makes it possible for his human creatures to serve and to obey him but does not compel them to do either. Human beings are endowed with freedom to choose whether they will accept or reject the revelation. Learning to answer the question which Jesus asked his followers remains one of the main tasks for education that is authentically Christian.

And Jesus went on with his disciples, to the villages of Caesarea Philippi; and on the way he asked his disciples, 'Who do men say that I am?' And they told him, 'John the Baptist; and others say, Elijah; and others one of the prophets'. And he asked them, 'But who do you say that I am?' Peter answered him, 'You are the Christ'.[3]

THE PRINCIPLE OF REINTERPRETATION

These beliefs have been reinterpreted throughout the course of Christian history. What might be termed 'the principle of reinterpretation' is one of the most basic principles of Christian education. It derives from Christian belief in creation, revelation and personal freedom. It works in such a way as to conserve what has been revealed, and to encourage an exploration of the accruing tradition by involving individual members of *this* generation with the *present* significance of events from an increasingly distant past. 'Tradition', as G. K. Chesterton once observed, 'is the democracy of the dead.' This principle not only safeguards the knowledge and experience which previous generations have built up but also enables the tradition itself to be renewed and expanded. Its usefulness in Christian education is that it suggests a method for determining whether a particular development in Christian life and thought is *authentic* (in that it is consistent with both the original revelation and the subsequent tradition), or *inauthentic* (in that it is consistent with neither).

From a Christian point of view, God is the source of all knowledge and wisdom. In creating human beings God endows them with a desire for knowledge and a freedom to pursue it. The creation myths in the book of Genesis establish the correct order of going, in which God grants to human creatures a measure of control over the creation, albeit within limits.

So God created man in his own image . . . , male and female he created them. And God blessed them, and God said to them, 'Be fruitful and multiply, and fill the earth and subdue it. . . . You may freely eat of every tree that is in the garden [of Eden]; but of the tree of the knowledge of good and evil you shall not eat, for in the day that you shall eat of it you shall surely die.'[4]

For Christians, in other words, there are always choices to be made about the limits of human freedom and responsibility. Christian education proceeds from the belief that without God there can be no true knowledge, and no true freedom. In the theory and practice of Christian education the principle of re-interpretation is useful in two specific ways. First, it introduces a dynamic rather than a static approach to the past, giving rise to an expectation that the Christian tradition will not be preserved in a merely mechanical way, out of uncritical conformity with the past. Students and teachers will be obliged to use their freedom to think for themselves. Second, it helps to filter out anything which is alien to the living tradition and which, if allowed to pass unobserved, might result in the gradual development of a world-view that it would be meaningless to continue to call Christian.

Human thought has swayed over the centuries between the extreme of realism, the belief that the visible world is all that exists, and the extreme of idealism, that the visible world does not really exist at all except in so far as our minds give it a certain brief and illusory reality. Christian thought rejects both these extremes. The world, and man within it, has reality, has existence. But this is a wholly dependent reality and existence. Nothing in the world, and least of all man himself, can be explained in terms of forces and principles solely within this world. There is a beyond, in dependence on which the world exists and man can find his freedom. If we wish to go a step further and put the matter theologically, we cannot think as Christians at all without the concept of creation; we take our stand on the first verse of the Bible: 'In the beginning God created the heavens and the earth'.[5]

THE PRINCIPLE OF TRANSFORMATION AND INTEGRATION

Christian education is a lifelong process of transformation. Christians believe that God is a *purposive* creator and re-creator.[6] The events of history are neither illusory nor infinitely recurring. The purpose of God is being worked out despite the existence of evil in the world, and despite the mystery of suffering. The Creator of all things is a God who reveals his will for the creation in many ways. That the purposes of God have been revealed (and can be known) is not a uniquely Christian claim. That God can be known uniquely, through the ministry of Jesus as well as through a study of the evidence furnished by the created natural order itself, is the distinctive Christian claim. The aim of Christian education is thus to disseminate this knowledge of the purposes of God. Important as it is for Christians to find (or to make) opportunites for this work in schools and other educational institutions, it is clear that Christian education is a lifelong process that continues long after formal education is over. Every experience in life is potentially an opportunity for acquiring deeper knowledge of what God has revealed.

Orthodox Christian belief acknowledges that the educative activity of God is not limited to this life. Education does not end at the moment of death, given that beyond this present life there are possibilities for further progress. This word *possibilities* reminds Christians that progress is conditional, in that it depends upon the readiness of the individual to cooperate with the Creator. Answering the question, 'What, in a word, would you as Headmaster be educating him for?', Dr Alington is said to have replied to the mother of a potential pupil, 'In a word, madam, for death'. The answer was neither flippant nor macabre. Christian education is not preoccupied with the subjects of death and the next world, but in preparing students for life in this world it can never treat death as a taboo, still less as the end of purposeful existence.

It is only in a preparatory sense that Christian education can be limited to institutions in which the quest for knowledge is, quite reasonably, initiated and informed. This formal education complements, ideally, the educational influences of the home and the church, making for the harmonious integration of individual physical, social, intellectual, moral, aesthetic and spiritual qualities. Christian education is a continually *transforming* and *integrating* process, first of individuals and then of the societies to which individuals belong. It cannot be used to shore up existing social arrangements without ignoring its essentially subversive function. Nor can social changes, however desirable at the time, remain free from its critical scrutiny in due course. This is an important consideration in education for cultural diversity.

THE CALL FOR MORE 'CHRISTIAN EDUCATION' IN SCHOOLS

Experienced teachers, whether Christian or not, will recognize the criticism from certain quarters in this country to the effect that there is not sufficient 'Christian education' in our schools today. It is said that the way to rectify the situation is to enforce the existing law with regard to education (especially the law which deals with statutory requirements for *religious* education), and to marshal parental opinion (claimed to be generally in favour) in support of the ensuing campaign. Despite the recent growth of religious and cultural diversity in Britain, the critics claim that it is *Christian* education or, more vaguely, education in the *Judaeo-Christian tradition*, which needs to regain the dominant position it once held in the nation's schools. The campaign, in essence, would seek to ensure the inculcation of Christian values and beliefs in schools. Would this amount to authentic Christian education, even if it is thoroughly Biblically based, and even if children become word-perfect in some revised catechism?

The disposition to dismiss alternative views of the world out of hand, or to disregard them as unworthy of serious attention, is common enough. The question to be asked at this point is whether Christian education has anything to offer in promoting a sensitively critical understanding of religious convictions and of cultural diversity. This applies just as much inside as outside the ranks of Christian believers. How successfully can Christian approaches to education minimize the human tendency in teachers to indoctrinate? This, again, is a question for Christians to consider inside their own church communities, as well as in the wider world of educational institutions. For centuries the means of inducting the young into Christian belief and behaviour was catechesis. The catechism, or oral instruction, is almost as old as Christianity. It was used to instruct children, and to test would-be converts in their knowledge of the faith. Later the oral instruction was transferred into written forms, employing the methods of question and answer in a rather formal way.

Martin Luther's *Small Catechism* of 1529 was an attempt to provide religious education for children. The *Heidelberg Catechism* of 1563 was devised for use by Calvinists. Members of the Dutch and German Reformed communities, Presbyterians and Anglicans, as well as Roman Catholics, all adopted one form of catechism or other at different times, for similar purposes. What place can catechism have in Christian education? The word *catechize* is of Greek origin, and its root meaning is scarcely reassuring in view of the comments already made in this chapter about personal freedom and autonomy. The Greek word means 'to make (the catechumen, i.e. the person under instruction) hear'. Authority on the part of the teacher and submission on the part of the taught would appear to be the necessary qualifications for participation in catechesis. Catechumens may be preparing for baptism before being admitted to full membership of the church, and may thus be presumed to be willing to accept the discipline of instruction as a test of obedience. But even in this situation catechesis can only be described as an instrument of authentic Christian education if it allows freedom for individuals to explore the tradition without compulsion.

Demands for more 'Christian education' in schools are seldom accompanied by constructive suggestions for making teaching more effective, and very often come from individuals or groups whose knowledge of contemporary educational theory and practice is limited. Dissatisfied with what they consider to be the betrayal of Christian values and beliefs in the curriculum of state schools, some Christians (inside as well as outside the schools) are already insisting on changes of a blatantly sectarian kind. In such instances the critics tend to overlook the educational issues which need to be considered.

It is sometimes argued that the solution to the problems associated with *confessional* teaching (that is to say, teaching designed to inculate certain beliefs and values) is to exclude denominational teaching of all types from county schools, leaving it to synagogues, churches and mosques to cater for their own special confessional interests. From a Christian perspective this may be no more than a falsely comforting half-answer, for if an approach to education has to be excluded from schools on the grounds that it is prevents individuals from thinking for themselves, and thus from choosing a way of life for themselves, then it would be more consistent to challenge it wherever it is to be found, in denominational schools, mosques, synagogues and churches, and for the same educational reasons.

FEATURES OF CHRISTIAN APPROACHES TO EDUCATION

Christian education is *directive*, in that it both points to a clear goal and enables students to advance towards it. Teachers and pupils alike are encouraged to aim towards the same goal, which is to know God in Christ. Christian education is *purposive* to this extent, even instrumental. It is form of *self-discipline* which yields results only to those who are prepared for the necessary effort. It is *conservative* in that it seeks to preserve and to transmit a received tradition. At the same time Christian education allows for, and encourages, a measure of freedom for teachers and pupils to explore the tradition for themselves. Christians can agree with Muslims about the truth of the Qur⁾ānic words to the effect that there is (or better perhaps, there can be) no compulsion in religion, given the freedom with which the creator has invested his human creatures.[7] This point is well illustrated in the Gospel narratives, in which Jesus himself teaches his followers by way of personal example, precept and parable. There is no compulsion in his teaching methods. He invokes the tradition and reinterprets it. Every new generation inherits the accumulated Christian tradition, but there is always room for fresh insights.

Christian education would appear to have three essential features. To begin with, it establishes faith in Jesus Christ as the foundation and guide for correct thinking and right action. Second, it is integrative, in that it serves to harmonize elements which may otherwise tend to be fragmented in individuals and in society. It is thus concerned with human beings 'whole and entire', and at each succeeding stage of life. Third, it enables individuals to decide for themselves whether they will believe or not, by exercising their capacity for reason as well as for faith.

From an educational point of view there is one aspect of Christian education which is of special interest in a situation where the unity of any society threatens to crack along the fault-lines of cultural diversity. It may be that the most significant task for Christian education at the present time is to provide bridges, not cement. Ideally, if not always in practice, Christian education promotes more than an understanding of one particular kind of religious faith. At the same time as Christians have encouraged the search for new knowledge, it has to be noted that there has been a consistent emphasis on the limits of useful knowledge, and on the foolishness of pursuing knowledge for its own sake. Few Christians have put this more clearly than the fifteenth-century Augustinian monk, Thomas à Kempis.

It is natural that man should desire knowledge; but what doth knowledge avail him without the fear of God? An humble rustic that serveth God is better than a proud philosopher who, neglecting the good life, contemplateth the courses of the stars. He that knoweth himself well groweth ever more conscious of his own sinfulness, and findeth no delight in the praises of man. Were I endowed with all the knowledge in the world, and lacked love, what would that avail me in the sight of

God, who will judge me according to my deeds?

Restrain thyself from an inordinate desire for knowledge, for therein lurk great distractions and delusions. The learned are well pleased to seem so to others, and to be accounted wise, but much that is to be found in learning little profiteth the soul. He that is intent upon things other than those that will help his soul's salvation is lacking in wisdom. Words will not satisfy the soul; but a good life giveth comfort to the mind, and a pure conscience affordeth great confidence in the sight of God.

The greater thy knowledge and the better thine understanding, the more rigorously wilt thou be judged, unless thy life be also most holy. Be not therefore exalted in spirit because of any skill or knowledge thou mayest possess, but rather let the knowledge thou hast been given make thee humble and cautious. If thou thinkest that thou knowest and understandest many things, remember also that there are still more which thou knowest not. Be not high-minded, but rather acknowledge thine own ignorance.[8]

At the heart of the Christian religion there is the passion of Jesus Christ. His suffering on the cross drew from him words which have been variously interpreted by Christians as both a cry of dereliction that God had apparently abandoned him, and as a cry of faith in God's providence. 'My God, my God, why hast thou forsaken me?' From this has developed the theology of dereliction which is at the heart of Christian faith and experience. Christian education proposes an understanding of human vulnerability and *difference*. It encourages the exploration of pluralism, with regard to doubt as well as to faith.

The Christian image of Jesus as the suffering God is a powerful icon. It expresses something of the vulnerability, as well as of the love of God, as Christians have come to understand it. The lesson is not without its implications for Christian approaches to education. Christian education ends where it begins, with the enigmatic figure of Jesus. In every generation it focuses attention on a startling claim which might otherwise remain unknown. This claim is that in Jesus, crucified and risen from the dead, the whole of creation is provided with a unique vision of the purposes of God. A knowledge of this divine initiative is 'necessary for salvation', as Christians might say, however variously they might interpret the word *salvation* in this context.[9]

THE PLACE OF JESUS IN THE CHRISTIAN TRADITION

Christian attitudes to knowledge, and to the acquisition of knowledge, are influenced primarily by the revelation contained in the Christian scriptures, although it is clear that pre-Christian cultures have also influenced the development of Christian opinion on many issues. In the first of the two quotations at the head of this chapter one of the characters of Pasternak's novel, in conversation with the principal character Yury Zhivago, acknowledges the debt which Christians owe to the classical civilizations of Athens, Jerusalem and Rome – but especially to the Jews, in whose traditions Jesus was nurtured.[10] Christians claim to inherit the Jewish tradition. For this reason they include the Jewish Bible in their own scriptures as the Old Testament.

Care was taken when discussing Jewish approaches to education in Chapter 3 to use the word *Bible* in its Jewish sense. In this chapter equal care is taken to use the word in its Christian sense. The Old Testament revelation is supplemented and fulfilled (as Christians would see it) by the New Testament. It is because this second part of the Christian scriptures describes in some detail the teaching of Jesus and records the impact of his life, death and resurrection on the early communities of Christian believers that it can never cease to be a primary source for studying the principles of Christian education.

Christians make unique claims about Jesus, describing him as God in human form, as the Saviour of the world, and as the Lord of life. He has other important titles in the Christian tradition, but the ones mentioned are sufficient to show that the importance of Jesus for Christians is quite different, for example, from the importance of Muhammad for Muslims. No comparison is intended between the former, who is worshipped as the Word of God by Christians, and the latter, who is honoured by Muslims because God sent him to bring the Word of God in the form of the Book, the Qur°ān. It is interesting to recall that, though honoured in Islam as a messenger of God, Jesus can never be worshipped *as* God by Muslims in the way which is distinctive of Christian orthodoxy.

Christians may allow familiarity to obscure the unique status of Jesus in their own tradition. If and when they do it may take a reminder from someone outside to set the record straight. It was at a conference on world religions several years ago, attended by members of different faiths, that the author listened to a Muslim chiding the Christians present for failing to make a single reference to Jesus in the course of their contributions to the debate about education. His complaint was not just that the name of Jesus had not been mentioned, but that the *divinity* of Jesus, strongly denied by an orthodox Muslim like himself, had not been admitted as a distinctive Christian belief which would inevitably influence the ways in which Christians would approach educational questions.

THE IMPORTANCE OF SCRIPTURE AND TRADITION

What is contained in the Biblical revelation is clearly normative for Christian beliefs and values. This is not to say that all Christians would agree that only what is explicitly scriptural is determinative for Christian education – or for Christian doctrine, for that matter. From the beginning Christian experience has continued to develop and to find expression in changing circumstances in different cultures, as the Good News (Gospel) of Jesus spread throughout the world. Christian tradition, therefore, gradually comes to assume an influential role, alongside the scriptures, in deciding on questions which affect the Christian way of life.

The New Testament includes a passage in which Jesus is recorded as making a promise to his disciples shortly before his arrest and crucifixion. The promise reflects his own developmental, rather than static, view of God's revelatory activity. The importance of this promise of Jesus for Christian approaches to education lies in the encouragement it gives to students to explore the world around them, confident that any new knowledge and new insights which emerge will not require them to abandon the tradition but to develop it.

I have yet many things to say to you, but you cannot bear them now. When the Spirit of truth comes, he will guide you into all the truth; for he will not speak on his own authority, but whatever he hears he will speak, and he will declare to you the things that are to come. He will glorify me, for he will take what is mine and declare it to you.[11]

CHRISTIAN MISSION AND CHRISTIAN EDUCATION

The marked loss of confidence in the status of Christian orthodoxy in some quarters, noticeable inside as well as outside the churches, has had its effects on Christian attitudes to education. At a time when the claim that 'Christianity is the true religion which stands in opposition to all false religions and ideologies' is increasingly disputed, it is not surprising that Christians are re-examining their understanding of the relationship between faith and knowledge in a pluralist society. Yet Christianity remains a *missionary* faith, which is to say that, despite profound differences of belief among Christians (differences which have made of contemporary Christianity a notable example of religious and cultural pluralism at work), the followers of Christ are under an obligation to support activities which can be described as educational in the broadest sense.

From the earliest times Christians have been encouraged to share their faith so that others have an opportunity to accept it for themselves. The resulting mission of the church has been world-wide in consequence. The author of St Matthew's Gospel concludes his account of the ministry of Jesus with some verses which have provided the basis for Christian education for centuries. These words have been interpreted as an instruction to succeeding generations of Christians. It does not matter here whether the words of what has come to be known as 'the Great Commission'[12] are to be taken as words which Jesus actually uttered, or whether they express the understanding of the teaching of Jesus on the part of the earliest Christian communities. The point is that, from the beginning, Christians have held to the belief that their mission was universal: 'Go therefore and make disciples of all nations, baptizing them in the name of the Father and of the Son and of the Holy Spirit, teaching them to observe all that I have commanded you; and lo, I am with you always, to the close of the age.'[13]

The literature of Christianity is full of references to the light of Christ which dispels the darkness of ignorance, a light which may be ignored but which cannot be extinguished. Knowledge, for the Christian, consists of a growing awareness, an increasing illumination, of the purposes of God as revealed in the person of Jesus. *Christian* education is a lifelong quest for this unique knowledge in which the significance of the events recorded in the New Testament is reinterpreted in the further light of present experience.

In the beginning was the Word, and the Word was with God, and the Word was God. He was in the beginning with God; all things were made through him, and without him was not anything made that was made. In him was life, and the life was the light of men. The light shines in the darkness, and the darkness has not overcome it. . . . And the Word became flesh and dwelt among us, full of grace and truth; we have beheld his glory, glory as of the only Son from the Father.[14]

In the inclusive sense of Christian education to which reference has just been made, the key to understanding is provided by the disposition of the individual believer to acknowledge (however fearfully) the hand of God in all the events and experiences of life. As in the case of Islam, discussed in Chapter 2, Christianity includes every aspect of human existence, so much so that some might feel that there is no need for education in a Christian community to be characterized as Christian unless the integrity of the community is threatened for some reason, in which case the phrase 'Christian education' begins to assume a distinctly defensive quality.

But there is this important difference between Islam and Christianity. In Islam there is nothing which corresponds to what Christians know as the doctrine of *original sin*. In simple terms this means that Muslims repudiate the suggestion that new-born children are adversely affected by the failures of their parents, still less by the disobedience of their remote ancestors. Each newly born infant starts with a clean slate. Parents may wilfully, or unintentionally, deprive their children of their rightful spiritual patrimony – that is, Islam – but there is nothing inherent in the birth of children which requires some form of divine redemption. In Islam no primordial alienation from God complicates the essential difference between the creator and those whom he has newly created.

In orthodox Christian language faith is a gift from God, but Christians have insisted that the preparation of the heart, mind and will in one who does not yet believe is part of the long-term strategy of Christian education in a narrower sense. For anyone to be in a position to accept what is a gift it is necessary that there be an awareness that such a gift exists, together with a willingness not to reject the gift out of hand when it is offered. The educational task of preparing individuals to receive the gift of faith remains the critical problem for Christian teachers. It would be as unrealistic to deny that Christian teachers have used their positions to influence less mature minds in favour of Christian commitment, as to require them to undertake never to do so.

Christian teachers are themselves in pursuit of the knowledge of God, which is to say that they are constantly learning more about the creative, re-creative and redemptive activity of God. They have to be not only willing, but also prepared (in every sense) to hand on to others what they know. It is clear that this requires both a readiness to bear witness to the truth as Christians see it, as well as the gift of quiet advocacy. In another part of the passage in St John's Gospel from which the last quotation is taken, there are references to John the Baptist. He was the one sent by God 'to bear witness to the light' – that is, to Jesus, the Christ. 'He was not the light, but came to bear witness to the light'.[15]

THE BIBLE AS AN EDUCATIONAL SOURCE-BOOK

The concept of education in the Jewish Bible has already been considered, so there is no need to cover the same ground again in this chapter. In this chapter the word *Bible* is used in its Christian sense. It has to be remembered, however, that the writers of the New Testament are inheritors of the Jewish tradition. Their understanding of education was demonstrably influenced by the history of their own Jewish culture. In the course of time the Jewish Bible became an integral part of the sacred scripture of Christians, for whom the two parts of the Bible, the Old Testament and the New Testament, comprise an organic unity of divine revelation. The first part, the Old Testament (or the Jewish Bible) records the early history of God's dealings with his chosen people, the Jews. The second part, the New Testament, reveals Jesus as the fulfilment of the promises made by God to the Jews, and as the light for the illumination of everyone in the world, Jew and non-Jew alike.[16]

In the New Testament, as in the Old, God shows himself in history, but there is a change of emphasis. In the light of Christian experience (notably so in the case of Paul, whose conversion is described in Acts 9: 3–6), that which was implicit in the Old Testament becomes explicit in the New.[17] God's loving concern for his human creatures is universal and inclusive, without regard to differences of race. Occasionally there is still reference to the Jewish Law, but that Law is now fulfilled by Jesus. In the Sermon on the Mount Jesus is recorded as saying to his disciples: 'Think not that I have come to abolish the law and the prophets; I have come not to abolish them but to fulfil them. For truly I say to you, till heaven and earth pass away, not an iota, not a dot, will pass from the law until all is accomplished.'[18]

The law of God which Jesus fulfils is described as a yoke that is easy. In the Christian tradition Jesus is not only an exemplary servant of God, but an exemplary *teacher* by virtue of his obedience to the will of God: 'Come to me, all who labour and are heavy laden, and I will give you rest. Take my yoke upon you, and learn from me; for I am gentle and lowly in heart, and you will find rest for your souls. For my yoke is easy, and my burden is light.'[19]

There is a clear account in the New Testament of the education of one of the earliest Christian missionary teachers, St Paul. To begin with this was a Jewish education. Later it assumed a different character as a result of his Christian beliefs and convictions. Paul's is an interesting case-study of the development of Christian education in the early Christian period. When he was eventually brought to trial in Jerusalem he addressed his critics in Hebrew, telling them,

I am a Jew, born at Tarsus in Cilicia, but brought up in this city at the feet of Gamaliel, educated according to the strict manner of the law of our fathers, being zealous for God as you all are this day. I persecuted this Way [i.e. this *Christian* Way] to the death, binding and delivering to prison both men and women, as the high priest and the whole council of elders bear me witness.[20]

Paul's attitude to the Jewish Law is interesting. He looked upon the old Mosaic Law as a kind of *pedagogue*, a teacher, who guides the pupil to one (Jesus) whose knowledge of God is unique.[21] Paul, well-versed in the Judaism of his own day, noted that even the best of pedagogues, guardians, custodians or teachers cannot teach as intimately as a father can teach his children by personal example and by fidelity to the new law which God has revealed in Jesus. In the figure of Jesus Paul recognized one through whom we are taught to become the children of

God.[22] There is, thus, both continuity and discontinuity between the Old and the New Testaments with regard to an understanding of God's educative work. There is continuity by virtue of the acceptance on the part of Christians of God's earlier promises, recorded in the books of the Old Testament. Discontinuity comes with the Christian interpretation of the life and ministry of Jesus. This is important for a proper understanding of the New Testament pre-suppositions about Christian education.

A feature of this is the emphasis on the educative significance of suffering. The subject of suffering is by no means neglected in the Old Testament, but in the New it is picked up rather differently. Suffering is part of the learning process, but not in a fatalist or abstract way. The teacher himself (Christ) exemplifies the teaching. The suffering of Christians is linked to the sufferings endured on their behalf by Christ. The love which God has for his children is demonstrated in Jesus. However imperfect the analogy may be it illustrates the fatherly concern that God has for his children. Whenever children neglect what is provided for their welfare they must expect correction. Obedience to the law of God is as much a part of the teaching in the New Testament as in the Old. The education of the Christian in the law of God is a means to an end. The end, or the reward for faithful service, is the privilege of sharing to some extent in the holiness of God.

We have had earthly fathers to discipline us and we respected them. Shall we not much more be subject to the Father of spirits and live? For they disciplined us for a short time at their pleasure, but he disciplines us for our good, that we may share his holiness. For a moment all discipline seems painful rather than pleasant; later it yields the peaceful fruit of righteousness to those who have been trained by it.[23]

This goal is, as Paul notes, unattained, but it is attainable: 'I press on toward the goal for the prize of the upward call of God in Christ Jesus. Let those of us who are mature be thus minded; and if in anything you are otherwise minded, God will reveal that also to you. Only let us hold true to what we have attained.'[24]

Paul develops his educational theme in other letters, noting that God continues to test his children to see if they are able to endure until the goal is attained. What we have to learn is what God has given to us in Christ. And on those who know about this gift there is placed an obligation to teach it to others.[25]

For the grace of God has appeared for the salvation of all men, training us to renounce irreligion and worldly passions, and to live sober, upright, and godly lives in this world, awaiting our blessed hope, the appearing of the glory of our great God and Saviour Jesus Christ, who gave himself for us to redeem us from all iniquity and to purify for himself a people of his own who are zealous for good deeds. Declare these things; exhort and reprove with all authority. Let no-one disregard you.[26]

According to Paul, Christians will find in scripture that which is 'profitable for teaching, for reproof, for correction, and for training in righteousness, that the man of God may be complete, equipped for every good work.'[27] Some have seen in texts such as this a confirmation of the inerrancy and verbal inspiration of the scriptures. Biblical fundamentalism, or Biblicism, is very influential in some educational circles, notably in the southern United States, and is present in Britain as well. To the extent that it inhibits the development of the critical faculty in students, and even excludes teaching material which is thought likely to promote critical attitudes, it cannot reasonably be described as Christian.

TEACHING METHODS

Christian parents are responsible for the education of their children in a direct way which they cannot wholly delegate to others. What methods should they be using themselves, and what methods would they be likely to approve in the work of other teachers? This responsibility is all the more difficult to discharge when the state requires attendance at schools where the prevailing values are different from, or in some cases inimical to, the values of the home. As previous chapters have indicated, the problem of a clash between the values of the home and those of the school is not limited to families with Christian convictions. Teachers have been invested with considerable powers of influence and persuasion by the state, powers which have been arrogated by legislators on behalf of society rather than delegated by parents, although it is true that few parents are heard to object.

Nevertheless, silence may conceal a profound level of parental disquiet, at the immediate prospect of divided loyalties. Children may fall victim to intellectual as well as social pressure when two sets of values, neither of which can be understood in terms of the other, begin to conflict. The difficulty is that it now seems to be taken for granted that when the educational values of minority religious groups conflict with the values of professional educators it is the former values which are held to be deficient. A case in point is the suggestion that *Christian* education (appropriate enough, perhaps, in the privacy of Christian communities) is conducted by methods of initiation and catechesis that are inadmissible in the wider world of educational orthodoxy. This kind of paternalism is a potential threat to cultural diversity.

Fathers are not to provoke their children to anger but yet 'to bring them up in the discipline and instruction of the Lord'.[28]

Christian education is, in this view, nurture in the faith. It is instrumental, though not necessarily indoctrinatory, because it encourages individuals to think for themselves and to reflect about the faith handed on to them in the light of their own experience. This point is an important one because it bears on the question of teaching methods. A careful reading of the New Testament shows that although Christian education is primarily concerned with nurture, this need not compromise the rights of individuals to make their own decisions after considering the evidence. For, if the Christian way of life is to be accepted either by children whose parents already belong to the Christian community, or by anyone outside the community of faith, Christian education must be characterized by the sensitivity of its methods. Two examples can be quoted from different authors in the New Testament. 'Have nothing to do with stupid, senseless controversies; you know that they breed quarrels. And the Lord's servant must not be quarrelsome but kindly to everyone, an apt teacher, forbearing, correcting his opponents with gentleness.'[29]

A similar approach is taken by another New Testament writer in a passage to which the title of this chapter alludes: 'In your hearts reverence Christ as Lord. Always be prepared to make a defence to anyone who calls you to account for the hope that is in you, yet do it with gentleness and reverence.'[30]

These two statements are of considerable importance in locating the distinctive features of Christian approaches to education. What makes them useful, as distinct from merely interesting, is the way in which they link teaching methods to subject-matter. In Christian education the subject-matter must always be related in some recognizable way to the life of faith which it serves. In Christian education that faith cannot fail to be at the centre of the enterprise without misrepresentation and loss. The crucial question is concerned with method. Much could be said about this by way of practical advice for teachers whose perspective on education is influenced by Christian belief. In summary it might be put like this.

Controversy for its own sake is to be avoided because it is potentially divisive and fruitless. But it is to be noted that one form of educational escapism is to conceal differences of opinion and of belief, or to exclude controversial issues from the classroom, in what are held to be the interests of tolerance. As distinct from this, one of the principal objectives in Christian education is to enable students to cope with controversy in a reasoned and reasonable manner. Ignorance – whether it be of the Christian view of life, or of any other view of life – is to be replaced by knowledge. Factual errors are to be corrected. Prejudice and misunderstanding are to be challenged. Above all, from a Christian point of view, students are to be enabled to give a reasoned account of the hope that is in them, but without giving offence gratuitously. Faith and reason are inseparable in Christian education. The teacher's approach should be exemplary with respect to both.

The idea that Christian education may have something unique to contribute to the debate about what are commonly called standards of social morality and religious belief in a pluralist society is easily overlooked or simply disregarded. On the other hand, the notion that Christian education is for ever tied to a particular set of social and religious values is too often assumed without any attempt at critical re-evaluation. The general principle which Christians are encouraged to apply to their own circumstances is expressed in a New Testament passage which, without some form of critical scrutiny, begs a number of important questions: 'Finally, brethren, whatever is true, whatever is honourable, whatever is just, whatever is pure, whatever is lovely, whatever is gracious, if there is any excellence, if there is anything worthy of praise, think about these things.'[31]

The development of the critical faculty to the point at which it becomes possible to 'give a reason for the hope that is in you' (or – what may be equally important from an educational point of view – a *reasoned* account for a rejection of any religious beliefs) becomes a major objective in Christian education.[32] Truth is to be distinguished from falsehood. Error is to be repudiated, not just avoided. False teachers and their teaching are to be exposed.[33] More immediately in relation to the words just quoted, Christian education becomes a joint enterprise in which teachers and students learn the art of patient discrimination. The attempt has to be made to *dis-cover* what is true, honourable, just, pure, lovely, gracious and excellent, and to distinguish those things which merit such epithets from those things which do not.

Not all Christians, perhaps, would be prepared to agree over points of detail with the eighteenth-century Christian writer William Law, but few would dispute that his effort to interpret the link between faith and life in his own day was a legitimate application of the general principle mentioned earlier:

An education under Pythagoras or Socrates had no other end but to teach youth to think, judge, act, and follow such rules of life as Pythagoras and Socrates used.

And is it not as a reasonable to suppose that a Christian education should have no other end but to teach youth how to think, and judge, and act, and live according to the laws of Christianity?

At least one would suppose that in all Christian schools the teaching of youth to begin their lives in the spirit of Christianity, in such severity of behaviour, such abstinence, sobriety, humility, and devotion, as Christianity requires, should not only be more, but a hundred times more, regarded than any or all things else.[34]

PERSONAL FREEDOM, SELF-DEVELOPMENT AND AUTONOMY

Christians commonly hold to the belief that they, like all other human beings, are subject to the revealed will of the creator, but at the same time are invested by God with a freedom not only to accept the revelation for themselves but to reject it. The eighteenth-century Enlightenment gave a fresh impetus to the pursuit of self-development and autonomy in education, understood as liberation from the restrictions placed upon the individual by authoritarian systems of belief. One is obliged to say 'a fresh impetus' in order to question the assumption that the kind of education which grew up in Europe and elsewhere as a result of Christian initiatives before the Enlightenment inhibited a spirit of free inquiry.

In the eighteenth century Rousseau, for example, maintained that the role of the teacher was to draw out of children what is latent in them, to foster its development, and thus to encourage the free development of individual human potential. He resisted the notion that education was a process by which uncouth children were filled up with external knowledge to make them 'civilized', or to prepare them to accept the restrictions placed upon them by society. But he was not the first to insist on the importance of child-centred education, or on the capacity of children to surprise their teachers with what they already know if encouraged to express it in their own way.

At that time the disciples came to Jesus, saying, 'Who is the greatest in the kingdom of heaven?' And calling to him a child, he put him in the midst of them, and said, 'Truly, I say to you, unless you turn and become like children, you will never enter the kingdom of heaven. Whoever humbles himself like this child, he is the greatest in the kingdom of heaven'.[35]

Emphasis on the uniqueness, individuality and potential of the person is at the heart of Christian education. This is not to deny that personal freedom can be abused by teachers who profess the Christian faith but rather to conclude that, whenever they refuse to respect the integrity of the person, agents of Christianity act in ways which are unchristian. From a Christian perspective there are limits to human freedom. Conformity to the will and purposes of God, revealed in the person of Jesus, ultimately decides the measure of freedom which men and women may enjoy. It is both the privilege and the obligation of human beings to be obedient to God, 'whose service' (in the words of the well-known Christian prayer) 'is perfect freedom'. The reinterpretation of this paradox is one of the contributions which Christian education might make to the life of a pluralist society, at a time when personal freedom is variously understood in different cultures. But compulsion merely converts service into bondage. It has no more respect for human rights than the varieties of ideological indoctrination.

To enable pupils and students to make choices for themselves (not just in the case of a specific world-view, whether Christian or not), Christian teachers are faced with two unavoidable long-term tasks, both of which call for *collaborative* efforts that are likely to involve different teachers in different subjects over extended periods of time. The first is to make accurate information available to students in ways suited to their needs and aptitudes. The second teaching task is evaluative. In the end it may be more important than the first, for if students are to be in a position to make choices for themselves, their capacity to arrive at reasonable critical judgements based upon the evidence adduced needs to be *exercised* as well as informed. This calls for practice, at however elementary a level, from the time that children begin to be capable of reflecting about their own opinions.

The temptation for the teacher is to assume that the readiness of children for this evaluative exercise is dictated by chronological age, without taking the trouble to investigate individual cases. The task of helping to develop the critical faculty cannot be left for the arrival of unspecified points in the future when students 'can decide for themselves'. Help with decision-making is part of a child-centred education at every stage of development. From a Christian point of view, knowledge is a gift, and there are varieties of gifts, but this does not release the teacher from the obligation to assist children to identify the particular gifts that are in them. It is easy to be cynical at this point, but it is because of the Christian insistence on the unique value of each individual that liberties cannot be taken with even the most intractable human material.[36]

There may be nothing uniquely Christian about this responsibility of the teacher for ensuring that talent is not wasted. In the selection of material to be presented to students, Christians might conceivably have a different perception of what is appropriate for the task from their non-Christian colleagues, however. In a genuinely pluralistic society this is more than likely to be so, and for that reason (presumably) to be considered sympathetically. Teachers are obliged to be selective about the material they present. There are several practical constraints. Lack of personal knowledge, lack of confidence in tackling certain topics, shortage of resources and shortage of time limit the possibilities to be considered. Although the process of selection is properly described as a matter for professional judgement, it can scarcely be denied that in practice the personal convictions and tastes of teachers sometimes bring the selection of material to be taught in the classroom (as well as the material to be excluded) perilously close to censorship. To some extent this is inevitable. The tendency to favour certain ideas at the expense of others appears to be a universal human characteristic.

THE END OF CHRISTIAN EDUCATION

Christian education is unintelligible without reference to Christian beliefs about divine initiatives and human responses. It is clear that on the one hand the appropriate responses to God's revelation are obedience and compliance – logically it could not be otherwise without trivializing the revelation. On the other hand, authentically Christian approaches to education in a secular, pluralistic country must leave room for the *exercise* of the freedom to decide, with which Christians believe all human beings have been endowed by God. Neither teachers nor students can legitimately be required to submit to authority in advance of the inquiry. This applies just as much to the teaching given within Christian communities as to the teaching in a secular environment. The decision is, in any case, a crucial one. To enable students to make a reasoned decision calls for considerable attention to detail, and for perseverance. It also requires attentiveness to the uniqueness of human relationships which for Christian teachers is a form of concentrated prayer.

The key to a Christian conception of studies is the realization that prayer consists of attention. It is the orientation of all the attention of which the soul is capable towards God. The quality of the attention counts for much in the quality of the prayer. Warmth of heart cannot make up for it. . . . For an adolescent, capable of grasping this truth and generous enough to desire this fruit above all others, studies could have their fullest spiritual effect, quite apart from any particular religious belief.[37]

However, there is another sense in which it is appropriate to speak of the end of Christian education. In this sense it is rather like the raft which the traveller uses to cross a raging stream. Having reached the safety of the other side the traveller abandons the raft. The function of the raft is well understood in Buddhism. Christian education is not an end in itself. Like the raft it is only a means to an end. It may in fact be an error to think in terms of fixed principles in relation to Christian education. The spirit of God blows where it pleases, to the surprise (and sometimes to the delight) of teachers and students. The following words from the pen of an eminent Jewish authority show that religious and cultural differences need not necessarily stand in the way of common educational goals.

When all 'directions' fail there arises in the darkness over the abyss the one true direction of man, towards the creative Spirit, towards the Spirit of God brooding on the face of the waters, towards Him of whom we know not whence He comes and whither He goes. That is man's true autonomy which no longer betrays but responds. Man, the creature, who forms and transforms the creation, cannot create. But he, each man, can expose himself and others to the creative Spirit. And he can call upon the Creator to save and perfect His (that is God's) image.[38]

These are fine words which breathe a spirit of humility and tolerance. Both qualities are indispensable at the present time. Even so, there is something much more explicit which must remain the final measure of Christian education. All authentically Christian approaches to education will be seen to combine an understanding of the beliefs of others (and of the freedom of individuals to make their own decisions) with the clearest possible presentation of the claims of the Christian Gospel. From first to last Christian education is an exploration of the implications of the claim that, 'in Christ God was reconciling the world to himself'.[39]

NOTES AND REFERENCES

1. Pasternak Boris 1958 *Doctor Zhivago* (translated from the Russian by Max Hayward and Manya Harari), Collins, London, p 101. Novels, poems and much more mundane forms of contemporary literature provide rich sources of material for teaching that can be suitably adapted for presentation to students of different ages and aptitudes
2. 2 Corinthians 4: 6. (All quotations from the Old and New Testaments are from the Revised Version text in *The New Oxford Annotated Bible, with the Apocrypha*, 1977 May. Herbert G and Metzger, Bruce M (eds) Oxford University Press, New York.)
3. St Mark 8: 27–29
4. Genesis 1: 27–28; 2: 16–17
5. Neill Stephen 1970 *Christian Faith and Other Faiths: the Christian Dialogue with Other Religions*. Oxford University Paperbacks, 2nd edn, p 7
6. 'Behold, I make all things new.' Revelation 21: 5
7. Qurʾān 2: 256. In Chapter 2 I have suggested several useful and available English versions of the Qurʾān
8. Kempis Thomas à, 1957 *The Imitation of Christ*, translated from the Latin by Maine George F. Collins, pp 34–35
9. This paragraph is substantially the same as one I included in another essay, 'Christian Education in a Multi-cultural Society', in a book of that title, edited by McLelland V A 1988, Routledge, pp 80–100
10. See Vermes Geza 1973 *Jesus the Jew*. Collins
11. St John 16: 12–14

12. See, e.g. Warren M A C 1976 *I believe in the Great Commission.* Hodder & Stoughton
13. St Matthew 28: 19–20
14. St John 1: 1–5, 14
15. St John 1:7–8
16. The words of Simeon made this clear when the infant Jesus was brought by his parents to the Temple in order to meet the requirements of the Jewish law. See Luke 2: 29–35; and cf. Isaiah 49: 6.
17. Paul's own account of his conversion is given in Galatians 1: 13–17; cf. Acts 9: 1–31
18. St Matthew 5: 17–18; cf. St John 1: 17–18
19. St Matthew 11: 28–30
20. Acts 22: 3–5
21. Galatians 3: 23–29
22. Galatians 4: 4–7
23. Hebrews 12: 9–11
24. Philippians 3: 14–16
25. Cf. 1 Timothy 4: 6–16; Ephesians 4: 11–16
26. Titus 2: 11–15
27. 2 Timothy 3: 16–17
28. Ephesians 6: 4
29. 2 Timothy 2: 23–25
30. 1 Peter 3: 15. This text is a useful starting point for what has recently come to be called 'faith-sharing' in Christian approaches to education. One such approach lies behind the publication of an approved Roman Catholic programme of religious education, prepared by A. Patrick Purnell, with the title *Our Faith Story*, Collins paperback, 1986. This particular approach has been criticized by some readers because it is too personalist, and because it appears to reduce the Christian faith to what is subjectively experienced
31. Philippians 4: 8
32. Hulmes Edward 1982 'Developing the critical faculty in religious education', Farmington Occasional Paper, Oxford
33. 2 Peter 2: 1–3
34. Law William 1978 *A Serious Call to a Devout and Holy Life.* Stanwood Paul G (ed). Classics of Western Spirituality, Paulist Press, New York, p 250
35. St Matthew 18: 1–4
36. 1 Corinthians 12: 4–31
37. Weil Simone 1965 'Reflections on the right use of school studies', in *Waiting on God* (translated by Craufurd Emma). Collins Fontana Books, pp 66, 76
38. Buber Martin 1961 'Education', in *Between Man and Man*, translated and introduced by Smith Ronald Gregor. Fontana Books, p 131
39. 2 Corinthians 5: 19

African perspectives: 'The lore of the land is beyond the knowledge of many fathers'

Rapid changes are taking place in Africa, so that traditional ideas are being abandoned, modified or coloured by the changing situation. At the same time it would be wrong to imagine that everything traditional has been changed or forgotten so much that traces of it are not to be found.[1]

Wisdom is like a goatskin bag; every man carries his own.[2]

THE ANTIQUITY AND DIVERSITY OF AFRICAN EXPERIENCE

Use of the phrase 'African perspectives' in the title of this chapter is an acknowledgement of the antiquity and diversity of the world-views that have influenced the lives of African peoples over a long period of time. In different ways three major systems of religious belief and social organization have emerged in Africa over the course of many centuries as agents of initiation, conservation and change – not least in education.

The first is characterized by perceptions of the universe (and of the place of every form of life in the created order) that can be subsumed under the phrase 'African Traditional Religion', despite local differences of emphasis.[3] The beliefs and values associated with African Traditional Religion are to be distinguished from those which derive from Christian or Islamic beliefs, but this is not to deny that both Christianity and Islam are firmly rooted in African soil: 'Both Christianity and Islam are "traditional" and "African" in a historical sense, and it is a pity that they tend to be regarded as "foreign" or "European" and "Arab".'[4]

Yet long before the advent of Christian or Islamic monotheism in Africa it was an alternative world-view which regulated human relationships in many parts of that continent. Communities which were in many cases widely separated geographically held to similar principles of belief and action, despite local differences of language and custom, and despite the inevitable incidence of inter-tribal conflict when there were clashes of interest. These religious beliefs, customs and traditions gave expression to a world-view that can be identified as essentially *African*: rooted in antiquity, but still resilient.

The second major influence has been that of Christianity. It is sometimes stated that Christianity is an alien world-view in Africa, imposed on subject peoples during the period of European colonial activity. But the impact of Christianity on Africa has a much longer history, which goes back to the beginnings of the missionary work of the church, as recorded in the New Testament.[5] This has ensured that there is a uniquely *African* dimension to the development of Christian theology, Christian social teaching and Christian education, but which is not recognized as widely as it might be.

The third major influence has been that of Islam, an influence that began in the first century of the Islamic era (the seventh century AD), shortly after the beginning of the prophetic mission of Muhammad, when Muslims ventured into Africa taking their way of life with them and making converts. Some moved west across the North African littoral, and south across the trade-routes of the Sahara. By the fourth Islamic century (the eleventh century AD) Muslims had established a flourishing civilization in West Africa. Though based upon Islamic principles, it was a culture which was able to adapt to the beliefs and social patterns of the indigenous peoples. In this respect it was less potentially disruptive of traditional African values than Christianity. One of the most spirited discussions of the impact of both Christianity and Islam on the peoples of Africa was provided almost a hundred years ago by the black scholar Edward Wilmot Blyden.[6]

THE SCOPE OF THIS CHAPTER

The principles which govern the relationship between religious belief and educational practice in Christianity, Islam and Judaism have already been discussed in previous chapters. In consequence, attention focuses in this chapter on 'African Traditional Religion'. This may be intrinsically interesting to students of cultural diversity, but there is an additional factor to be considered. The influence of African Traditional Religion is being felt in Britain today not as an external pressure but as an internal force. The reasons for its presence in British society have to be understood if this aspect of cultural diversity is to be used effectively in education. Some reference to Britain's colonial and post-colonial relationships with Africa must, therefore, be made as the chapter proceeds.

It is true that rapid political, economic and social changes have already taken place in several African countries. It is clear that even more significant (and probably disturbing) changes cannot be long delayed elsewhere in Africa – notably in the southern parts of the continent. The struggle for independence is sustained by promises of change, and by the expectation that injustice will be removed. Whether or not these promises are being realized is for Africans themselves to decide.[7] From a practical point of view, with effective teaching in mind, there is a link (if not an entirely happy one) between their recent history and ours that bears directly on the recognition of the educational implications of cultural diversity.

The western world has been influenced by African culture in a variety of ways. The proximity of the North African coast to the southern shores of Europe across the Mediterranean ensured cultural exchanges long before the first European attempts to colonize parts of the African continent. Other routes linked Africa to the ancient civilizations of the Fertile Crescent, and then to Asia, providing further opportunities for the meeting of cultures. Still later, the inhuman trade in black slaves from Africa to the New World led to the widespread dissemination of African religious and cultural values in the Americas. In all of this movement African ideas, music and art have influenced the development of western civilization in areas of life as apparently unrelated as European painting and American jazz.

During the period of European colonial administration in Africa Britain played a major role in opening up what was mistakenly called 'the dark continent' to the influence of non-African cultural beliefs and values. By the end of the nineteenth century vast areas in East and West Africa, for example, had been explored and incorporated into the British empire. Less than a hundred years later most of these once-dependent colonies had assumed the status of independent sovereign states.[8]

The problems associated with intolerance are universal, giving a much wider currency to concepts such as *independence, self-determination, liberation, freedom* and *autonomy* than is often suspected. The relevance of such concepts makes it easier for teachers to tackle the social aspects of pluralism by drawing attention to common interests rather than to destructive divisions, although the latter cannot be ignored. The African experience reveals what can happen when one culture is disrupted (or displaced) by another through outside interference and exploitation. The impact of European colonialism on Africa was disruptive, despite the best efforts of European administrators, entrepreneurs and Christian missionaries. Africans themselves are prepared to acknowledge these efforts but insist that European standards of administration, education, medicine and commerce were inevitably imposed upon subject peoples during the colonial period.

The continuation of British influence on African life is nowhere more apparent than in education. Africans have shown a passionate interest in acquiring knowledge from British teachers, and a great aptitude for learning. They have been quick to seize opportunities for self-advancement through education, and to adapt to changing circumstances. Does this mean that they have abandoned their traditional values? The answer seems to be No, even when those with African cultural roots are obliged (for whatever reason) to live in western, secularized, pluralistic societies.

On the whole I am more a pagan than a Christian, and is that such a bad thing to be? In the tribe I learned discipline and the law of the tribe. The old women told me that I was always being watched, in the day-time by the big light, the sun, and in the night by the small lights, the moon and the stars; whatever I did would be known, and, if I broke the law of the tribe, what I had done would certainly come to light. Was that a bad way of educating the conscience of a boy?[9]

AFRICAN TRADITIONAL RELIGIOUS BELIEFS AND VALUES

The individual and the community

Traditional African societies bear witness to a conviction that a religious view of life provides the community not only with a sense of spiritual and social coherence but the means of realizing them. Alternative world-views are unlikely to satisfy the deepest needs of the African spirit if they fail to enable individuals to recognize and fulfil their communal responsibilities. From an educational point of view the implication of this is clear. What is necessary for the health of the African spirit may also be necessary for others. African Traditional Religion[10] is not *dead* religion, although its existence is always being threatened by the claims of secularism.

For many decades black African students have been coming to the West for higher education. All of them have, to a greater or lesser extent, experienced the dislocations caused by culture shock. In order to be successful in their studies they are obliged in most cases to assimilate the values of the western intellectual tradition. This adaptation is not easy for them to make, as any-one who has ever worked with them can confirm. They live be-tween two worlds, that of their African roots, and that of their western mentors. One point of difference between these two worlds concerns the relationship of the individual to the com-munity. In an African society every aspect of existence is under-stood in a religious sense as part of the corporate life of a com-munity, linking the past with the present: 'Failure to realize and appreciate this starting point has led missionaries, anthropologists, colonial administrators, and other foreign writers on African religions, to misunderstand not only the religions as such but the peoples of Africa.'[11]

The emphasis given in the West to the uniqueness of the individual, and the attention given in western education to the concept of autonomy, are alien to the indigenous African traditions with which we are concerned here. Descartes' personalist dictum, *cogito ergo sum* ('I think, therefore I am'), has thus to be modified by those who have experience of both European and African ways of life. This requires that the African experience of *community* be acknowledged as a source of educational wisdom. '*I* am, because *we* are. And since *we* are, therefore *I* am', is an African variant of Descartes' philosophical point of departure.[12] This variant may be used to counter a prevalent European attitude which emphasizes the importance of individual rights, very often at the expense of community obligations and interests. This is an attitude which Africans consider to be misguided. From an African point of view it is the conformity of the individual to the beliefs and customs of society which makes for the stability of the community. In return, it is the stability of the community which protects the rights of the individual.

A coherent view of life

In his book *Introduction to African Religion*,[13] John Mbiti shows where African attitudes to the life of society find expression. His analysis provides teachers with one of the most useful guides to effective teaching in this area. The key to the enterprise is African religion, which

evolved slowly through many centuries, as people responded to the situations of their life and reflected upon their experiences. Many factors must have played a part in its development. This includes the geographical environment – mountains, rivers, deserts and forests – the change of the seasons, the powers of nature (such as earthquakes, thunderstorms and volcanoes), calamities, epidemics, diseases, birth and death, and major historical events like wars, locust invasions, famines, migrations and so on. To these must be added man's reflection on the universe, the questions about its origin, the earth and the sky, the problem of evil and suffering, the phenomena of nature, and many other problems.[14]

A sense of the coherence of life and of the intimate relationship between every aspect of human existence, though typical of African culture, is not unique to it. A comparable sense of wholeness is, of course, to be found in the world-views considered in previous chapters, but what becomes clearer from a study of the African experience in particular is that a way of life which is *comprehensively religious* in character is easy to disrupt in the assumed interests of pluralism. This presents a curious paradox at a time when great efforts are being made to preserve minority rights. There is, therefore, all the more reason in a *pluralist* society to consider the claims of such an alternative world-view.

Approaching traditional African beliefs and values

(a) *Making a start*   Africans retain their own distinctive cultural patterns. The expression of African cultural diversity is to be found in a wide variety of forms. Each of them offers a rich source of teaching material. The list of topics might include such headings as the following: beliefs and customs; rituals, ceremonies and festivals; shrines, sacred places and religious objects; proverbs, riddles and wise sayings; myths and legends; art and symbols; music and dance.[15]

Teachers who are interested in considering African perspectives with their students may, at first sight, be daunted by the amount of material available. Suggestions which may be used as the basis of straightforward schemes of work are required at this stage. Teachers in 'pluralist' countries such as Britain are now obliged to confront the issues of *mutual* enrichment and *inter*dependence in order to test their intentions about pluralism. Space must be provided for members of ethnic minorities, as for others, to discuss the issues which actually affect their daily lives.

All teachers have some responsibility for ensuring that this space is provided. It is said that this cannot be done with the 'hard' scientific subjects. Teachers of science and science-related subjects might care to question this, but the task can certainly be attempted in the humanities. This is particularly true in the case of religious education, and this is one of the principal reasons why the subject is so important at the present time. But what kind of a starting-point is available?

If the testimony of some anthropologists is to be accepted, it is to parts of East Africa (in Kenya and Tanzania) that the origins of mankind are to be traced. Human artefacts, such as tools and weapons, and the remains of bones said to be in the order of two million years old have been discovered. In that sense it may be true that 'man was born in Africa'.[16] The Bushmen of the Kalahari desert are a people who have roamed the deserts of southern Africa for thousands of years. Their way of life is threatened with extinction by the values of a modern technological world. This endangered community is perhaps the best-known, if the least understood, example of the antiquity of human social organisation in Africa.

Laurens van der Post has written about the impact of alien cultural values on this largely forgotten African community, the aboriginal inhabitants of Namibia (formerly South West Africa) and Botswana: 'I have an inkling now of the almost paralytic effect our mere presence can have on their natural spirit.'[17]

Yet the charge of disrupting an ancient culture is not only to be laid on Europeans, or whites of European descent: 'I find the thought of what black and white did to the Bushmen almost more than I can endure.'[18]

(b) *The concept of time* The African understanding of *the significance of time in the life of the community* provides a useful starting-point for preparing a scheme of work. Its usefulness lies in the fact that it affords an interesting alternative approach to the mystery of time for students who may never have thought consciously about the subject, or who may think about it only in conventional western terms. Time is the continuum in which events occur. There is something important to be learned from the African experience of *contemporaneity*, and from the African understanding of time which goes beyond the mere recognition of duration. That which has happened has a profound significance for the present life of the community. That which is happening *now* involves the individual directly in a re-interpretation of the story of the collective life of the community. The distant future lies not only beyond the knowledge of human beings but outside their present interest.

According to traditional [African] concepts, time is a two-dimensional phenomenon, with a long *past*, a *present*, and virtually *no future*. The linear concept of time in western thought, with an indefinite past, a present, and an infinite future, is practically foreign to African thinking. The future is virtually absent because events which lie in it have not taken place, they have not been realized, and cannot, therefore, constitute time. If, however, future events are certain to occur, or if they fall within the inevitable rhythm of nature, they at best constitute only *potential time* not *actual time*. . . . *Actual time* is therefore what is present and what is past. It moves 'backward' rather than 'forward'; and people set their minds not on future things, but chiefly on what has taken place.[19]

This African understanding of the significance of time is not 'backward-looking' in common western parlance. On the contrary, it links the present generation directly to the experience of the past, and revivifies the life of the past in the present. This attitude is evident in the words of the proverb quoted in the title of this chapter. 'The lore of the land is beyond the knowledge of many fathers.' It is the cumulative tradition that is normative for present thought and present action. Religious and social values are thus conserved, and the collective wisdom of ancestors is handed on in a way which provides for a measure of stability and continuity.

The principle of democracy is extended to the 'living' dead. In all of this there is a lesson for any advanced technological society, in which a sense of the continuing importance of the past has been lost, and in which there appear to be no comparably effective mechanisms for conservation, continuity and change. In an African community untouched by the 'benefits' of a modern lifestyle, the long-established rhythms of nature provide a sufficient promise for the needs of the immediate future, beyond which it is neither necessary nor prudent to speculate. Another religious tradition expresses a similar sentiment: 'Do not be anxious about tomorrow, for tomorrow will be anxious for itself. Let the day's own trouble be sufficient for the day.'[20]

(c) *God and creation*   Throughout Africa it is believed that the universe was created. It did not just happen of itself, and it has not always existed. There are many different accounts of creation, but they all tell stories about contingency. God, the creator, stands outside what he has created, yet he is closely associated with its destiny. God preserves its existence. This view is essentially religious because it recognizes a unique relationship.

How did the world come to be? How do we account for the existence of the sun, the moon, the stars? Where did everything come from, and for what purpose? What happens after death? There are many myths and legends that can be used to illustrate the answers, as well as the further questions, that come from these African sources. The function of these religious myths is not to provide satisfactory scientific answers to difficult questions, but to preserve characteristic African beliefs about the contingency of the created order, and about the total dependence of individuals and communities on the creator.

So, for example, 'God created man so that the sun would have someone for whom to shine'. In several cases male and female appear together as husband and wife, at the end of God's creative activity. All kinds of plants and fruits, the animals and birds, and the fish in rivers and oceans are there to serve the needs of mankind. Or again, 'The Lozi narrate that God was still on the earth when he created man after creating all the other things. He went on to make different peoples, each with its own customs, language, and manners.' To express the creative work of God, various metaphors are used in the narratives. God is the potter who throws men and women from clays of different colours. Mankind's original state on earth was one of bliss, but disobedience brought suffering and death. Smoke from fires 'created on earth by friction' rose into the sky to make God withdraw, at least partially, from the human scene.[21]

The created order is not self-sufficient but dependent. It is not the planet Earth which is the centre of things. Pride of place goes to men and women. Everything exists for the sake of mankind. In principle this enlarges the African perspective of creation, making the defence of any outdated cosmology unnecessary. In the design of the creator the universe is not, and never was, *geocentric* but *anthropocentric*.

African people consider man to be at the centre of the universe. Being in that position he tries to use the universe or derive some use from it in physical, mystical, and supernatural ways. He sees the universe in terms of himself, and endeavours to live in harmony with it. . . . In this way the visible and invisible parts of the universe are at man's disposal through physical, mystical, and religious means. Man is not the master in the universe; he is only the centre, the friend, the beneficiary, the user. For that reason he has to live in harmony with the universe, obeying the laws of natural, moral, and mystical order. If these are unduly disturbed, it is man who suffers most.[22]

Belief in a creator God who sustains and controls the creation is universal in traditional African societies, whatever reasons may be suggested to account for it, from a feeling of human dependence to a fear of the uncontrollable forces in nature. No one has seen God, but a knowledge of his will has been built up over long periods of time by careful observation. His attributes, and aspects of his activity, are recalled by means of many of his other names. He is spoken of as if he had human qualities. These elements of anthropomorphism are inescapable. In addition to being addressed as 'Creator' he may be called Father (in some cases as Mother) by his children, thus uniting the community as an extended family. He is King, Chief, Ruler, Judge and the truest Friend of mankind.

As a *person* God both sees and hears. He is able to touch, to taste and to smell. He is capable of speech, of joy, of anger, of remembering good and evil deeds, of eating and drinking, of sleeping, of playing. God is holy, merciful, compassionate, just and good. He provides, protects, forgives, punishes, rewards. Nature reflects the activities of the creator at every turn. The sun and moon are the eyes of God. Nothing escapes his gaze at any time. His favour ensures the succession of day and night, the proper course of the seasons, the fertility of the land, and the creativity of the womb. His disfavour is expressed in punishments which may bring famine, drought, disease and death. Yet even in these cases the ears of God are not deaf to petition or sacrifice.

(d) *Prayer*   Prayer, has always been a highly important part of African daily life. It has been described as 'the central phenomenon in the religious traditions of Africa'.[23] This is all the clearer now that the work of writing up the oral tradition, and of translation, is going ahead. Many illustrations of this could be given. The following example serves to show how a typical prayer ritual of the Igbo people in Nigeria provides an opportunity for uniting the members of a family, together with any guests who may be present:

The [morning] prayer falls into four main parts. The first is a recognition of the presence of God and the departed members of the family (the living dead). The man greets God and the living dead, and then gives them the kola nut. Usually the kola nut is split into two, one part is given away and the other is retained by the giver. The nut, and the act of sharing it, symbolize friendship, hospitality, welcome, and unity; they are the signs of removing distance, belonging together, establishing and renewing friendship.

The second part of the prayer asks for forgiveness for any evil which the man and his family may have done. Then he asks for long life, food, children, and rich harvests, all of which are valued very highly in African societies.

The third part deals with the relationships in the community of neighbours and other people. The man wants only what is good to prosper. Therefore he invokes God, and the spiritual powers, to deal with those who propagate evil. He invokes formal curses on those who do evil to him and the community.

The concluding part is often used in Igbo prayers: 'Let the kite perch, and let the eagle perch, whichever says that the other must not perch, let its wings break off!' This means that all creatures should live peacefully with one another, for there is room for each one. But they have to live in peace and justice, without one pushing out another.[24]

The appropriateness of the preceding paragraph for present purposes is obvious. African prayers express the sense of unworthiness and uncleanness which human beings have in the presence of the holy God. Wherever there is impurity it must be ceremonially removed. Without the act of purification the community suffers; the life of its people its animals and its land is endangered. In preparation for acts of ritual cleansing, designed to restore harmony, wholeness and health to the community, individuals must approach God in humility, expressing their confidence in his providence.

Societies which are threatened by internal divisions have something to learn from the emphasis on peace and love which is to be found in many African prayers. The notion of peace carries with it the sense of tranquillity, quietness, freedom from disease and danger, contentment, happiness and the removal of all forms of evil. It is comprehensive peace, directed towards individuals, the community, the country, nature at large. It can be said that peace and tranquillity are the final end of prayer. A good illustration of this comes from a litany in which the leader calls for peace, and the people respond by calling for peace:

Leader	*Other People*
Say peace!	O peace!

Leader	*Other People*
Peace to children!	O Peace to children!
Peace to the country!	O Peace to the country!
Peace to the gardens!	O peace to the gardens![25]

(e) *Intermediaries*   When confronted by the awesome power of the Supreme God many worshippers are too conscious of their own insignificance and unworthiness to approach God directly. At such times God is approached through intermediaries who may be divinities, spirits or other human beings. There are spirits of the sky, spirits of the earth, and spirits of nature. Recourse to spirit intermediaries does not compromise the essential monotheism of African belief because spirits are themselves subordinate beings, subject to the Supreme God. In any case, belief in these lesser divinities tends to be localized.

Human intermediaries include kings, elders of the tribe, priests, diviners, healers and rain-makers. They act on behalf of individuals, and of their own communities, to protect (or restore) the relationship between God and his people. The supervision of ritual offerings, sacrifices and prayers is their responsibility – one that includes the giving of counsel and the interpretations of dreams and portents to those who solicit advice.

The intermediaries who are believed to be spiritual beings include 'the living dead'. Members of a family will invoke the help of their own ancestors. The community will preserve the names of former leaders and other important figures of the past. This does not make African traditional religion a system of ancestor worship; the departed are not worshipped. Their graves are respected, shrines are built for them and food is offered to them, in the belief that their influence on the community, and their care for its welfare, did not come to an end with physical death.

It is believed that they have easier access to him than ordinary people, although anybody can approach God directly if they have need to do so. The idea of intermediaries fits well with the African view of the universe, which holds that the invisible world has its own life and population. The life of this invisible world is in some ways higher than that of man, but God is higher still. In order to reach God effectively it may be useful to approach him by first approaching those who are lower than he is, but higher than the ordinary person.[26]

(f) *The problem of evil*   Mention of intermediaries in considering African religious perspectives raises an important question. It is clear that belief in God is rooted in the conviction that God seeks to provide for the well-being of his creation. But are all the agents of God benevolent? Are there *bad* as well as *good* spirits? Or is their favour, like the much more important favour of God himself, conditional? In other words, are the spirits sometimes well-disposed to human beings, and at other times not? Does disobedience to the higher powers bring evil in the form of natural disaster, sickness or death to individuals and communities?

Some spirits are manipulated by human agents in the benign work of healing, or divination, for instance. But the power of mediums, diviners and medicine-men may be used in less benevolent ways. A sorcerer or a witch may be consulted by one member of the community to direct malevolent spiritual powers against an enemy or rival. The suspicion on the part of the potential victim that misfortune, or even death, may follow the linking of secret animosities and private rituals leads to countervailing measures in which another cultic figure is employed to solicit the protection of the spirit world. The phrase 'preventive medicine' takes on a different meaning.

To Africans of every category, witchcraft is an urgent reality. . . . African concepts about witchcraft consist in the belief that the spirits of living human beings can be sent out of the body on errands of doing havoc to other persons in body, mind, or estate; that witches have guilds or operate singly, and that the spirits sent out of the human body in this way can act either invisibly or through a lower creature – an animal or a bird.[27]

To western eyes this presents a less attractive aspect of the African world-view. The manipulation of powers in the spirit world to settle private scores seems to be inconsistent with belief in a beneficent creator who provides for the daily needs of all his children. Fear, rather than love, appears to be the motivating force here. That fear continues to dominate daily life despite a loving and caring providence may have something to do with the fact that in African traditional religion there is literally *unfinished* business. Reference to the two-dimensional concept of time that governs life in traditional African societies was made earlier. The future dimension of time is shadowy and unreal. The present assumes its importance because of the past when, according to many accounts, mankind enjoyed a state of bliss that has since been lost. But what will fulfil the *present*? Can such a loss ever be made good in the future? One of the best-informed African authorities on the comparative study of religion arrives at the following assessment of the capacity of African Traditional Religion to provide satisfactory answers to the most pressing human questions.

It is perhaps here then, that we find the greatest weakness and poverty of our traditional religions compared to world religions like Christianity, Judaism, Islam, Buddhism, or Hinduism. These traditional religions cannot but remain tribal and nationalistic, since they do not offer for mankind at large a way of 'escape', a message of 'redemption' (however that might be conceived). Is it in this very issue, then, that these other religions have made a universal appeal and won adherents from all mankind? . . . Such 'redemption' involves rescue from the monster of death, regaining immortality, and attaining the gift of the resurrection. . . . Only a three-dimensional religion can hope to last in modern Africa which is increasingly discovering and adjusting to a third dimension of time.[28]

EDUCATION AS INITIATION INTO THE COMMUNITY

Education, in a formal sense, is initiation in traditional African societies. It is part of the process of moving from childhood into full membership of the adult community. To prepare for this transition the young person usually goes into seclusion, to be taught the lore of the land by elders appointed for the task. The period of intensive preparation includes education in the history of the community, its beliefs and customs, and the obligations of marriage and of family life. The initiate undergoes physical testing as well, designed to teach the virtues of obedience, courage and endurance. Frequently this involves the inflicting of pain that leaves scars which are signs of tribal identity, marking off the members of one community from the members of another. The sense of shared identity that follows initiation rarely extends beyond the members of a single tribal community.

The positive side of this is that it formally acknowledges inclusion within the community. The negative side is that it isolates the members of one community from those of another. Divisions are created *within* a community by the special loyalty for one another felt by members of groups who undergo their rites of initiation at the same time. In other cases divisions inside a community are perpetuated by the existence of exclusive secret societies. As a result there is little evidence to suggest that African experience might provide models for the construction of complex multi-cultural societies. Recent events show that the pursuit of social harmony on the basis of mutual tolerance and respect between races is being challenged in Africa – as elsewhere – by sectional interests.

CONTINUING THE SEARCH: EDUCATIONAL IMPLICATIONS

What has been described and discussed so far in this chapter is sufficient to show the nature of the African perspective. It is enough to encourage teachers to look carefully at African experience, and to make further explorations of their own into what may well be unfamiliar territory. The African experience is interesting in its own terms, and also for the fresh light it sheds on universal human problems. For these reasons it may be commended as a potentially rich resource for teachers working in a culturally diverse society. But in this country there is another reason for exploring the African experience in education in a culturally diverse society. It has to do with the welfare of significant minority groups in Britain today.

Some of these minority groups in Britain trace their cultural roots directly to the continent of Africa, others to Africa indirectly, through more distant ancestors who were transported to the islands of the Caribbean, or to the southern states of the USA, as slaves. In recent years considerable numbers of immigrants from Africa and the West Indies have arrived in Britain, and have added distinctive elements of Afro-Caribbean culture to public and private life. Other members of the black community in Britain have no direct knowledge of life outside Britain. They were born here, as were their parents. They have never seen the African or West Indian homelands of their ancestors. To continue to call them *immigrants* is as inaccurate as it is discriminatory. Irrespective of the lawful routes by which they, or their forebears, have come to this country, they are entitled to share the responsibilities and benefits of citizenship without fear of discrimination.

The tensions between *some* white and *some* black citizens in Britain today cannot be understood without reference to British colonial history in Africa. By the end of the eighteenth century many European whites were profiting from the transportation of blacks across the Atlantic to the New World. The compliance on the part of those who condoned the slave-trade in principle, no less than the direct involvement of the slave-masters themselves, inflicted humiliation on generations of black men, women and children, who were taken into slavery in the Americas under inhuman conditions. At the same time it has to be noted that without the cooperation of other Africans in rounding up potential victims, the slave-trade might have been brought to an end much earlier.[29] More compassionate whites eventually took the initiative in abolishing slavery, but Europeans continued to enjoy a privileged status in Africa as a result of their post-slave-trading activity. With the best of intentions it is likely to take a long time for the memories of this form of racial discrimination to mellow in Britain among the descendants of victimized communities.

Britain, in fact, is also home for minority groups whose world-view is still influenced by elements of African traditional beliefs. Some of these beliefs may appear strange to westerners unfamiliar with either the cultural history of Africa or the tenacity with which deported African slaves clung to their traditions on foreign soil.

It might be argued that the presence in Britain of minority groups with African cultural roots is one of the indirect consequences of British colonialism. Educators might ask what it is that such groups can uniquely contribute to the *corporate* life of a society that is said to be culturally diverse. What importance is attached in decisions about educational policy to the *experience* as well as the *aspirations* of such minority ethnic groups, whose attitudes are still (at least partially) formed in a different cultural milieu? There is a temptation to dodge the real issue by seeking to make special *temporary* provisions for minority groups who (it is anticipated) will lose their distinctive cultural identity through assimilation within a couple of generations. This is to miss the unique opportunities presented by cultural diversity in a pluralist society. The question is, rather, to what extent may our common understanding of human relationships be *permanently* enriched by African perspectives?

The exuberance of charismatic Christian churches of West Indian origin, for instance, is a striking reminder of the liturgical and theological diversity that is to be found within Christianity, provided that a sufficiently wide-ranging approach to Christianity as a *world* religion is admitted in education. The mingling of different religious and cultural traditions is also exemplified by the Rastafarian life-style.[30]

Discrimination on grounds of racial origin persists in Britain, however, on both sides of the black/white racial divide, to the disadvantage of everyone concerned. Any attempt to benefit from past experience, with the intention of promoting social harmony in a post-colonial pluralist society must take account of the existing legacy of human relationships distorted by an obsolete theory of race. That theory of race was the product of an earlier age in which it was assumed (or even held to be divinely ordained) that some were born to enjoy privilege, and others to accept subservience, on grounds of colour.

COPING WITH INTOLERANCE

One of the most important tasks in education today is to help students to understand what may be lost when different cultures clash. In this task teachers have a further obligation: to present an accurate picture of the problems which face newly independent African countries in maintaining their drive towards self-determination, without romanticising the record of Africans themselves. It is now beginning to be possible to assess the records of independent black African and Caribbean governments with regard to questions of human rights. It transpires, as many observers (black as well as white) have already pointed out, that white colonizers were not the only oppressors seen in Africa. No race has a monopoly on virtue. It is unreasonable to hold any society collectively responsible for the inhuman acts of some of its members. The difficulty is that criticism of the achievements of independent African nations, coming primarily but not exclusively from former colonialist sources, is understandably perceived by Africans and people of African descent to be evidence of renewed racial hostility. To be even-handed in these matters a teacher must be unusually sensitive and patient. But wherever black and white citizens are brought together in this country for the statutory years of education in schools there are opportunities for encouraging the growth of such sensitivity and patience. This would seem to be the only way by which some of the former mistakes identified by a modern African writer can be rectified.

The substitution of European for African values was carried out everywhere [i.e. in colonial Africa], not just in the schools. African values were derided and attacked. . . . Thus did the colonial schools manufacture meek, grateful and loyally submissive Africans, in many of whom every desire for that cultural and political sovereignty their ancestors had fought to keep had been abolished.[31]

The problem of European cultural dominance and ascendancy continues even after self-rule and independence have been won. And it may continue in the post-colonial period when British citizens whose cultural roots lie in what were once colonial dependencies now seek to adjust to British social pressures. This factor has an important bearing on the present discussion because cultural imperialism may still be found in unexpected places. It may turn up, for example, in the educational system of a country which prides itself on its readiness to recognize pluralism and to appreciate all the manifestations of cultural diversity.

NOTES AND REFERENCES

1. Mbiti John S 1977 *African Religions and Philosophy*. Heinemann, p 11
2. In recent years several books, critical of aspects of the colonial period, have been written by African scholars. References to some of these studies are made in the notes which follow. These books shed light on African perceptions of the European colonial legacy. More recently another kind of book has begun to appear, written by Africans attempting to understand their post-colonial heritage. In the West these books, chiefly novels, are less well known. Their interest lies in the fact that they reflect dissatisfaction with African traditional beliefs and customs, and criticism of the injustices

inflicted on blacks by blacks in modern Africa. For French-speaking readers in Africa and elsewhere, Bolya Baenga's prize-winning novel *Cannibale* is an example

3. The use of the phrase *African Traditional Religion* indicates a shift in European attitudes. But the phrase can be misleading if it suggests to western readers a monolithic system of beliefs and values. Its usefulness lies in the way in which it displaces terms previously employed to describe aspects of African culture in a rather patronizing, not to say disparaging, manner. As a result, words such as *primitive, native, savage*, are heard less frequently. The student of African religion is confronted with 'a bewildering variety' within 'a basically more or less homogeneous system'. See E. Bolaji Idowu, 'The nature of African traditional religion', in *African Traditional Religion: a definition*, p 108. There is something to be discussed here, however; is the ambiguous phrase 'more or less homogeneous' merely a polite way of describing what elsewhere might be described in divisive and sectarian terms?

4. Mbiti *African Religions and Philosophy*, p 12

5. The story of Philip's meeting with the Ethiopian servant of Queen Candace on the road from Jerusalem to Gaza is recorded in Acts 8: 26–40

6. An interesting case-study for teachers to consider is that of the eminent and controversial black teacher Edward Wilmot Blyden (1832–1912). His best-known work is *Christianity, Islam and the Negro Race*, London, 1887, which contains several essays on the impact of Christianity and Islam upon traditional African communities. The book was re-published by Edinburgh University Press in 1967, with an introduction by Christopher Fyfe. Blyden campaigned for African peoples in the light of his understanding of many of the issues discussed in this chapter. His life and career will suggest several possible lines of further inquiry for teachers who may be looking for suitable material from Africa on which to base their schemes of work on the issues raised in this book.

Blyden, born on the island of St Thomas in the Caribbean, described himself as a man 'of ebony hue', and was proud to claim that he came from Ibo stock, which is to say that his ancestors came from what is known as Cross River State in eastern Nigeria. In 1850 he was refused entry to Rutgers College, New Jersey, because of his colour. He concluded that the United States was no country for those like himself whom he invariably called *Negroes*. In 1851 he arrived in the recently created state of Liberia, West Africa. His subsequent career in Africa was brilliant, if stormy at times. As a scholar, politician, diplomat, and a tireless campaigner on behalf of the cause of 'Negroes' he became an exemplary champion of black emancipation, meeting his white contemporaries on equal intellectual terms.

His intellectual achievements were impressive:

Blyden was easily the most learned and articulate champion of Africa and the Negro race in his own time. To his educated Negro contemporaries his achievements as litterateur, educator, theologian, politician, statesman, diplomat, and explorer were the most convincing refutation

of the oft repeated white charges of Negro inferiority. His teachings, incessantly propounded, that Negroes had a history and a culture of which they could be proud, and that with the help of New World Negroes a progressive civilization could be built in Africa, gave members of his race a new pride and hope, and inspired succeeding generations of African nationalists and New World leaders.
(Hollis R, Lynch *Edward Wilmot Blyden, Pan-Negro Patriot 1832–1912*. Oxford University Press, 1970, p vii)

7. Chinua Achebe 1978 *Arrow of God*. Heinemann African Writers rev. edn, p 16. In the same passage of the novel Achebe uses the African proverb quoted in the title of the present chapter
8. At midnight on 6 March 1957 Kwame Nkrumah became leader of the newly independent state of Ghana, known during the period of British administration as the Gold Coast. Ghana was the first black African state to emerge from British colonial dependency. In his address to the crowds gathered to celebrate the event, Dr Nkrumah commented, 'At long last the battle has ended.' The thirty years that have elapsed since then have confirmed that in Ghana, as in other newly independent African states, the ending of alien colonial administration only marks the beginning of more protracted struggles for freedom and independence
9. The words of Okot p'Bitek, a Kenyan student studying in Canada, quoted by Stephen Neill 1984 *Crises of Belief: the Christian dialogue with faith and no faith*. Hodder & Stoughton, pp 177–78
10. The phrase 'African Traditional Religion' is really an umbrella term covering a wide variety of beliefs and customs which are related but distinct. It is not possible here to give a comprehensive picture of the multiplicity of such beliefs and customs in Africa. See E. Bolaji Idowu 1973 *African Traditional Religion: a definition*. SCM Press, p 10:

The world outside Africa has still to wake up to the fact that African traditional religion is *the* religion which resulted from the sustaining faith held by the forbears of the present Africans, which is being practised today by the majority of Africans in various forms and various shades and intensities, nakedly in most cases; but also, in some cases, under the veneers supplied by Westernism and Arabism; it is also a religion which is receiving a new vitality in certain areas in consequence of nationalism plus inspiration by other religions.

See also Lamin Sanneh 1983 *West African Christianity: the religious impact*, Orbis Books, Maryknoll, New York, pp 210–41
11. Mbiti *African Religions and Philosophy*, p 15
12. Mbiti J S 1978 *Prayer and Spirituality in African Religion*. Charles Strong Memorial Trust, Flinders University, South Australia p 9. The passage continues:

Nobody can exist and survive on his own. Individuals interdepend on others at the social and biological level; they also depend in another direction, on God as their Father and Creator, as well as the departed and the ancestors. . . . In African prayer, people are not embarrassed about speaking to God as 'You our Father', and 'we your children' [or by] telling the living dead not to forget their children. Humility has also respect, love, honour, admiration, and adoration, towards God, and sometimes towards the living dead

13. Heinemann, 1975. In the Preface the author describes his book as an introduction to the subject, and 'therefore written in a fairly simple style'. It was written as a textbook for use in secondary schools
14. Ibid., p 14
15. John Mbiti considers these topics in a different order in *Introduction to African Religion*, pp 19–30. Other sources of useful teaching material on the topics listed include two titles by E G Parrinder: *African Traditional Religion*. SPCK 1961; and *African Mythology*. Hamlyn, London, 1967
16. Maquet Jacques *Civilizations of Black Africa*, revised and translated by Joan Rayfield, Oxford University Press, New York, 1981, p 37
17. van der Post Laurens 1965 *The Heart of the Hunter*. Penguin Books p 13. In an earlier book (*The Lost World of the Kalahari*. Penguin Books, 1962) van der Post describes his journey into the deserts of South West Africa in search of the few remaining Bushmen and their distinctive way of life
18. van der Post *The Heart of the Hunter*, p 56
19. Mbiti *African Religions and Philosophy*, p 17
20. St Matthew 6: 34
21. The chapter on 'The creation and original state of Man' in John Mbiti's *African Religions and Philosophy* (pp 92–99) gives several examples of creation myths from different parts of the continent.
22. Mbiti *Introduction to African Religion*, p 39
23. Shorter Aylward 1975 *Prayer in the Religious Traditions of Africa*. Oxford University Press, New York, p 4. A wide range of prayers is to be found in J S Mbiti's collection. The *Prayers of African Religion*, SPCK, 1975, which includes prayers for such different situations (some repeated daily, others each month, or annually) as help on the journey of life from birth to death, and after death; for the gifts of life, health, wealth, prosperity; and for success in growing crops, in collecting food, in hunting and fishing. Other prayers are offered in praise and thanksgiving to God; as part of sacrificial rituals; as blessings, or as curses; for safety when travelling; for deliverance in times of war or natural catastrophe; for a proper relationship with the spirits
24. The English translation of the prayer referred to here is given in Mbiti's *Prayer and Spirituality in African Religion*, pp 2–3. 'After such a prayer', the author notes, 'the man and his family are ready to go through the day with a good will and good spirit.'
25. Ibid., p 10
26. Mbiti *Introduction to African Religion*, p 63
27. Idowu *African Traditional Religion*, pp 175–76
28. Mbiti *African Religions and Philosophy*, p 99
29. The Emir of Kontagora, when captured by the British at the beginning of the twentieth century in what is now one of the northern states of Nigeria, is reported to have said, 'Can you stop a cat from mousing? I shall die with a slave in my mouth' (quoted in J D

Anderson 1972 *West Africa in the Nineteenth and Twentieth Centuries.* Heinemann, p 36).

Samuel Ajayi Crowther (1806–91), who was to become the first black African bishop of the Anglican communion in 1864, and a group of others from his village were captured by Yoruba Muslims in 1821. They were roped together and marched south to Popo, at that time centre of the Portuguese slave-trade. The ship taking them across the Atlantic was intercepted by a British naval vessel. Crowther and his companions were liberated and taken to the colony of Sierra Leone. See P R McKenzie, *Inter-Religious Encounters in West Africa: Samuel Ajayi Crowther's attitude to African traditional religion*, Leicester Studies in Religion (1), 1976

30. A development of the 1930s in Jamaica, Rastafarianism owed much to the inspiration of the black leader Marcus Garvey (1887–1940). Garvey's message to blacks who were still suffering the indignities of racial discrimination in the Americas, long after the abolition of slavery, was 'back to Africa!' In essence it was the same message of black Zionism, or Ethiopianism, as that of his Afro-American predecessor Edward Wilmot Blyden (1832–1912). Ethiopia, with its ancient independent *African* civilization, was seen to represent the aspirations of blacks as a whole, freed from alien cultural domination.

    The coronation of Ras Tafari as Emperor of Ethiopia in November 1930 was the event for which Garvey and his supporters had been waiting. The new Emperor took the name Haile Selassie ('Power of the Trinity'). He is believed by Rastafarians to be the incarnation of the living God for black people, just as Moses was for Jews and Jesus was for Christians. From Judaism and Christianity Rastafarians took the Commandments given to Moses in the Old Testament, and the two Great Commandments mentioned by Jesus in the New Testament. More controversially, Rastafarians insist on the use of *ganja* (marijuana) as an aid to reasoned thinking. With their 'dreadlocks' they constitute an easily recognizable black ethnic minority group in Britain. For thirty years their numbers have been growing, reflecting the need of some black people to identify themselves with specific African roots, and also to challenge the assumptions of western society ('Babylon') which the righteous God will destroy by fire. It is scarcely surprising that their beliefs and life-style are subjects of interest

31. Chinweizu 1975 *The West and the Rest of Us: white predators, black slavers, and the African elite.* Vintage Books, Random House, New York, pp 77–78. On p xxiii the author quotes an African saying which ironically expresses an attitude towards the European exploration and exploitation of Africa: 'When they [the Europeans] first came they had the Bible, we had the land. We now have the Bible and they have the land.'

CHAPTER 6

Indian perspectives: 'Education is integrally connected with the dharma of a community'

There is no pure unalloyed Indian. He can be a Dravidian, an Aryan, an Austroloid or a Mongoloid. His hair may be fair or dark, straight or curly, the skin very fair or wheat-coloured, beige, brown or ebony. For India has always accepted races, tribes, ways of thought and life, without demanding from them conformity which would negate individuality, yet stamping on them the unmistakable mark of Indianness.[1]

So long as one does not become simple like a child, one does not get divine illumination. Forget all the wordly knowledge that thou hast acquired and become as ignorant as a child, and then thou wilt get the divine wisdom.[2]

CHARACTERISTIC CONCEPTS OF INDIAN THOUGHT AND BELIEF

The study of the different religious beliefs and cultural attitudes which have their origin in India is no longer an exotic study in Britain. Apart from Muslims, whose way of life has already been considered in Chapter 2, there are many other British citizens whose cultures developed in the subcontinent. Britain has a population of well over 300,000 Hindus. Of this number almost 70 per cent have a Gujarati and 15 per cent a Punjabi cultural background. The remaining 15 per cent consists of minorities who look to areas in Maharashtra, West Bengal, Uttar Pradesh and Tamil Nadu for their cultural roots.[3]

The existence of these communities in Britain would be a sufficient reason for taking an interest in their traditional ways of life, but their special needs are already the subject of detailed investigation and study elsewhere.[4] The purpose of this chapter is to consider some of the characteristic concepts of Indian thought and belief, in order to find out how these ideas might contribute to a wider understanding of the meaning and purpose of education in a culturally diverse world. What does education look like through Indian eyes? What lies behind the statement, 'Education is integrally connected with the *dharma* of a community'?

Because there is so much material that might be considered under this heading, the scope of this chapter has to be limited.

The words *India* and *Indian* are used here with particular reference to Hinduism, and to that part of the subcontinent which has
formed the state of India since independence from Britain (and
partition from Pakistan) in 1947. Given the range of religious and
cultural diversity in India, and the impracticability of considering
more than a part of it here, the best course is to single out some
of the characteristic concepts of Hindu thought and belief which
add an Indian dimension to the discussion of the role of
education in a culturally diverse society.

As in previous chapters, the community and its relationship
with the individual are considered from a particular viewpoint.
From an Indian point of view the life of an individual is determined by several factors that have a special bearing on education,
to be considered later in the chapter. Among them are the
concepts of *dharma, moksha (mukti), karma, saṁsāra,* and
sādhanā. In view of the extended time-scale that is a characteristic of Indian thought it would be more accurate to say that the
successive lives of an individual are determined by these factors.
Education, in so far as it is instrumental in assisting an individual
to reach higher stages of existence is, for this reason, a matter
of *ultimate* concern. It is also a protracted and disciplined vocation, both for teachers and for students.

THE MEETING PLACE OF CULTURES

Modern India is a secular state which continues to provide a
model for other countries with pluralist aspirations, despite the
difficulties it is having in resolving the internal conflicts between
some of its own diverse cultural communities. Cultural diversity
is no new phenomenon in India. The state of India may be a
comparative newcomer in international politics, but the cultural
life of its people has a long history. Commenting on the antiquity
of Hinduism and its associated ways of life, K. M. Sen wrote,
'Unlike other world religions such as Christianity, Islam, or
Buddhism, Hinduism did not have any one founder. It grew
gradually over a period of five thousand years absorbing and
assimilating all the religious and cultural movements of India.'[5]

British rule brought to India administrators, soldiers, entrepreneurs and Christian missionaries, with ideas for the transformation of society. As privileged representatives of the imperial
power they could hardly fail to advocate the values of their own
culture. In much the same way as in other countries subjected
to European colonialism, India felt the impact of western
educational theory and practice. The influence of European ideas
was not eliminated at independence. Indeed, India continues to

capitalize on the educational legacy of its former expatriate rulers. But it is not with any such assimilated, and no doubt appropriately modified, ideas about education that this chapter is concerned; focus of interest is the indigenous tradition which was inevitably obscured for Europeans by the long period of colonial rule, though never lost, and which continued to develop in harmony with its own ancient spiritual ideals.

This is not to deny the importance of other religious and cultural traditions in modern India. Buddhists, Jains, Parsees, Christians, Muslims, Sikhs, for instance, all contribute to the richness of India's cultural life. The attitudes of Muslims, however, have already been considered in a previous chapter. Buddhist approaches to cultural diversity, though clearly Indian in the sense already mentioned, must lie beyond the scope of the present chapter, for reasons of space. Similarly, Sikh ideas and ideals will not be discussed despite the importance of the Sikh community in the life of modern India, and the increasingly prominent role now being played by Sikhs in Britain. Nevertheless the importance of these other traditions in the developing story of Indian society cannot be ignored, not least because the relationships between members of different cultural and ethnic groups in India have often been under strain. Social harmony has frequently been disrupted by claims of sectional interest.

Demands for autonomy have recently led to conflict between central and state governments in India, to civil disturbances inside the country, and even to acts of terrorism beyond its borders as activists drew attention to their causes on the wider international stage. Conflicting national interests may yet lead to further hostilities between India and Pakistan. Another bitter conflict is developing between opposing ethnic groups in Sri Lanka. It has already cost many lives, and has created its own refugee problem. It is a conflict that also affects the lives of many people in Tamil Nadu, in south India. Demands for the creation of an independent Sikh state of Khalistan in the Punjab have repercussions not only in India, but also in other parts of the world, including Britain, where Sikh and Hindu communities are to some extent caught up in a nationalist controversy. It is futile to attempt to predict the likely outcome of these disagreements that seem to have cultural differences as their basis.

For Muslims in India there is the opportunity, at least in theory, to follow the Islamic way of life in the separate Islamic state of Pakistan. But it was only after considerable blood-shed and despite strenuous efforts of some Muslims and Hindus to prevent it that Muslims secured for themselves in 1947 the right to establish Pakistan as a community founded upon Islamic principles, quite independent of the Hindu community.[6] For Pakistan the break-up went further: East and West Pakistan, already separated physically by the northern provinces of India, were soon embroiled in civil war. The result was independence for Bangladesh, formerly East Pakistan, in 1971. A precedent for separation, and for separate development, was thus set in India in 1947. This is not to deny that the state of India provides for many more Muslims to follow their own distinctive way of life without official hindrance inside India, but from the Islamic point of view the practice of Islam is inevitably impeded in a secular, pluralist state.

The insistence on separate development, to the point of independence, raises questions about the capacity of an avowedly pluralist society to cope with the potentially divisive tendencies of cultural diversity. It also raises questions about the status and rights of minority groups in India, where the contrast between the peaceful, non-violent support of cultural difference is increasingly being challenged by expressions of violent sectarian interest. In the opinion of a close friend, a distinguished Indian teacher, this should surprise no one in the West, apart from those who are incurably romantic about his country where, to use his own words, 'violence is endemic'.

DHARMA

The pursuit of knowledge and wisdom in India is time-consuming in a way that is almost inconceivable in the West. Throughout the various successive stages of existence the concept of *dharma* is all-pervading. This can be said by way of drawing attention to the various meanings of the Sanskrit word *dharma*. In the attempts to define the term it has often been remarked that *dharma* and religion are not the same, and that *dharma* has more to do with the behaviour of human beings than with their religious beliefs. Hinduism is less a system of orthodoxy than of orthopraxis. *Dharma* influences the form and content of Indian education in the broadest sense because it provides for the regulation of both individual and community life.

Dharma is the unalterable moral law in the universe. Teaching students to conform to the demands of such a moral law is the major task of education. Disobedience to its requirements has among its effects the distortion of social relationships. The correct discharge of religious and moral duty, in ways that are appropriate to the different stages and states of existence, helps to preserve cosmic order and balance. Ignorance of sacred, law, tradition, duty, moral norms – in short, ignorance of 'what is right'[7] – disturbs the balance of things. In consequence, each individual also bears some responsibility for the well-being of the community as a whole. In India Hinduism is known as '*sanātana dharma*' and '*vaidika dharma*'. '*Sanātana dharma*' expresses the idea that as a way of life, Hinduism is eternally true, and not rendered obsolete by the passage of time; '*vaidika dharma*' confirms that *dharma* is also a codified system of faith and practice, a sacred law, founded upon the ancient Hindu scriptures known as the Veda. The word *dharma* implies a way of life based upon righteous action.

Education, in its successive stages, retains a normative function, and is primarily concerned with the search for enlightenment and for truth, not the pursuit of self-interest. The responsibility for performing one's duty, for fulfilling one's *dharma* in the service of the community, is at its best dissociated from any thought of the personal benefits that might accrue to the individual who performs it. The lesson to be learned is that progress towards *moksha* (liberation) is, ideally, incidental to the selfless performance of duty for its own sake. This is one of the major themes of the *Bhagavadgītā* ('The Song of the Lord'), one of the most popular of the sacred writings of India, which has been influential far beyond its borders.

A gift is pure when it is given from the heart to the right person at the right time and at the right place, and when we expect nothing in return.

But when it is given expecting something in return, or for the sake of a future reward, or when it is given unwillingly, the gift is of *Rajas*, impure.[8]

SAMSĀRA AND MOKSHA

The pursuit of truth is a task which occupies not one lifetime but many. Indian attitudes to education are thus conditioned by concepts of time (and of timing) that are disconcerting to western minds. There is also an overwhelming sense of the illusoriness of human existence, experienced in the continuous cycle from birth to death, and from death to re-birth, known as *samsāra*. The promise is that by means of discipline, self-control and devotion, and by the diligent and selfless performance of duty, liberation (*moksha*) from an endless cycle of lives can finally be achieved.

The chief purpose of education in the Hindu tradition is to lead individuals from the Unreal to the Real, from ignorance to true knowledge, from darkness to light, and from bondage to freedom, no matter how distant a prospect that liberation may be. This provides a powerful motivation for education because everything possible is to be done to equip individuals to secure release from the bondage of human existence. In the words of the sixteenth-century Indian poet Rajjab, learning to 'give form to the yet unformed' and 'to speak out and express' may be identified as two of the principal aims of education in which teachers, by means of their own knowledge and experience, provide an example for their students to emulate.

According to Hindu teachings, every individual soul must pass through this cycle of births and deaths before it is finally reunited with the One, the undifferentiated Reality, which is Brahman. In Hindu belief it is not the true destiny of human beings to be separated or alienated from the ultimate source of Being. Until the moment comes, however long delayed, when the differentiation between the individuated soul and Brahman is obliterated, human beings have something for which to strive – namely, *moksha*, 'liberation' from reincarnation. In the vastness of time and space the image is that of individual droplets of spray that fall back into the ocean and immediately lose their identity in an undifferentiated whole.

In the Upanishads, the ancient sacred texts which date from about 800 BC, there is the affirmation of a relationship that is unique. Two concepts are brought together and equated. The first is Brahman, already mentioned above, and meaning the all-pervading, undifferentiated Reality. The second is *Ātman*, which means 'self'. The affirmation is that Brahman is *Ātman*. This Upanishadic teaching identifies the true goal of every individual 'self' in the Sanskrit phrase, *tat tvam asi*, which means 'That art thou'. In this phrase the word *that* refers to Brahman (the universal being), the word *thou* to *Ātman* (the individual self). This idea is not easy for western minds to grasp. It does not mean that union with Brahman (that is to say, union with the Absolute, or with God) is the goal to which individuals ultimately *progress*. Instead, it affirms what *is*, and what always has been: namely, that there exists no 'Absolute' over against the 'individual self'. This is such an important point that it calls for a quotation from one of the Upanishads:

There was Shvetaketu, the son of Uddalaka Aruni. To him his father said: 'O Shvetaketu, live the disciplined life of a student of sacred knowledge (*brahmacarya*). No-one belonging to our family is unlearned in the *Veda* and remains a *brāhmaṇa* only by family connections as it were'.

He [Shvetaketu], having approached a teacher at the age of twelve, and having studied all the *Vedas*, returned at the age of twenty-four, conceited, thinking himself to be learned, stiff. To him his father said: 'O Shvetaketu, since you are now conceited, think yourself to be learned, and have become proud, did you also ask for that instruction whereby what has been unheard becomes heard, what has been unthought of becomes thought of, what has been uncomprehended becomes comprehended?'

'How, sir, is that instruction?' asked Shvetaketu.

'Just as through the comprehension of one lump of clay all that is made of clay would become comprehended – for the modification is occasioned only on account of a convention of speech, it is only a name; while clay, as such, alone is the reality. Just as through the comprehension of one ingot of iron all that is made of iron would become comprehended – for the modification is occasioned only on account of a convention of speech, it is only a name; while iron, as such, alone is the reality. . . . So is that instruction.'

'Now those venerable teachers did not know this; for if they had known it, why would they not have told me?' said Shvetaketu. 'However, may the venerable sir tell it to me.'

'So be it', said he. 'In the beginning this world was just *Being*, one only, without a second. Some people say: 'In the beginning this world was just non-being, one only, without a second; from that non-being, Being was produced.' But how could it be so? How could Being be produced from non-being? On the contrary, in the beginning this world was Being alone, one only, without a second. Being thought to itself: 'May I be many; may I procreate.' It produced fire. That fire thought to itself: 'May I be many. May I procreate.' It produced water. Therefore, whenever a person grieves or perspires, then it is from fire [heat] alone that water is produced. That water thought to itself: 'May I be many. May I procreate.' It produced food. Therefore, whenever it rains, then there is abundant food; it is from water alone that food for eating is produced. . . .

'That divinity [Being] thought to itself: 'Well, having entered into these three divinities [fire, water, and food] by means of this living Self, let me develop names and forms. Let me make each one of them tripartite.' That divinity, accordingly, having entered into those three divinities by means of this living Self, developed names and forms. . . . It made each one of them tripartite. . . .

'Bring hither a fig.' 'Here it is, sir.' 'Break it.' 'It is broken, sir.' 'What do you see there?' 'These extremely fine seeds, sir.' 'Of these, please break one.' 'It is broken, sir.' 'What do you see there?' 'Nothing at all, sir.'

Then he said to Shvetaketu: 'That subtle essence which you do not perceive – from that very essence does this great fig-tree thus arrive. Believe me, that which is the subtle essence – this whole world has that essence for its *Self*; that is the *Real*; that is the *Self*. *That* subtle essence *art thou*, Shvetaketu.'[9]

RELIGIOUS STRIVING: SEARCHING FOR TRUTH

The testimony of the wisest Indian teachers is that there is no easy way to truth. But truth, in the Indian perspective, is no mere figment of the imagination. Truth can be grasped and, ultimately, realized. The continuing search for truth calls for the development of many personal qualities, not the least of which is perseverance. The word *sādhanā*, 'religious striving', expresses the kind of personal effort that is necessary. The meaning of *sādhanā* is similar in many respects to the meaning of *jihād*, the Islamic concept of 'striving', considered in an earlier chapter.[10] It is not enough to experience awe and wonder in the presence of mystery, or to speculate about the human condition. There is a code of moral behaviour to be learned and practised, *dharma* to be understood and implemented:

> Every religion tends to find a conflict between what men do and what, according to its values, men ought to do. This conflict is closely linked with man's concept of the nature of the universe. Once men are recognized to be the creation of the Supreme and all men are recognized to be brothers, the ideals of selfless service and sacrifice become obvious.[11]

It is *self*-deception and personal indolence which postpone the moment of illumination, and thus awareness of the truth. This is the testimony of the anonymous Indian sages of antiquity, as well as of better-known modern teachers such as Mahatma Gandhi. Gandhi's teaching with regard to *satyāgraha*, 'holding to truth' by non-violent methods of personal advocacy and persuasion, was a practical interpretation of the significance of *dharma* in the light of present needs. In his example of 'righteousness', in conformity with the revealed moral law, Gandhi set out to provide confirmation in India of the truth of Plato's dictum that the creation (and re-creation) of the world of civilized order is the victory of persuasion over force.

'THERE IS NO EASY WAY TO TRUTH'

In its manifold aspects Hinduism is more than a religion in the western sense.[12] The Hindu view of life is at once inclusive, tolerant and disciplined. The universal appeal of the inclusive, tolerant ideals of Hinduism has attracted many twentieth-century seekers after truth to the Indian sub-continent. The ordered relationships of organized social life and the disciplined fulfilment of duty (*dharma*) appropriate to each stage of Hindu life have been greeted with less enthusiasm by western pilgrims, many of whom have failed to note the insistence of their hosts on the need for self-discipline, dedication and application in the pursuit of truth. The freedom to be tolerant can only be exercised within the framework of *dharma*. Outside that framework tolerance degenerates into licence and chaos, both of which are antithetical to *dharma*.

The extract below reminds readers that western misconceptions about Indian religion can lead to unfruitful encounters between East and West. The writer describes what happened when two western 'seekers after illumination' met an Indian teacher in a remote part of India. Behind the verbal exchanges there lies a western misconception; namely, that Indian religion is preoccupied with a discussion of the unreality of the world, and with

speculation about how release from the bondage of illusory existence is to be achieved. The notion that the Indian teacher has
important things to say about social obligations, and about the
performance of duty in this *present* world, has fewer attractions
for the students in question. The extract illustrates both the limits
of tolerance on the Hindu side, and the naïve western assumption
that education rewards the self-indulgent with its choicest fruits.
The passage comes from a book that is not as well known as it
deserves to be:

'Do you like our temple? Where do you come from?'
The boy replied, 'I am from the States, and my (girl) friend is from
London.'
'Why have you come to India?' asked the holy man.
'We want to reach . . .'
'I beg your pardon. I did not understand. Please say it again.'
The boy blushed and said, 'You know, enlightenment, release . . .'
'Ah, you mean you wish a revelation of God, or as we say, to be
absorbed in unity.' The old seer sat back, pleased to have understood,
but the boy and girl were distressed.
'No, no, enlightenment, nirvana, release into nothing, like in the old
books, you know.'
'But enlightenment is recognition of unity, or in your tradition, knowl-
edge of God.' The old man stated this flatly.
'No, we learned all about it, the big self and the little self, and finding
nothingness.'
But my young friend, the great self is the Universe, or God, and
absorption into that unity is what we are all seeking.'
'We spent time in Rishikesh with a guru,' the girl tried to explain.
'He said we had to meditate to make ourselves empty.'
'Yes, as vessels for the god, or unity, within and without.'
'No, to be not attached to life, so we can be released. You know,
initiated.'
'But you are young, you have not yet begun to live, this is not the
time to be released. You must wait until you are old like me, and all
your duties done, then you can go out to seek release.' The old man
changed his attack. His audience was growing and they murmured
approval at this remark.
'We have no duties, we just want to get released.'
'Of course you have duties: to learn, to work, to marry and have children, to raise them as best you can. Then when they have children you
can choose to take this path.'
'But we don't want all that. We don't have to do it. We want to get
released now.'
'My friend, I do not understand this phrase "get released". Here we
view enlightenment as an achievement of study, discipline and devotion.
One earns release, or revelation, one cannot be made aware by any
other agent than one's mind, or the tools of one's spirit. First you must
master the languages of revelation, either in our tradition or in your
own, and then you must practise hard until you are able to reach that
one moment of joy. Nothing can obtain it for you except work and

constant awareness.' The small man was revelling in the phrases of the foreign language . . .

'But does not a guru do that? He releases you and you get enlightened. It is not hard, they said so in Rishikesh. We have been looking for a guru who will take us together.' The boy put his arm around the girl. . .

The old teacher smiled and then his face grew sad. Slowly he withdrew into himself and the Indians knew that the interview was over. The couple looked confused as people started to walk on and as the old man began to murmur, oblivious of them all.

'Why did he stop talking like that? Why did he look so sad?'

The couple turned to the remaining watchers. A studious-looking man looked at the holy man and at the boy's honest bewilderment. Finally he spoke:

'I think he fears that you have only disappointments ahead, and he does not wish you to go from our country with this disappointment. There is no easy way to truth.'[13]

The lesson of the final sentence of this extract from Heather Wood's record of her travels in India is clear enough. Without personal effort and the performance of duty there can be no progress towards enlightenment. The Hindu approach to life is realistic as well as visionary. It accepts individuals as they are, without denying what they may ultimately become. Their desires are needs to be met, although these desires confirm the fallen state from which individuals have ultimately to raise themselves. Part of the explanation for this apparently permissive approach is to be found in the Indian concept of time, and in the doctrine of reincarnation which gives fresh opportunities for redeeming past mistakes in a succession of future lives.

The truth that pleasure-seeking, for example, gives no lasting satisfaction will eventually become self-evident to everyone. The point is reached when further pleasures of the same order begin to pall and fail to satisfy. This is where the Hindu approach to life is not only realistic and practical, but visionary. Experience shows that all desires except one, however refined they may become in human terms, eventually pall. The single exception is the desire to be released from *saṁsāra* and to be reunited with the Absolute. This is no doubt part of universal human experience, but what characteristics the Hindu attitudes to human aspirations and desires is its readiness to allow individuals to discover this truth for themselves:

In the telling words of Bhartrihari, 'What if you have secured the fountain-head of all desires; what if you have put your foot on the neck of your enemy, or by your good fortune gathered friends around you? What, even, if you have succeeded in keeping mortal bodies alive for ages – *tatah kim*, what then?' The successes of the material world, great as they are, are not considered sufficient, and it is here that the ideal of *moksha* or *mukti* comes in. This ideal of liberation is not a negative state. It is a state of completeness, of fullness of being, free from the bondage of *karma*, and, thus, free from re-birth.[14]

DIFFERENT PATHS TO THE TRUTH

To insist that there is only one true religion is, from a Hindu point of view, a sign of ignorance and self-deception. God is known by different names. There are many paths to God, to ultimate reality, to the truth. There is the path of *karma* (work and action); there is the path of *jñāna* (knowledge); there is the path of *bhakti* (devotion to a personal Lord). All these paths lead to the same destination as different routes lead to the summit of a mountain. Such was the ancient Hindu belief, expressed again by the nineteenth-century Indian teacher Sri Ramakrishna,[15] who claimed to know this from personal experience.

Wherever I look I see men quarrelling in the name of religion – Hindus, Mohammedans, Brahmins, Vaisnavas and the rest, but they never reflect that He who is called Kṛṣṇa is also called Siva, and bears the name of Primitive Energy, Jesus and Allah as well – the same Rama with a thousand names. The tank has several *ghats*. At one Hindus draw water in pitchers, and call it *jal*; at another Mussalmans draw water in leathern bottles, and call it *pani*; at a third Christians, and call it *water*. Can we imagine that the water is not *jal*, but only *pani* or *water*? How ridiculous! Then Substance is One under different names and everyone is seeking the same substance; nothing but climate, temperament and name vary. Let each man follow his own path. If he sincerely and ardently wishes to know God, peace be unto him! He will surely realize Him.[16]

These sentences express some of the most fundamental Hindu beliefs. During the past hundred years or so they have attracted attention wherever dissatisfaction with dogmatic religion has been felt. Yet here Ramakrishna goes considerably beyond an appeal for tolerance in the common good: he only resorts to what can be called a dogma of Hinduism when he insists that all paths lead to God. His statement reflects a point of view that is both generously tolerant and yet effectively exclusive. This ambivalence is because the limits of tolerance, from a Hindu point of view, have to be drawn at just the point where those of different convictions may be unable to agree, namely, that 'all paths lead to God'. To agree *without* persuasion would be to compromise without conviction.

As one can ascend to the top of a house by means of a ladder or a bamboo or a staircase or a rope, so diverse are the ways and means to approach God, and every religion in the world shows one of these ways. Different creeds are but different paths to reach the Almighty. Various and different are the ways that lead to the temple of Mother Kali at Kalighat (Calcutta). Similarly, various are the ways that lead to the house of the Lord.[17]

In saying this Ramakrishna reveals himself as one who inherited an ancient Hindu tradition, who sought to interpret it for his contemporaries, and who then proceeded to advocate its principles of tolerance by combining precept with practice. This bears strongly on the *exemplary* role of the teacher in education, for if teachers are unable (or unwilling) to demonstrate how *mature* persons cope with the practical problems of cultural diversity, it is less likely that students will take the issues very seriously. The example of Ramakrishna illustrates that it is not just a detached readiness to accept that others are entitled to pursue their own ways to the truth as they see it; there is an additional element, to the development of which teachers can usefully direct some of their effort. This additional element is better described as a social skill that has to be acquired in a pluralist society. It has to do with an individual's capacity to *affirm*, not just to accept, or to tolerate, the experience of others.

The evidence does not show that such a skill occurs naturally. This suggests an important task for teachers in a pluralist society. It is not an additional so much as a complementary task, the key to which may be an educational principle that can be called 'the principle of affirmation'. This principle applies to questions of religious and cultural difference. It operates in a world of experience that admits no straightforward distinctions between what is verifiably *factual* and what is factually *inaccurate*. The principle affirms that, when it comes to private judgements, religious beliefs, interpretations, cultural values (and the ability to express them), the only thing to be denied is denial itself, as shown later.

Another Indian teacher, Rabindranath Tagore,[18] sought on one occasion to express his own experience of truth in the form of a prayer which he offered for his country, and for anyone who realizes that there is something of universal significance to be learned from the accumulated wisdom of India:

Where the mind is without fear and the head is held high;
Where knowledge is free;
Where the world has not been broken up into fragments by narrow domestic walls;
Where words come out from the depth of truth;
Where tireless striving stretches its arms towards perfection;
Where the clear stream of reason has not lost its way into the dreary desert sand of dead habit;
Where the mind is led forward by Thee into ever-widening thought and action –
Into that heaven of freedom, my Father, let my country awake.[19]

Tagore's testimony was in line with that of many other mystics whose spiritual experience appears to rise above differences of name and form. To recognize the underlying unity in all the manifestations of religious and cultural diversity, however, truth-seekers do not have to abandon the particularity of their own traditions. They have to learn to affirm the experience of others who belong to different traditions.

The ability to 'pass over' into another belief system, to share the values of another culture, was demonstrated by Gandhi even though he always insisted that his chief loyalty was to the traditions of his own land, in accordance with his understanding of the concept of *swadeshi*.[20] In outlining his views about the importance of community life in the Sabarmati ashram,[21] he noted that children who came from Hindu, Muslim, Parsee or Christian cultural backgrounds must be taught not only about their own tradition but about the traditions of their neighbours. Education was to be a 'training of the spirit' as well as an activity for the formation of character. Among other things emphasized by Gandhi in education at the ashram were

physical labour, industriousness, simple living, and self-control (*swaraj*). Other things stressed by Gandhi were punctuality, concentration, the memorization of verses, and correct pronunciation. The ashram vows sent to members of the Sabarmati ashram while Gandhi was in jail included allegiance to truth, non-violence, continence, non-possession and non-stealing, and Gandhi regularly made these the subject of his discourses. The remaining vows enjoined control of the palate, fearlessness, removal of untouchability, bread labour, equality of religions, and *swadeshi*.[22]

What is interesting about these educational directives (they can scarcely be described as recommendations for open-ended group discussion) is Gandhi's insistence on self-discipline. The values mentioned are to be acquired, not merely admired. The tolerance which he advocated, and learned to practise, was more than an inoffensive indifference. It was, in fact, a highly subversive instrument for the exposure of every form of intolerance.

All this was intended to nurture an outlook which went beyond family attachments. From his letters the reader gets the impression of a man who knew very well how many frictions arise when people live in a community. For example he advised: 'The first step in purifying oneself is the admission and the eradication of whatever bad feelings one might have about others.' This is the first step in what Gandhi called the education of the heart, something, incidentally, which he thought intellectuals were particularly in need of. There is a New Testament ring to the following: 'Speak with one who does not speak with you; visit those who do not come to you; make up with someone who is angry with you.'[23]

It is neither synthesis nor conversion but affirmation that may be the key to unity in a culturally diverse society. The examples of Indian teachers such as Ramakrishna, Tagore and Gandhi help to formulate more precisely the principle of affirmation that was mentioned earlier. Teachers at all levels of education who advocate the acceptance of cultural diversity in a pluralist society need to recognize that it is example, not precept, that is crucial. The working principle for all teachers is, *We are right to affirm experience; the experience of others as well as our own. We are wrong only in what we deny.*

SOCIAL DIVISIONS IN INDIA: VARṆA AND JĀTI

In the Indus valley a highly developed urban civilization flourished between 4000 and 2200 BC at places like Mohenjodaro, Harappa and Kathiavar. Its influence, moreover, extended beyond the comparatively small area in the north-west out towards the Ganges and other northern parts of the country. Various artefacts, seals and statuettes have been excavated since archaeological work began in 1921.[24] Cultural enrichment of a different kind came as a result of invasions and migrations in the second millennium BC. Aryan invaders, members of a Caucasian race from the Iranian plateau to the north-west, brought with them their own language, religion and way of life. Their word *Hind* came to be used of the land east of the Indus River (in Sanskrit *Sindhu*). Later, in its derived forms, the term was applied to the subcontinent as a whole, India; to its way of life, Hinduism; as well as to the Indus that once formed its western border.

The arrival of Sanskrit-speaking Aryans from the north-west in an area that was already the home of an ancient civilization introduced vigorous new elements of cultural diversity. The invaders brought their own religion and their own traditions. They came as conquerors, and no doubt felt themselves to be superior and more powerful than the Dravidian peoples they met. It is clear that considerable mingling of cultures took place over a long period. One of the most lasting results (and, incidentally, one of the features of Indian life to be criticized most frequently outside India) was the division of society into exclusive and self-contained groups. Much later the word *caste* was applied by Europeans to the rigid system of social divisions that seems to have originated in the understandable attempt to introduce a coherent division of labour centuries before.

Every society is divided into groups enjoying different levels of privilege. Initially, there were four castes in Indian society. In time they became rigidly separated from one another, each with its own responsibilities and privileges. The castes were hereditary, and stringent internal laws forbade marriage between members of different castes. First in order of social precedence were priests and scholars. Next came princes and warriors. After them came landowners, merchants and traders. The fourth group consisted of workers and servants. But these four groups did not include the countless numbers of those who found themselves classless in the basest sense; these were the outcastes, the 'untouchables', who enjoyed no privileges. It is obvious that in a social order which institutionalized such divisions education served different ends than it does in a pluralist society which is founded upon principles of equality. Members of a caste learned to fulfil the duties and to enjoy the privileges of their own class, and to keep clear (literally, in some cases) of members of other castes.

The words *varṇa* and *jāti* are the Sanskrit terms used with reference to the multiplicity of divisions which eventually emerged some 500 years before the birth of Christ. But even at that time there was strong opposition to the divisiveness of caste inside India. Siddharta Gautama, who became known as the Buddha ('the Enlightened One'), lived in what is now north-east India from 563 to 483 BC. He rejected the inequality of caste, as his followers have undertaken to do ever since. In modern times Gandhi's approach to India's social needs, while not rejecting the idea of caste (which has a Vedic scriptural foundation) did not tolerate 'untouchability' (castelessness) that had no such scriptural authority. His respect for those who were beyond the pale of every caste – so-called *vrātyas*, 'outcastes' – prompted him to call them *harijans*, 'children of God'. In his regard for the needs of India's 'untouchables' he did no more than reflect the teaching of some of the most ancient Hindu scriptures. For if the Upanishadic teaching about the identification of *Brahman* and *Ātman* is accepted, no divisions of caste can be allowed. Yet these groups were not originally intended

to be warring communities but complementary classes. If the hands quarrel with the stomach or the head, it is not the stomach or head alone that suffers but the entire body including the hands. The head cannot claim superiority over the feet simply because it trails in the air while the latter tread the dust; the feet are as essential to the body as the head. It is the principle of integration and co-ordination that weighed with the builders of caste.[25]

The fourfold division of Hindu society noted earlier is associated with the word *varna*, the root meaning of which is 'colour'. This suggests that the notion of racial superiority on grounds of colour was not entirely absent in the days when Aryans, Greeks, Parthians, Huns and others, crossed the Indus River and invaded the land to the east. With the passage of time, however, *varṇa* may have assumed a meaning more in keeping with the description of a person's character than of his skin pigmentation. The Sanskrit terms for the four divisions of caste are, *Brāhmaṇa* (priests and scholars), *Kshatriya* (princes and warriors), *Vaiśya* (landowners, merchants and traders), and *Shūdras* (workers and servants). The responsibilities of each caste were described in the Vedic scriptures.

The duties of the castes are these. The *Brāhmaṇa* is the custodian of the spiritual culture of the race. His first duty is to specialize in spiritual ideas and broadcast them. He is the friend, philosopher and guide of humanity. He is not to burden himself with worldly goods; and the society will keep him above want. . . .

The *Kshatriya* is the guardian of society, its protector and preserver. He is the soldier who fights for the freedom of the race, and the prefect who keeps the peace of the land. He has to save the social polity from alien domination and internal dissensions. . . .

The *Vaiśya* is the expert in economics. His is the duty of arranging for the production and distribution of wealth. . . .

The *Shūdra* is the worker, the manual labourer. His place in society is no less important than that of the other three classes.[26]

These divisions, important as they are, appear to have been less significant in the everyday life of India's masses than those which belong to a different class structure, that of *jāti*. The establishment of craft guilds, for instance, introduced elements of organization and social differentiation which reflected, and helped to preserve, the range of technical skills practised in society. Each of these sub-groups protected its own interests and made arrangements for the transmission of its own values. But for every specialized craft there were numerous unskilled occupations. *Jāti* is a term that covers the multiplicity of all these functional divisions. In practice many of these groupings became exclusive. Social barriers were erected between the various occupations, and special rules applied to marriage (for example) and to the preparation, eating and sharing of food.

In all of these divisions of caste, both *varṇa* and *jāti*, it remains one of the most intriguing paradoxes that a society which allowed so much tolerance with regard to religious belief and philosophical thought should erect so rigid and intolerant a system of social relationships. In this respect the distinction between the ideal and the real has nowhere been more pronounced than in India.

THE THEORY OF KARMA[27]

The theory of *karma* calls for some explanation. *Karma* means 'work' or 'action', but it has a more technical sense; it also means the 'law of the cause of action, and of the effect of action'. Every action that occurs is both an effect of a previous action (or sequence of actions) and a cause of subsequent actions. Every act is determined by previous acts, and is potent with energy for future action. The work of every individual has its correlated effects on the life of the community as a whole. Further, the law of *karma* applies not just to human beings but also to the whole of creation – to animals, to the Earth, to the planets and even to the gods.

The concept of *karma* is clearly linked to the two concepts of *dharma* and *saṁsāra*, which have already been considered. With reference to *dharma* Hindus believe that human beings ought to be ethically responsible (or can be taught to be ethically responsible) for their personal actions. This conviction is present in all the shades of meaning of *dharma*, whether it be understood as a collection of sacred lore in the Vedic scriptures to be honoured, or as a moral law at work in the universe to be acknowledged, or as a duty appointed for individuals to fulfil according to their positions in the community. In consequence, it is freedom, not determinism, that is at the centre of Hindu ethics, for if men and women are not free to exercise moral choice then they cannot be held to be responsible for their actions. Without freedom to choose their courses of action human beings would be trapped in an arbitrary universe. If there were no good grounds for believing that personal duty, selflessly performed, would find its proper reward in higher forms of existence, the notion of *saṁsāra*, the cycle of re-births, would be merely debilitating.

At first sight it would appear that the theory of *karma* contradicts the freedom of the will. How can anything with the force of an inescapable law of the universe allow for the exercise of personal freedom? To this Hindus might reply that the law of *karma* is indeed inexorable: we are now reaping the rewards, or suffering the punishments, for past deeds. The law of *karma* establishes the present stage of existence in which individuals find themselves. We are, in short, what we have deserved. But this does not deny to human beings their duty to use present opportunities for making progress towards their ultimate goal. By building up good *karma* in this life individuals ensure progress in the next. T. M. P. Mahadevan put it this way:

It is in the Upaniṣads that the law of *karma* is formulated with a fair measure of precision. '*Karma*' used in this context means not only 'deed' but also the result of deed. According to this law there is nothing chaotic or capricious in the moral world. . . .

The *karmic* law applies the principle of cause and conservation of energy to the moral world. There is conservation of moral values, just as there is conservation of physical energy. Nothing is lost which has been earned by work; and nothing comes in which is not deserved. Every action has a double effect; it produces its appropriate reward, and it also affects character. It leaves behind an impression in the mind of man. It is this impression that is responsible for the repetition or avoidance of the same action. While character informs conduct, conduct in turn moulds character. 'A man becomes good by good deeds and bad by bad deeds.'

. . . *karma* does not bind man entirely. The cycle of *saṁsāra* has not the inevitability of a fate. Man has the freedom to get out of the vicious circle; and if he has the will, *karma* will help and not hinder his progress. In the words of Dr S. Radhakrishnan, 'the cards in the game of life are given to us. We do not select them. They are traced to our past *karma*, but we can call as we please, lead what suit we will, and as we play, we gain or lose. And there is freedom.'[28]

But if the law of *karma* operates in this way, what room is left for compassion when confronted by the needs of others in *their* present condition? It might be argued that the suffering they are enduring now is no more than the just reward of their past actions, and that it would be improper to attempt to interfere. To this possible criticism of Hindu ethics, Mahadevan also has a reply:

Under the rigid law of *karma*, it is said, there is no room for social service; for it does not allow of interference with the working out of a man's *karma*. This is a gross mis-reading of the law. It goes against the grain of Hinduism to suggest that each individual is an independent entity. The individual is not unrelated to society. He acts on, and is acted upon, by those who surround him. And naturally he has to share their joys and sorrows. If he brings succour to the suffering it is in part to his own advantage. Social service is not only consistent with the law of *karma* but is also enjoined as a means to release from *saṁsāra*. Work, when selfish, forges the chains of bondage, and when selfless, makes for freedom from fetters; just as a poison which ordinarily kills becomes a means of cure when it has been medically purified. 'In this way, and not otherwise it is', says the *Iśa Upanisad*, 'that *karma* does not cling to you.'[29]

THE ĀŚRAMAS, OR STAGES OF LIFE

It has already been emphasised that Indian perspectives on the pursuit of liberating truth are broad as well as long. With sufficient imagination one can see that the goal of all our 'religious striving' (*sādhanā*) will ultimately be gained, despite temporary set-backs and the lengthy cycle of re-births. Existence itself is the learning process. Education never ends until its final object is attained. There are, none the less, distinct stages of life which follow recognized and recurring patterns, and which reflect the degree of knowledge and experience which an individual has acquired. These stages of life are known as *āśramas*, and there are four of them. Each has its own set of duties (*āśrama-dharma*).

The first stage is that of *brahmacarya*, the stage of studentship, which covers the period of adolescence. From the details given in a text written in the fifth century BC, we get an idea of the way in which the tradition was passed on to succeeding generations by means of a common language and a common discipline. After initiation, which entitled him to wear the sacred cord of the twice-born, a boy from one of the three upper divisions of caste was expected to go to live with his teacher. This was a time for studying the sacred texts under the guidance of a teacher (*guru*), and for the practice of celibacy. The committing to memory of selected Vedic texts was an important part of education. Archery, the art of war, astrology and music also featured in his studies. When this stage of his education was completed he returned home.

Twelve years (should be) the shortest time (for his residence with his teacher).

A student who studies the sacred science shall not dwell with anybody else than his teacher. . . .

He shall obey his teacher, except when ordered to commit crimes which cause loss of caste.

He shall do what is serviceable to his teacher, he shall not contradict him.

He shall always occupy a couch or seat lower than that of his teacher.[30]

The second stage of life is that of the *gārhasthya*, of the house-holder and active worker. The central importance of the married state and of family life is thus emphasized. In the normal course of events one should marry, and assume the responsibilities of this second stage of life, as soon as the student stage is completed. Marriage is a form of sacrament. Ideally, it is for life. This stage of life is of the greatest importance in that it ensures the stability of society. Furthermore, the worldly success of the 'active workers' provides for the material needs of those at other stages of life. Without the industry and diligence of the house-holder, the lives of others would be much more difficult. The chief duties attaching to this stage are the five great sacrifices that are made to Brahman through study of the Veda; the sacrifice of offerings each day to the domestic gods; that of gifts made in honour of departed relatives; the sacrifice of service to domestic animals by caring for their needs; and the sacrifice of service to humanity by offering hospitality to guests, and help to those in need.

The third stage of life is that of *vānaprasthya*. The married state is not an end in itself. When the family has been reared, and its members themselves move into the second stage of life, it is time for both husband and wife to begin a new stage of life which marks a disengagement from former activities, and a retreat to the forest for the 'loosening of bonds'. Not necessarily together and no longer, necessarily, a literal withdrawal from society into the forest, man and woman enter a probationary period of asceticism to devote themselves to study.

When a householder sees his skin wrinkled, and his hair white, and the sons of his sons, then he may resort to the forest.

Abandoning all food raised by cultivation, and all his belongings, he may depart into the forest, either committing his wife to his sons, or accompanied by her. . . .

Let him be always industrious in privately reciting the Veda; let him be patient of hardships, friendly towards all, of collected mind, ever liberal and never receiver, and compassionate to all beings.[31]

The final stage of life is that of *sannyāsa*. This is the life of a hermit. The *sannyāsin* is one who spends his life in contemplation, renouncing everything but the final pursuit of *moksha*, liberation. Family, home, wealth and position in society are all abandoned in order to devote oneself to meditation, until the moment of death. The hermit is the one who retains no desires, and has no wants. This final stage of life is never completed until individuals are ready for release from the last of their cycle of re-births, and their education is finished.

THE PRICE OF TOLERANCE

The paragraph quoted at the beginning of this chapter was written by Mrs Indira Gandhi when she was Prime Minister of India. Her words capture the spirit of tolerance and mutual respect that has come to be identified in the western world as uniquely Indian. Yet even in India tolerance and mutual respect are social objectives, not realized goals.

Only a few years after she had completed a book on India giving an account of her country's tolerant attitudes to cultural diversity[32] Indira Gandhi was assassinated by disaffected political opponents.[33] And Mahatma Gandhi, whose teaching was founded upon the principle of non-violence (*ahiṁsā*), was himself a victim of the forces of intolerance against which he campaigned. He also met a violent death, shot at prayer in New Delhi by a Hindu who was angered by Gandhi's concern for the welfare of Muslims in India.[34] Yet the example of Gandhi lives on and is still the inspiration behind many movements for peace and justice throughout the world.

This chapter has attempted to identify some of the key elements in what might reasonably be called Indian attitudes to education. From time to time it has been necessary to comment on the empirical reality, as well as to admire the ideal. The fact is that the pursuit of tolerance in a culturally diverse society is often costly. In assessing the lessons for education in a pluralist society which the Indian experience provides, it is the apparent failures that are often more instructive than the ideals themselves.

NOTES AND REFERENCES

1. Gandhi Indira 1980 In the Preface to *Eternal India*, George Allen & Unwin, p 7
2. Sri Ramakrishna, from *The Sayings of Sri Ramakrishna*, compiled by Swami Abhedananda, The Vedanta Society, New York, 1903, quoted by Robert O. Ballou (ed.) in *The Bible of the World*, Kegan Paul, Trench Trubner & Co., 1946, pp 165 and 172
3. Knott K 1981 'Statistical analysis of South Asians in the UK by religion and ethnicity', *Community Religions Project*, Paper no. 8, University of Leeds
4. See, for example, the work of the *Hindu Nurture Project*, under the aegis of the Department of Arts Education, University of Warwick, Coventry CV4 7AL; see also Richard Burghardt (ed.) 1987 *Hinduism in Britain: the Perpetuation of Religion in an Alien Cultural Milieu*. Tavistock
5. Sen K M 1965 *Hinduism: the World's Oldest Faith*. Penguin Books, p 7
6. See Khan Mohammad Ayub 1967 *Friends Not Masters: a political autobiography*. Oxford University Press:

We crossed a river of blood to achieve independence. People were uprooted and driven like millions of dry leaves by a turbulent gust of fanaticism and blind passion. They were trampled and crushed under the feet of communal fury. Hundreds of thousands of men, women, and children were butchered and the sub-continent was engulfed in a bloody civil war. (p 48)

7. The phrase is used by Mahadevan T M P 1956 in *Outlines of Hinduism*. Chetana Ltd, Bombay, p 302:

Hindus can point to no single founder of their beliefs or way of life. The authority of Hinduism is derived from the testimony of countless ancient sages whose religious experience helped to formulate the tradition. Much of this experience is embodied in the four collections of *Vedas*. The word *Veda* means 'knowledge', specifically, knowledge of the Truth

8. Bhagavadgītā, xvii, 20–21, pp 113–14, in the translation by Juan Mascaro, Penguin Classics 1962. The *Gītā* takes the form of a dialogue between the warrior Arjuna and Krishna (an incarnation of deity) on the eve of a great battle. In the course of the discussion much is said by Krishna about the selfless performance of duty. This famous Sanskrit devotional text may date from the 6th century but is generally considered to have been written down between 400 and 200. It forms part of the great epic, the *Mahābhārata*. In its 90,000 couplets the *Mahābhārata* tells the story of a conflict between two branches of the same family. Relatives, as the epic points out, frequently understand each other least

9. *Chāndogya Upaniṣad*, VI 1–14, given in Embree Ainslie T 1972 *The Hindu Tradition: Readings in Oriental Thought*. Vintage Books, Random House, New York, pp 59–61
10. See Chapter 2, pp 38, 50
11. K M Sen *Hinduism: the world's oldest faith*, p 13
12. See Sarvepalli Radhakrishnan 1931 *The Hindu View of Life*. London
13. Wood Heather 1980 *Third-Class Ticket*. Routledge & Kegan Paul, London, pp 61–62
14. Sen *Hinduism: the world's oldest faith*, p 23
15. Sri Ramakrishna Paramahansa lived from 1836 to 1886:

He was born into a poor Bengali family. In 1855 he became a devotee of the Hindu goddess Kali, spending the rest of his life serving the Universal Mother as a priest at the Dakshineswar Temple outside Calcutta. For him the image of Kali was more than a stone statue. It was a living form of the divine principle. For fifteen years he demonstrated his mastery of the various techniques of Hindu Yoga, and claimed to have had mystical experiences through Christian and Islamic worship as well. His conclusion was that all forms of religion can lead to the highest experience of God, and he preached a universalism that was founded upon his own experience.

He became renowned for his saintliness and spiritual wisdom. After his death his widow and disciple, Sri Sarada Devi, began to spread his teachings. His gospel of the universal religion was carried to the West by his disciple, Swami Vivekananda, who founded the Ramakrishna Mission to further the teachings of the master. His followers seek to combine meditation and social action in monastic communities established in various parts of India, Europe, and the United States

16. Quoted in Ballou Robert O, 'The sayings of Sri Ramakrishna', in *The Bible of the World*, p 161
17. Quoted by Mahadevan T M P in *Outlines of Hinduism*, pp 221–22
18. Rabindranath Tagore lived from 1861 to 1941. Born in Calcutta, he came from a wealthy Bengali family. In 1877 he began legal studies in England, but soon returned to India to manage his father's estates. At first he was interested in the cause of Indian nationalism, but subsequently repudiated nationalism and denounced violence. He campaigned against the Indian caste system. In 1901 he founded a school at Bolpur, north-west of Calcutta, which became known as *Shantiniketan* ('dwelling of peace').

During the course of his life he wrote many novels, plays, books of verse, devotional songs (to some of which he added music), essays and philosophical works, which drew on the ancient scriptures and mythology of India. His written works were universally popular in India. He wrote them in Bengali, but translated many of them into English.

In 1913 he was awarded the Nobel Prize for Literature. For all this work he was revered as a teacher and a sage. He lectured in many parts of the world. His attitude to western values was ambivalent. He admired the practical and technological expertise of the West, but deplored the spiritual emptiness and wastefulness he saw there. In 1915 he was knighted. In 1922 the school founded earlier at Bolpur (*Shantiniketan*) became the Visva-Bharati University. Social reform, international cooperation and unity, and rural reconstruction, featured prominently in the new curriculum, attracting students from far beyond the borders of India

19. Tagore Rabindranath, quoted by Indira Gandhi, *Eternal India*, p 250
20. *Swadeshi*, a term used by Gandhi, means adherence to the traditions of one's own land, or loyalty to one's own culture. It draws attention to the responsibility of individuals for preserving the welfare of their own community. Gandhi also emphasizes the importance of *swaraj* (self-control), and *swadharma* (the performance of one's own allotted duty), for similar reasons
21. The ashram was founded at Kochrab, near Ahmedabad, in May 1915. After an outbreak of plague it was transferred to a site near Sabarmati
22. Chatterjee Margaret 1983 *Gandhi's Religious Thought*. Macmillan, p 146
23. Ibid.
24. See Basham A L 1971 *The Wonder that was India*. Fontana Books
25. Mahadevan *Outlines of Hinduism*, p 70; and from one of the hymns of the *Rig Veda* ('To Purusha'):

When they divided Purusha (the first created person) how many portions did they make?
The *Brahman* was his mouth, of both arms was the *Rajanya* made.
His thighs became the *Vaisya*, from his feet the *Sudra* was produced

26. Mahadevan *Outlines of Hinduism*, pp 73–74
27. *Karma*: 'action'; the law of the cause of action, and of the effect of action. Not to be confused with *kāma*, meaning 'desire'
28. Mahadevan *Outlines of Hinduism*, pp 58–60
29. Ibid., p 61
30. Embree *The Hindu Tradition*, p 84
31. Ibid., pp 90–91
32. See note 1 above
33. On 31 Oct. 1984. Three Sikhs were subsequently charged, and convicted on 22 Jan. 1986. One had been a member of Mrs Gandhi's bodyguard
34. He was assassinated on 30 Jan. 1948. For a discussion of the development of his thought, see Gandhi M K 1940 *An Autobiography, or the Story of My Experiments with Truth*, Navajivan Publishing House, Ahmedabad, 2nd edn; also Margaret Chatterjee, *Gandhi's Religious Thought*

CHAPTER 7

Cultural diversity and the education of commitment

The problem of our youth is not youth. The problem is the spirit of our age: denial of transcendence, the vapidity of values, emptiness in the heart, the decreased sensitivity to the imponderable quality of the spirit, the collapse of communication between the realm of tradition and the inner world of the individual. The central problem is that we do not know how to think, how to pray, how to resist the deceptions of too many persuaders. There is no community of those who worry about integrity.

The problem will not be solved by implanting in youth a sense of belonging. Belonging to a society that fails in offering opportunities to satisfy authentic human needs will not soothe the sense of frustration and rebellion. What youth needs is a sense of significant being, a sense of reverence for the society to which we all belong.[1]

People should not be able to say of anyone that he is a mathematician, or a preacher, or an eloquent man, but that he is a man. Only this universal quality pleases me. . . . For this universality is the finest thing. Undoubtedly this universality is also the only key to one culture, because culture is harmony, or the co-ordination of parts in an all-pervading unity.[2]

Over a hundred years ago J. H. Newman commented that 'it is almost thought a disgrace not to have a view at a moment's notice on any question'. The subject which he was discussing was university education. In the middle of the nineteenth century, when Newman was at work, formal education was far less comprehensive – in every sense of the word – than it is today. The provision of universal primary and secondary education and the development of higher education lay some distance ahead. Newman was aware of the neglect of education, even in the universities. Education then was not so controversial, nor so potentially divisive, as it is in a culturally diverse society today. He was aware of certain tensions in education, especially where differences of religious and cultural diversity appeared to make a common approach to education impossible.[3]

Newman set himself the task of examining, among other things, the function of education in helping to develop a common approach to critical inquiry among individuals and groups with very different convictions about how education should be conducted. He maintained that the best kind of education is that which is founded upon, and nourished by, the Christian religion. For him the Christian faith (and, more especially, the Roman Catholic version of it) offered satisfying answers to the most profound human questionings. Needless to say, not everyone agreed with him then. There might be fewer still to agree with him today, even if they took the trouble to follow his argument. Yet none of his critics could fail to note that his position had been carefully and systematically worked out.

The common prejudice to which Newman draws attention in the sentence quoted above presents a problem to any thoughtful teacher. How is education to be seen as a process in which prejudice is identified, and commitment subjected to critical scrutiny, without giving cause for offence? How does the dissemination of information *about* various aspects of cultural diversity begin to stimulate and to sharpen the critical faculty? When religious beliefs are under scrutiny the problem is even more acute. How does the teacher approach *this* task, given the assumption that in liberal education individuals are to be enabled to choose for themselves? What happens when, in the exercise of that right to choose, a member of a minority group begins to voice criticism of that group, and even seeks an opportunity to break away from it? In the religious education competition organized in 1983 by the Birmingham local education authority, and mentioned in Chapter 2, page 29, one of the Muslim entries in the 16–17 age-group was singled out in the published report for the following comments by a Muslim reviewer. The subject of the essay in question was 'Belonging to a faith community in Birmingham today':

One young man is particularly critical of the community, and poses questions which are related to the need on the one hand of having a faith, and on the other, the difficulties in the modern age, of following a formal religious life. He questions the religiosity of many of his co-religionists whom he dubs as hypocrites, who, he alleges, go to the mosques to 'gain respect in the social structure'. 'I suppose', he continues, 'this is true for every religious community, bad and good all together. However, I can say there are people who justly command respect, and so they should – who are honest in their dealings both with God and man. Unfortunately, I have to say for the majority, religion is just a weapon in social fields, to re-inforce futile arguments. . . .

Clearly there is much in the failings and mis-management of the Muslim community affairs in this country which the young people here should be critical of. The Muslims are not a united community. They are divided into sects and allow their sectarian objectives to take precedence over the wider interests of the community, or the truly Islamic ideals. There have been bitter sectarian disputes between rival factions in matters of the control of mosques and even police have been called to ensure law and order.[4]

The great religions of the world continue to make staggering affirmations about the nature of reality, and about the purpose of human existence. Non-theistic attitudes such as are to be found among secular humanists reflect comparable, but contrasting, beliefs. To know nothing about these affirmations and claims and yet to venture an opinion about their worth is to deserve the criticism which Newman, and others, have repeatedly made. The essential function of education for cultural diversity is to remove some of this ignorance, as well as the dogmatism that springs from ignorance. It may be necessary to give a high priority, across the curriculum, to teaching methods which will inculcate a sense of mutual respect for what may be alien at first sight. What has to be resisted at every stage is the urge to deny the insights of others. There is an almost universal human tendency to repudiate what is unfamiliar.

THE EDUCATION OF COMMITMENT IN A CULTURALLY DIVERSE SOCIETY

The cultivation of informed opinions is one of the responsibilities of professional educators. There are two aspects to this. The first concerns the personal development of teachers themselves. It involves the deliberate attempt to bring their own prejudices, beliefs and attitudes to self-conscious awareness. The injunction 'Know thyself' is to be found in many different traditions. From an educational point of view this process of self-inquiry is a vital part of the teacher's preparation for the classroom. In that sense it is exemplary, and an encouragement to those who are less experienced in forming considered opinions. It seems reasonable to expect that teachers should continue to reflect on the ways in which they themselves develop informed opinions. How do *teachers* avoid prejudice and bias? What does it mean for *teachers* to be tolerant of the beliefs of others? What are the limits of tolerance, even in the pursuit of education for cultural diversity?

The second aspect of this responsibility follows on from the first. It concerns the personal development of pupils and students. Students may legitimately expect to find that their teachers are personally involved in the pursuit of the educational goals to which they are professionally committed. If students are required to learn how to formulate opinions and make choices on the basis of the kind of evidence which is provided during the course of supervised studies, then they, in turn, may reasonably expect to find that their supervisors have acquired some skill in formulating their own opinions. It is a teacher's responsibility to share the skill so as to encourage the development of a comparable skill in students. It is not a question of imposing the opinions of teachers on pupils; it is, on the contrary, a matter of exemplifying a method so that all forms of indoctrination, from whatever source, may be resisted.

Society is increasingly complex, and it is not unreasonable to suggest that during the course of their education students should be able to find some guidance and *practice* in coping with the levels of complexity. If the United Kingdom is to be anything more than a loose federation of religio-cultural minorities, or a predominantly secular society in which the majority of the population remains largely indifferent to the cultural eccentricities of isolated groups, it would seem that education as a whole stands in need of a thorough reappraisal. The problems raised in schools by pluralism and cultural diversity cannot be solved by a handful of enlightened teachers who happen to work in religious and moral education. It will be a joint effort on the part of all teachers who recognize a common responsibility which makes the difference.

This reappraisal is likely to require more than calculated indifference, or tolerance, or the agreement to differ. It will require of teachers and students alike the skill (by no means universally inherent, and thus worth cultivating) to acknowledge the extent of cultural diversity in Britain. The divisions in society are fed by passionate affirmations on the one side and by equally passionate denials on the other. This is apparent in many parts of the world today. Beirut is not the beautiful city it was once, and it is unlikely to regain its sophisticated harmony for the foreseeable future. The same is true of other parts of the Near East, of Iran, of Sri Lanka, of the Punjab and other parts of the Indian subcontinent, of areas in Central and South America – in fact, of a distressingly large number of places besides.

A major role for education in this country is to enable students to see that behind the affirmations and denials there may be common interests which only become apparent after careful and patient examination. No educational strategy which limits the pursuit of the common interests which may lie behind cultural diversity to specific areas of the curriculum is likely to succeed. The overall strategy may find special focus in religious and moral education, but what has been called *the education of commitment* on several occasions in this book calls for the support of every part of the curriculum. This is less idealistic than it may sound. It has the virtue of taking seriously the religious and moral bases of community.

Some years ago I received a note from a correspondent which concluded with the following words: 'I think it important even within Christianity but also much more so in cross-religious contexts to stress the proverb, "Never judge a man till you have walked a mile in his moccasins." Imaginative moccasin-walking is the greatest single skill that religious education can produce, I would say.' This is an open-hearted approach, and it is characteristic of the attitude of many teachers today. It is applied here specifically to religious education, but it can be applied equally to other subjects. Indeed, if it is not, there will be such a gap between the ideal and the real in schools that not even the most imaginative teachers of religious education will be able to bridge it.

We do need to approach the traditions and beliefs of others with respect. Without some *initiative*, without some first step, showing a willingness to understand what it feels like to belong to another community, it is doubtful that members of that other community will be disposed to reciprocate, especially if they belong to a minority group. Imaginative moccasin walking can be a rewarding activity. The notion that one cannot really understand another's way of life without sharing it, at least to some extent, helps to contain the spread of prejudice. But the chief difficulty with this inclination to walk in another's footsteps is that it tends to relativize culture. I respect my neighbour's traditions and beliefs because they are *his*, and not because they claim (or can ever claim) *my* allegiance.

All manifestations of cultural diversity are thus accorded a spurious parity of esteem. This is particularly the case with regard to the world religions which make universal claims. Is religion culturally conditioned? Is the exercise of personal choice with regard to religious or non-religious belief a real possibility or a self-deception? Would it not be more appropriate to say that the accidents of history and geography effectively determine the *choice* for us? If the making of a choice for ourselves is illusory, it would be more realistic to remove references to the development of autonomy in the individual student from the language of educational aims and objectives. On the other hand, if there is the chance that personal choice can be made in ways that are not merely arbitrary, or determined by historical and geographical accidents, then the task for teachers in a culturally diverse situation is to help students to evaluate the options which are now open to them.

It is just at this point that pupils and students in schools may be left intellectually defenceless in non-directive education. They are encouraged, either now or at some unspecified time in the future, to make decisions for themselves about a host of complex issues in the modern world. In the attempt to avoid value judgements, teachers are expected to resort to descriptive, rather than evaluative, methods. There is obviously a great deal of interesting material to be described in a culturally diverse society. So vast, in fact, is the amount of material that the task of describing (and of assimilating the descriptive detail) may become an end in itself, a lifelong pursuit. Who would presume to *choose* – that is, to make up his mind, to commit himself – without first considering all the evidence? And who, having studiously postponed a decision lest the choice be premature, is ever in a position to do much more than to follow sympathetically the footsteps of those who *have* committed themselves to a way of life?

EVALUATING PERSONAL COMMITMENT

Personal commitment, religious claims, attitudes and opinions are the raw material of education for cultural diversity. Without critical scrutiny all personal commitments, religious claims, attitudes and opinions, may be accorded an equal value, or dismissed as equally valueless. If this happens it will not be surprising to find that students remain indifferent to the claims of any of these lively options. Their induction into an uncritical kind of agnosticism will have been well started.

The great teachers of religion have always had to get rid of the useless lumber which accumulates in its progress – the rigid dogmatism, the narrow legalism, the mechanical rites, the silly superstitions which may become a substitute for religious life. But in our times there is a special need for intellectual honesty or intellectual scrupulousness. These words have to be used in no crude sense: they must not be taken to suggest that religious men, or religious leaders, are guilty of rank dishonesty or wilful unscrupulousness – that in short they are conscious hypocrites. This would be far from the truth and would be merely insulting.[5]

How is the student to distinguish the enduring truth of a religious claim from the patent falsity? In the wider sphere of opinions and attitudes, how is the student to distinguish between what is true and what is false? To remove what the author of the passage just quoted calls 'the useless lumber', 'the mechanical rites' and 'the silly superstitions' calls for a special kind of skill which remains untutored if teachers are preoccupied with purely descriptive methods. Each of these phrases contains a judgement of value. The philosopher-teacher who used them was prepared to give instances to support his opinions. To reach a point at which opinions can be both formulated and defended requires that description *and* evaluation go hand in hand at every step of education.

It is not enough to describe the various options that are available. Description precedes evaluation in most areas of life so that a better, or a more appropriate, way can be chosen for the completion of a particular task. Does this extend to culture, to religion, in a pluralist society? If so, how are choices made?

These are questions in which teachers may be presumed to have a lively interest. What is to count as evidence? What other approaches to knowledge, and to the acquisition of knowledge, can be considered? How have other societies in different places, and at different times in history, responded to the human condition? How is a personal search for meaning to be initiated, encouraged and sustained? How are students brought to the position where they see for themselves that the effort required to understand what the education of commitment in a culturally diverse society means is no less than the effort required to make progress in any other demanding subject?

These are not easy questions to answer. It is much easier to leave them unasked. Much, in any case, will depend on the quality of the teachers concerned, and on the resources (spiritual as well as material) which they can utilize. But there are some things which can be said. Taken separately, they may not provide the clues for which busy teachers are searching. Taken together, they may suggest some interesting possibilities for teachers with imagination. The first point to note is very practical. In any subject education needs to be systematic and sequential, taking the student into increasingly more complex fields of experience and study.

If this is not so, then students become bored by repetition, and frustrated by the absence of any challenge to their intellectual and imaginative powers. In the case of the education of commitment, it is inappropriate to speak of a single subject area. It has already been pointed out that the responsibility for introducing students to the complexities of cultural diversity under this heading rests, to some extent, on every teacher. Each successive stage in the school career of a student might usefully complement and extend those stages that precede it. More attention can be paid to developmental psychology in the planning of syllabuses in which every part is related to the whole.

The second point is this. It is obvious that as students are encouraged to move from pre-literacy and pre-numeracy to more advanced stages of literacy and numeracy in different subjects, they should see comparable prospects for progress in the education of commitment. This does not necessarily mean that there should be new teaching material at every stage. It means that material which has already been taught can be approached from different points of view, and at deeper levels of understanding than before. This is precisely where the claims of multi-cultural education can be tested, because familiar material can be seen from different perspectives through the lenses of other cultures. There is, of course, a real difficulty for schools in which teachers are more concerned with day-to-day survival than with teaching towards long-term ends. The suggestions which are now being made can only be tested in an environment of comparative stability and cooperation in the classroom.

It is difficult to predict the shape of education in the future. It seems that unless education is geared to cope with the cultural diversity to be found within society in terms of *opportunities* rather than *problems*, it may not be possible in the long term to preserve the equilibrium, stability and cooperation in schools, without which education degenerates into various forms of child-minding. But this means that controversy has to be faced courageously in the class-room. Controversial differences of opinion are the essential ingredients in the education of commitment. Controversial differences are to be welcomed and understood rather than avoided or concealed at all costs. Controversy can be ignored. That is a way of dealing with it which finds some support from those who argue for non-interference. But in a culturally diverse society this contributes to the problem rather than the answer. Something significant will have been lost if the *educational* opportunities for taking the measure of controversy are not seized.

It cannot be denied that the exploration of cultural diversity in the interests of what has been called here 'the education of commitment' requires a considerable degree of teaching skill, experience and imagination. Nor is it being suggested that teachers should go out of their way to provoke controversy. The fact is that it is already there in the classroom, barely concealed in many cases, and waiting for recognition. It is equally undeniable that there are easier ways to spend time teaching than in encouraging students to explore the uncharted seas of controversy. Children, it is often said, are not *ready* for that sort of thing in any case. Some teachers are more entertaining than others, but there is no satisfactory reason for proceeding as if education were another branch of show business, in which the actors are permitted to keep going as long as the audience finds the performance diverting. This analysis is by no means fanciful. Wherever courses and teachers are assessed by students, there is a tendency for education to be treated like other sections of the communications media, and for ratings to dictate both programme content and method. of presentation.

The future of education in schools (and in other educational institutions) is threatened just as much by soured human relationships which have unacknowledged cultural differences as their common cause, as by low salary levels for teachers, by lack of resources of one sort or another, or by technological developments which may make existing arrangements obsolete, and a good number of teachers redundant. There is, of course, just the possibility that by doing little or nothing by way of utilizing the living options which a genuinely pluralist society offers in education, these cultural differences will become so attenuated with the passage of time that they will linger only in folk-memory, to be recalled at moments when a community celebrates a half-remembered past.

Education for cultural diversity amounts to a carefully programmed induction into the complexity of society today, and lays the foundations for learning to cope with the complexities of tomorrow's world. There is an important working principle of effective teaching here. It might be termed *the principle of continuity and development*. It derives from a recognition of the importance of the past for an understanding of the present. It emphasizes the continuing significance of tradition for a sense of cultural identity. At the same time it allows for reflection, for adaptation and for changes to meet present needs. It allows, in other words, for decision-making, and facilitates personal choice. It is directed towards developing the critical and evaluative faculty in students stage by stage, so that the decisions they make and the opinions they come to hold are informed and reasonable.

These considerations suggest a second working principle of effective teaching which is of great practical value. This is *the principle of advocacy*. This is another aspect of the exemplary role of the teacher which was discussed earlier. It illustrates the ways in which every teacher can contribute to the education of commitment, whatever his or her special subject or special responsibility, may be. It is the responsibility of teachers of music, history, art, religious education, science or any other subject for that matter, to present their subjects as powerfully and as imaginatively as possible so that students may be encouraged to see at least two things: first, that with sufficient time and application they may emulate, and even excel, their teachers; second, that failure to reach high academic standards in a given field of studies need rob no subject of its intrinsic value, and no student of self-respect and human dignity.

In the education of commitment teachers can be advocates in several senses of the word. They can show how a subject may be worth studying for its own sake, as well as for the more immediate material benefits it may bring. In a world of frequently bewildering cultural diversity where *one* kind of knowledge seems to be the only kind which is respected for the material advantages it creates, room can be made, and a case argued, for different approaches to knowledge, and to the good life. It is just here that the principle of advocacy is so vital for the health of a *pluralist* society. When all the social pressures are acting to eliminate cultural distinctions in the name of some homogeneous technology, the teacher still has the chance to challenge the prevailing orthodoxy by introducing students to world-views of which they know nothing, or which they are in danger of forgetting. Whether it be ignorance or forgetfulness, students may have to rely on a few teachers (if it should come to that) to be the *only* informed advocates, whom they meet on a regular basis during the course of their school careers, of once major world-views.

Throughout this book, the practical needs of teachers facing the demands of an increasingly complex pluralist society have been kept in mind. Education for cultural diversity, with its emphasis on the education of commitment, does not fit neatly into present curriculum requirements, and provides a criticism rather than a confirmation of the dominant theory of knowledge. In such a case it is neither easy nor profitable to make extensive lists of suggestions which teachers can try out for themselves in the classroom. There are no simple solutions of that type to present problems. There is no substitute for careful reflection in which all the cherished educational aims and objectives are subjected to critical scrutiny. This can be a painful process for many teachers who would prefer to have a library of manuals full of useful tips. There may be a place for such a book, but not yet. Many fundamental issues have first to be thought through. This book has brought some of them into focus.

It has already been made clear that, for several reasons, the phrase 'multi-culture education' is not serving us very well as an umbrella term (see above, Chapter 1, pages 12–18). It might be better if the phrase were dropped, but it has developed a momentum of its own, and it will not be easy to draw attention to the logical difficulties it raises without risking a charge of insensitivity to real social need. The fact remains that those with cultural background in Asia, Africa, the Caribbean and elsewhere who have recently chosen to assume the responsibilities and privileges of British citizenship have different, and often *radically* different, ideas about the purposes of education. Agreement about first principles is, perhaps, impossible for cultural reasons. This is why it was pointed out earlier that the problem of education for cultural diversity is not just one which faces immigrant minorities in Britain. How many generations does it take for citizens to be called British rather than immigrants? It is a problem for longer established minorities, and for the majority too.

From whatever cultural background people have come – Jews, Christians, Muslims, Sikhs, Buddhists, non-believers (the list goes on in a pluralist society) – they show little inclination to delegate to politicians or teachers who proceed from other philosophical assumptions the right to *control* an over-arching educational system. Does this mean that nothing practical and realistic can ever be done because of the divisions and disagreements within various communities? In spite of the difficulties it is hard to be pessimistic. The way forward is by no means clear, but certain things are clearer than they once were. What is needed is an education which provides an initiation into pluralism first and foremost. It will involve every part of the curriculum, though not always explicitly or self-consciously. It will, nevertheless, involve teachers in a personal way by virtue of their exemplary role in formulating and changing attitudes to society as a whole, and to their own opinions and convictions.

Pluralism is not just an up-market word for *difference*. Pluralism has to do with differences which challenge the easy tolerance of *indifference*. There are important choices to be made. Islam (it is not the only example) confronts the individual with a very basic choice. The choice that is made has grave consequences for the individual concerned, and for the community. To ignore the claims of Islam is already to have made a choice. It is to have rejected the claims of the *true religion*, as Muslims repeatedly insist. In a school, the task of exploring the implications of pluralism cannot be delegated to departments of religious and moral education, though they may have an important coordinating role. Teachers have to provide the kind of education which encourages the development of the critical faculty, so that informed personal choices can be made throughout the course of life, and long after formal schooling is over. With new information, new evidence and new experience, choice can be re-affirmed, modified or re-made. And the exercise of the skill of *choosing* is founded upon something more solid than caprice.

It is the individual teacher whose influence and guidance is crucial and exemplary. Students and teachers alike need to be able to distinguish between what is reasonable and what is unreasonable so that they are able to widen their understanding of different kinds of evidence. Teachers and students are engaged in a common quest for knowledge which can never be said to be complete. This gives a spice to the search at each succeeding emotional and intellectual level. The hope that today will bring some new insight is sufficient to re-kindle enthusiasm for the discipline of teaching and learning. This is not faith despite the evidence, but a reasonable expectation for everyone involved in education.

COPING WITH THE DIVERSITY OF COMMITMENT IN THE CLASSROOM

This may be considered in at least two ways. It may refer to the diversity of commitment in the world *outside* school, thus raising the question of how to present this *external* diversity to students in the classroom. Or it may refer to a point of more immediate interest to teachers; namely, the diversity of commitment that is to be found *within* the classroom, raising the question of how those individual commitments are to be brought to self-conscious awareness. The word *commitment* may not feature prominently in the working vocabulary of teachers, but it is likely to be used increasingly wherever education (and not only Religious Education) is seriously discussed in the future.

When the word *commitment* is used in this context it assumes a special significance. To begin with, it is used in an inclusive, not an exclusive, way, which is to say that it refers to no specific kind of belief. The word has a general application: it is used in recognizing the existence of any set of assumptions and beliefs, explicit or implicit, which guides human action and influences attitudes. In any group of human beings there is a diversity of such commitment. This is part of the problem that faces teachers, especially in Religious Education, because the diversity of opinion, prejudice and belief is not limited to pupils and students.

How does a teacher cope with the diversity of commitment which influences actions and responses in a variety of ways within the classroom? There is no need to dwell on the difficulties created for teachers by hostile attitudes to what arc held to be matters of private beliefs, to Religious Education in general, or by dogmatic claims about truth, from whatever source. These different attitudes, so influential inside the classroom, reflect an inner commitment on the part of those who hold them which is rarely subjected to critical scrutiny.

Everyone connected with the work of schools can learn a good deal from the experience gained by teachers of Religious Education during the past two decades or so. During this period the whole approach to the subject has been reassessed, both with regard to syllabus content and to method. A new and different approach has been recommended along descriptive and inclusive lines, one which has generally found favour, and which has produced some interesting innovations and a plethora of new teaching material.[6] It recognizes the diversity of religious beliefs in the world, and encourages students and teachers to see for themselves, to think for themselves, and to make an appropriate choice when it comes to personal commitment.

This new approach is not without its critics who claim that by opening the subject to the beliefs and practices of Jews, Muslims, Hindus, Buddhists, Sikhs, secular humanists and others, the special position of Christianity in the school curriculum has been weakened. Others would argue that an inclusive programme of Religious Education, which does *not* neglect Christianity as a major world religion, ensures that the beliefs and practices of Christians receive a sympathetic hearing which they might not otherwise get. But the real challenge is not about the relative position of this or that religion in one subject in the school curriculum.

The education of commitment is unlikely to be effective if it is delegated (one might almost say 'relegated') to a single subject area. Other teachers will naturally, and mistakenly, think that it is not their business. *Effective* teaching on personal, social, religious and moral questions involves the *whole child*, and hence the whole curriculum. All the parts must contribute to the whole. Questions like *Is that feasible?* or *How is that to be done?* are fair, but the search for answers will inevitably be postponed until sufficient teachers pave the way for solutions by acknowledging a common educational objective, in the attaining of which all teachers have an essential part to play.

One of the most important tasks in education as a whole is to provide students with accurate information. But there is more to education than description, however accurate the detail. The phrase 'education of commitment' suggests an *inclusive* long-term educational strategy which is well suited to the needs of a modern culturally diverse society. It is designed to combine both the descriptive and the evaluative aspects of education in order to develop the critical faculty. This does not mask a confessional (or neo-confessional) intent. On the contrary, it recognizes the implications of all forms of commitment, and provides students with a mechanism for detecting the subtle pressures of a so-called neutral, value-free or objective approach to education.

The aim of such a strategy would be to encourage students to formulate carefully considered and informed judgements, continuously reassessed in the light of fresh information, new knowledge, and recent experience, on issues which are potentially divisive. This may not eliminate the divisions in society, but it may help a significantly greater number of students and their teachers to understand *why* differing beliefs, assumptions, attitudes and prejudices are divisive, with a consequential reduction in the level of misunderstanding and disturbance in society. The professional skills of teachers would be demonstrated in adapting this strategy to the particular needs and attitudes of the students they teach.

The comparatively short period spent in school can be used to lay the foundations for the education of commitment. An awareness of critical issues can be established quite early, so that when the time comes later in life for important personal matters to be decided, the individual can call on some practical experience, gained in school, of evaluating evidence. The education of commitment is a continuing process which is as much concerned with the considered reflection of teachers as with the responses of their pupils. In this sense it is a *joint* educational venture, in which teachers play exemplary roles, not only as teachers but as students. The education of commitment does not end when school days are over; it is lifelong activity.

Choosing is a difficult business. How are choices made? There can be no reasonable choice where there is ignorance of the available options. Accurate description is, therefore, a necessary preliminary. But there can be no sensible choice without the ability to discriminate. It is not for teachers to make invidious comparisons, nor to treat different cultures comparatively. A more fundamental educational point is at stake here. On the basis of what kinds of evidence are personal commitments made? How do those more experienced in these matters (teachers, for instance) come to retain certain beliefs and to abandon others? In a culturally diverse society these questions assume a special significance when they are linked to notions of personal choice. Cultural boundaries are not sacrosanct. If there are ways into a culture, there are also ways out. Freedom to choose means taking either course. In a pluralist society, children from one cultural background cannot be confined indefinitely by the traditions of their parents, even though some approaches to education would have it so, as earlier chapters in this book have attempted to show.

Some cultural boundaries cannot be crossed without preparation and initiation. Judaism is not a proselytizing culture, but the Gentile can become a Jew under certain circumstances. Conversion, a change of life-style, is the key to Christian culture and Islamic culture. Christianity and Islam are both missionary faiths with a world-wide appeal. With a similar objective in mind, but from a very different set of beliefs and attitudes, secular humanists appeal to their contemporaries to change course and accept a new way of life. Birth and re-birth are the gateways to Hinduism. In a culturally diverse society the process of conversion is often less deliberate. It is a gradual disengagement from within a community, an imperceptible drift from one type of commitment to another, a change of which little notice is taken and for which no account is thought necessary. But even this is choice of a kind. The education of commitment would provide some guidance for the reasonable exercise of choice.

Wherever education is perceived to be an enterprise, a process, which enables individuals sooner or later to reach a point at which they are in a position to decide certain matters for themselves, it follows that some guidance in choosing should find a natural place in the curriculum. Teachers know that, in practice, the different forms of commitment that are the most easily identifiable in schools are arbitrary, uninformed by systematic criticism, and apparently inaccessible to sensible discussion. This situation is likely to remain unchanged unless the attempt is made to develop other attitudes that are critically self-aware. Out of this mish-mash of prejudice arise many of the tensions and misunderstandings which bedevil the subject of cultural diversity.

In popular usage the word *commitment* is usually taken to mean a form of *religious* conviction. Few teachers will need to be reminded that there are other kinds of commitment, largely negative and irreligious in character, which children and adults (some of them teaching colleagues) find opportunities to express both inside and outside the classroom. Dogmatic assertions about racial and cultural supremacy or inferiority, or the assertion that this subject or that in the curriculum is 'a waste of time', illustrate, however crudely, a guiding inner commitment that might profit from exposure to a little critical scrutiny.

This scrutiny of unexamined beliefs, assumptions and prejudices can begin modestly enough inside the classroom. In the first place, the teacher's personal example is crucial. This is true in an obvious sense, but there is more to it. It is with regard to method in this context that the teacher's role is *exemplary*. The teacher can guide, suggest new ideas, encourage and inform, without ever wilfully imposing personal views. It is not a matter of peddling dogmatic certainties. But if the teacher gives an impression of indifference, poses behind a spurious neutrality, or is otherwise clearly uninvolved *at a personal level* in the 'long search', it is doubtful that the pupils will be.

Readiness for religion, and for the profound questions about human existence, appears at an earlier age than some are prepared to admit. The truth of this is illustrated by the kind of evidence, easily ignored in schools, which so often astonishes parents of pre-school children. The capacity of an individual to reflect, however simply in the first instance, about the most profound questions of human existence is not determined by chronological age.

I feel (and I daresay that you have the same feeling), how hard or rather impossible is the attainment of any certainty about questions such as these in the present life. And yet I should deem him a coward who did not prove what is said about them to the uttermost, or whose heart failed him before he had examined them on every side. For he should persevere until he has achieved one of two things; either he should discover, or be taught the truth about them; or, if this be impossible, I would have him take the best and most irrefragable of human theories, and let this be the raft upon which he sails through life – not without risk, as I admit, if he cannot find some word of God which will more surely and safely carry him.[7]

Note that the education of commitment in a culturally diverse society begins *inside* the classroom, with beliefs, prejudices and attitudes to life which are already to hand. It may be unwise to attempt to explore the wider world with its complex cultural differences and competing systems of belief before undertaking the immediate and local task of exploring the range of commitments to be found among the members of *this* particular class. It is tempting to divert attention from the existing tensions within a group, however small, by choosing teaching material which is distant from the student's own experience. The wider world may be dealt with later, but the point at issue here is one that is often raised by young teachers.

How does a teacher penetrate the cloud of apathy that all too frequently fogs the classroom, and get pupils interested in finding out more about what they think they know already? One way, and it is not suggested that it is the only one, is to start with the very indifference and apathy of a group, and to make of that unpromising situation a point of departure for an exploration of attitudes and prejudices. Other openings will follow. It is hardly necessary to add that when the right moment comes there is an undeniable place for a consideration of ideas that may be very strange and remote at first sight. The inclusion of teaching material from world religions (Christianity among them) as the foundations of different cultures, is appropriate here, and not only in Religious Education.

Tackling the education of commitment takes teachers to the stage of long-term preparation. Whatever else is attempted, it must be a long-term objective to enable *these students, this group*, to become more self-consciously aware of the beliefs which unite them and the differences which threaten good relationships between them. This may always have been the case in schools, but it is never more important than today, when the existence of cultural diversity among the members of a school community may be far greater than ever before. This may be a ground-clearing exercise that teachers are obliged to repeat, but it is essential. In the light of new information and knowledge, existing commitments may need to be modified, or even abandoned. There is nothing final in this process. It may just as well begin in school, where youthful enthusiasm and immaturity can, to some extent, be guided and informed, provided there are sufficient teachers with the sensitivity and the will.

NOTES AND REFERENCES

1. Heschel A J 1966 *The Insecurity of Freedom*. Farrar, Straus & Giroux, New York, p 39
2. Jaki S L 1966 *The Relevance of Physics*. University of Chicago Press, p 533, quoting Pascal, in the translation of J M Cohen, Penguin Books, 1961, pp 39–40
3. See Newman J H 1852 *The Idea of a University. Defined and illustrated in nine discourses and occasional lectures and essays*, re-

published with an introduction and notes by I T Ker, Clarendon Press, Oxford, 1976, p 13
4. Saqeb Ghulam Nabi 1983 in *Muslim Children present their Faith*, Jørgen Nielsen (ed.), Research Papers, *Muslims in Europe*, Centre for the Study of Islam and Christian–Muslim Relations, Selly Oak Colleges, Birmingham, no. 19, Sept. pp 33–34
5. Paton H J 1955 *The Modern Predicament*. Allen & Unwin, p 385
6. See, for example, Hull J M (ed.) 1982 *New Directions in Religious Education*, Lewes, Falmer Press
7. Simmias speaking to Socrates shortly before the latter's death, in *Phaedo*, translated by Benjamin Jowett, *The Dialogues of Plato*, 3rd edn, Random House, New York, vol 1, p 470

SOURCES OF ADDITIONAL INFORMATION

Africa Centre
38 King Street, London WC2 E8JT (tel.: 01-836 1973)

Alister Hardy Research Centre
Manchester College, Oxford OX1 3TD; office: 29/31 George Street, Oxford (tel.: 0865-243006)

American branch: The Alister Hardy Research Centre (USA) Inc., The Gallup Building, 53 Bank Street, Princeton, N.J. 08542, USA (tel.: 010-1-609 924 9600)

Founded in 1985, shortly before the death of Sir Alister Hardy, a pioneer in the scientific investigation of religious experience, the Centre includes in its various programmes a new project designed to gather accounts of religious experience from the adherents of all the major religious traditions, as well as from members of 'primal cultures', and from those with no formal religious affiliation. This will be 'a first step to exploring the possibility that religious awareness has a common biological or structural basis in all human beings'. The project is an interesting innovation, and may also attract the attention of many whose interest in the issues discussed in this book stops short of any formal religious commitment.

Bible Society
Stonehill Green, Westlea, Swindon SN5 7DG (tel.: 0793-617 381)

Board of Deputies of British Jews (Central Jewish Lecture and Information Committee),
Woburn House, 4th Floor, Upper Woburn Place, London WC1H 0EP (tel.: 01-387 3952)

Publishes *Finding out about Judaism*, and many other useful items of material about Jewish life and culture.

Board of Education (Church of England)
Church House, Dean's Yard, Westminster, London SW1P 3NZ (tel.: 01-222 9011)

British Buddhist Association
57 Farringdon Road, Hatton Garden, London EC1M 3JB (tel.: 01-286 5575)

British Council of Churches (Committee for Relations with People of Other Faiths)
1 Eaton Gate, London SW1 9BT (tel.: 01-730 9611)

Among its wide-ranging activities, BCC produces reports which deal with contemporary issues in education.

British Friends of Neve Shalom
24 Culverlands Close, Green Lane, Stanmore, Middlesex HA7 3AG
(tel.: 01-954 4487)
    This organization promotes friendship and cooperation in Israel
between Jews, Christians and Muslims.

British Humanist Association
13 Prince of Wales Terrace, London W8 (tel.: 01-937 2341)

Buddhist Society
58 Eccleston Square, London SW1V 1PH (tel.: 01-834 5859)

Catholic Education Council
41 Cromwell Road, London SW7 2DJ (tel.: 01-584 7491)

Catholic Truth Society
38–40 Eccleston Square, London SW1V 1PD (tel.: 01-834 4392)

Centre for Black and White Christian Partnership
Selly Oak Colleges, Birmingham B29 6LQ (tel.: 021-472 7952)

Centre for the Study of Islam and Christian–Muslim Relations
Selly Oak Colleges, Bristol Road, Birmingham B29 6LE (tel.: 021-472 4231)
    The Centre has an international reputation for its pioneer work in
this field. It has excellent library and study facilities.

Centre for the Study of Judaism and Jewish/Christian Relations
Central House, Selly Oak Colleges, Bristol Road, Birmingham B29
6LQ (tel.: 021-472 4231)
    The Centre aims, *inter alia*, 'to foster the appreciation of Judaism
as a living religion; to offer an experience of personal encounter
between Jews and Christians'.

Christian Education Movement
West London Institute of Higher Education, Lancaster House,
Borough Road, Isleworth, Mddx TW7 5DU (tel.: 01-847 0951)

Commission for Racial Equality
10–12 Allington Street, London SW1E 5EH (tel.: 01-828 7022)

Commonwealth Institute
Kensington High Street, London W8 6NQ (tel.: 01-603 4535)
    The Institute arranges exhibitions, lectures and seminars on the
cultural life of different parts of the Commonwealth. For permission
to borrow books and audio-visual material, apply to the librarian.

Culham College Institute
The Malthouse, 60 East Saint Helen Street, Abingdon, Oxon. OX14
5EB (tel.: 0235-20458)
    The Institute is concerned with church-related education.

Farmington Institute for Christian Studies
4 Park Town, Oxford OX4 6SH (tel.: 0865-57456)
    The Institute, founded in Oxford in 1974, has a special interest in
educational projects designed to promote a deeper understanding of

the nature of Christian education in a pluralist world. Information about its publications, courses for teachers and other activities is available from the Director.

Hindu Nurture in Coventry Project
Department of Arts Education, Westward Site, University of Warwick, Warwick CV4 7AL (tel.: 0203-523523)

India House
Aldwych, London WC12 (tel.: 01-852 1401)

Indian Buddhist Society of the United Kingdom
Nanda House, 9 Carlisle Road, Edgbaston, Birmingham B16 9BH (tel.: 021-455 7285)

Indian Government Tourist Office
21 New Bond Street, London W1 0DY (tel.: 01-437 3677)

Institute of Race Relations
247 Pentonville Road, London N1 9NG (tel.: 01-837 0041)

The Institute has a large library, with a useful children's section. Requests for information about the Institute's services and book-lists should include a stamped addressed envelope.

Islamic Cultural Centre, and London Central Mosque
146 Park Road, Regent's Park, London NW8 (tel.: 01-724 3363)

This is one of the most important centres of Islamic worship and study in Britain. It has a tradition of providing information about the Islamic way of life to serious inquirers.

Islamic Information Service Ltd
Trafalgar House, Waterloo Place, London SW1 (tel.: 01-930 8081)

Israel Government Tourist Office
18 Great Marlborough Street, London W1V 1AF (tel.: 01-434 3651)

Jewish Education Bureau, Leeds
8 Westcombe Avenue, Leeds LS8 2BS (tel.: 0532-663613)

Jewish National Fund (Youth and Education Department)
Harold Poster House, Kingsbury Circle, London NW9 9SP (tel.: 01-204 9911)

Provides Jewish speakers for schools and other groups, and an advisory service about Jewish life and culture.

Minaret House
A range of booklets and audio-visual material about Islam. Send a stamped addressed envelope for lists to 9 Leslie Park Road, Croydon, Surrey CR0 6TN (tel.: 01-654 8801)

Multi-Faith Centre and Resource Unit, Birmingham
1 College Walk, Selly Oak, Birmingham B29 6LE (tel.: 021-472 0139)

The Centre, which began its work in 1982, is described as 'an international foundation for education and citizenship'. Details of its activities are available from the Director.

Muslim Educational Trust
130 Stroud Green Road, London N4 3RZ (tel.: 01-272 8502)

National Christian Education Council
Robert Denholme House, Nutfield, Redhill, Surrey RH1 4HW (tel.: 0737-822411)

National Geographic Society
4 Curzon Place, Mayfair, London W1Y 8EN; (in the USA) P.O. Box 2895, Washington, DC 20013-9990

National Society Religious Education Centre (Church of England)
23 Kensington Square, London W8 5HN (tel.: 01-937 4241)

North of England Institute of Christian Education (NIECE)
Information about the work of the Institute can be obtained from its Director, School of Education, Carter House, University of Durham, Durham (tel.: 091-374 2000)

Open University Educational Enterprises Ltd
12 Cofferidge Close, Stony Stratford, Milton Keynes MK11 1BY (tel.: 0908-74066)

Ramakrishna Vedanta Centre
Blind Lane, Bourne End, Bucks SL8 5LG (tel.: 06285-26464)

Rastafarian Advisory Service
17a Netherwood Road, Hammersmith, London W14 0BL (tel.: 01-602 3767)

Religious Education Centre
Avery Hill College, Bexley Road, Eltham, London SE9 2PQ (tel.: 01-850 1199)

Royal Asiatic Society
56 Queen Anne Street, London W1 (tel.: 01-935 8944)

Members and library associates have access to material on the religions and cultures of the East.

School of Oriental and African Studies (University of London)
The Extra-Mural Department, Malet Street, London WC1E 3HP (tel.: 01-636 8000)

The Department arranges in-service courses for teachers on various topics related to the theme of this book.

Shap Working Party on World Religions in Education
Founded after a successful conference held at the Shap Wells Hotel in the Lake District in 1969, Shap continues to provide teachers with a wide-ranging service in the study of world religions. Conferences are devoted to aspects of religious belief and practice in different traditions. Among its most useful publications are: *World Religions: a handbook for teachers*, new edn, 1987; and the annual *Shap Mailing*. Both these publications contain a wealth of information for teachers. Further information is available from the Secretary of the Shap Working Party, Bishop Otter College, College Lane, Chichester, West Sussex (tel.: 0243-787911)

Sikh Missionary Society (United Kingdom)
Information about the Sikh religion and way of life is available from
10 Featherstone Road, Southall, Mddx UB2 5AA (tel.: 01-574 1902)

Society of Friends (Community Relations Committee, SRC)
Friends House, Euston Road, London NW1 2BJ (tel.: 01-387 3601)

The Society organizes conferences on education and community and
race relations, providing speakers from different religious traditions.
The Society has a long history of opposition to war and of support for
the cause of peace throughout the world.

Spalding Trust
The Trust was founded some 50 years ago by the late H. N. Spalding,
to promote in the western world a study of the great religions of the
East. Since then its work has grown to include all the religions of the
world. From the beginning the Trustees have taken an interest in
education, and have given financial support to a number of
educational projects. It also supports scholarly research in the field of
Religious Studies. The Trust is based in Oxford.

Further information is available from the Secretary to the Trustees,
Mrs. C. O. Kornicki, 56 Carlyle Road, Cambridge CB4 3DH (tel.:
0223-322054)

Standing Conference on Inter-Faith Dialogue in Education
c/o 33 Seymour Place, London W1 6AI (tel.: 01-723 4404)

Study Centre for New Religious Movements
Central House, Selly Oak Colleges, Bristol Road, Birmingham B29
6LQ (tel.: 021-472 4231)

The Centre has an unique collection of information and material
about new religious movements and cultural traditions in different
parts of the world, including the Pacific islands, many parts of Africa,
North, Central, and South America.

Union of Muslim Organizations of United Kingdom and Eire
This organization provides information about a wide range of Islamic
activity. Details can be obtained from the General Secretary, 109
Campden Hill Road, London W8 7TL (tel.: 01-229 0538)

Welsh National Centre for Religious Education
Details of available resources can be obtained from the School of
Education, University College of North Wales, St Mary's, Bangor
LL57 1DZ (tel.: 0248-351151 (2956))

West London Synagogue
33 Seymour Place, London W1 (tel.: 01-723 4404)

World Congress of Faiths
28 Powis Gardens, London W11 1JG (tel.: 01-727 2607)

The Education Committee of the World Congress of Faiths advises
teachers on material suitable for use in multi-faith education. WCF
publishes *World Faiths Insight* three times a year. Their *Interfaith
News* is also available on request. It contains details of local meetings
in different parts of the country.

York Religious Education Centre
The College, Lord Mayor's Walk, York YO3 7EX (tel.: 0904-656771
(209))

RECOMMENDED READING

(All places of publication are London unless otherwise stated)

Achebe Chinua 1962 *Things fall Apart*. Heinemann African Writers Series
Achebe Chinua 1978 *Arrow of God*. Heinemann African Writers Series, revised edn
Ahmad Khurshid 1968 *Principles of Islamic Education*. Lahore (and Ansari, Z I), *Islamic Perspectives*. Leicester, 1979
Ajayi J F A 1965 *Christian Missions in Nigeria 1841–1891: the making of a modern elite*
Alexander Philip S (ed. and translated) 1984 *Textual Sources for the Study of Judaism*. Manchester University Press
ᶜAli Abdullah Yusuf see under Qurʾān, al-
Arberry Arthur J (ed.) 1969 *Religion in the Middle East*. Cambridge University Press, 2 vols. see also under Qurʾān al-
Arnold Thomas and Guillaume Alfred (eds.) 1931 *The Legacy of Islam*. Oxford University Press, new edn., *see under* Bosworth C E
Asad Muhammad 1969 *Islam at the Crossroads*. Arafat Publications, Lahore
Asad Muhammad 1974 *The Road to Mecca*. Dar al-Andalus, Tangier
Askari Hasan and Hick John (eds) 1985 *The Experience of Religious Diversity*. Gower Publishing Company Ltd., Aldershot
Awolalu J Omosade 1979 *Yoruba Beliefs and Sacrificial Rites*. Longman
Ayandele E A 1966 *The Missionary Impact on Modern Nigeria 1842–1914: a political and social analysis*. Longman
Ballou Robert O (ed.) 1946 *The Bible of the World*. Kegan Paul, Trench Trubner & Co., Ltd
Barish Louis and Rebecca 1979 *Varieties of Jewish Belief: Questions and Answers about Basic Concepts of Judaism*. Jonathan David, New York
Barrett Leonard E 1976 *The Sun and the Drum: African roots in Jamaican folk tradition*. Kingston
Basham A L 1967 *The Wonder that was India*. Sidgwick and Jackson, 3rd rev. edn, 1971, Fontana Books
Bastide R 1971 *African Civilizations in the New World*. C Hurst
Beauchamp H K see under Dubois Abbé J A
Benvenisti Meron 1986 *Conflicts and Contradictions*. Villard Books, New York
Bible, The Revised Standard Version 1977 in *The New Oxford Annotated Bible with the Apocrypha*. edited by Herbert G May and Bruce M Metzger, Oxford University Press
Blackham H J 1968 *Humanism*. Penguin Books

Blyden E W 1967 *Christianity, Islam and the Negro Race.* Re-published by Edinburgh University Press, (first published in London, 1887)

Borowitz Eugene B 1969 *How Can a Jew Speak of Faith Today?* The Westminster Press, Philadelphia

Bosworth C E (ed.) 1970 *The Legacy of Islam.* New edition, Oxford University Press. See also under Arnold T

Bowen D G (ed.) 1986 *Hinduism in England.* Faculty of Contemporary Studies, Bradford College

Bowker John 1987 *Licensed Insanities: religions and belief in God in the contemporary world.* Darton, Longman and Todd

British Humanist Association 1975 *Objective Fair and Balanced: a new law for religion in education.* London

Brown Alan (ed.) 1986 *Festivals in World Religions.* Shap Working Party on World Religions in Education, Longman

Buber Martin 1961 'Education' and 'The Education of Character' in *Between Man and Man.* Translated by R Gregor Smith, Fontana pp 109–147

Burghardt Richard (ed.) 1987 *Hinduism in Britain: the perpetuation of religion in an alien culture.* Tavistock

Campbell Colin 1971 *Toward a Sociology of Irreligion.* Macmillan

Caporale and Grumelli (eds) 1971 *The Culture of Unbelief.* University of California Press

Cashmore Ernest 1979 *Rastaman: the Rastafarian movement in England.* Allen & Unwin

Cashmore Ernest 1984 *Dictionary of Race and Ethnic Relations.* Routledge & Kegan Paul

Casse Pierre 1981 *Training for the Cross-cultural Mind: a handbook for cross-cultural trainers and consultants.* 2nd edn, SETER (Society for Inter-cultural Education, Training and Research) Washington, D C

Chaikin Miriam 1981 *Light another Candle: the story and meaning of Hanukkah.* Clarion Books, Ticknor & Fields, New York

Chaikin Miriam 1983 *Make Noise, Make Merry: the story and meaning of Purim.* Clarion Books, Ticknor & Fields, New York

Chaikin Miriam 1985 *Ask Another Question: the story and meaning of Passover.* Clarion Books, Ticknor & Fields, New York

Chatterjee Margaret 1983 *Gandhi's Religious Thought.* Macmillan, Library of Philosophy and Religion

Chauduri Nirad C 1979 *Hinduism: a religion to live By.* Chatto & Windus

Chinweizu 1975 *The West and the Rest of Us: white predators, black slavers, and the African elite.* Vintage Books, Random House, New York

City of Birmingham Education Committee 1975 *Living Together: a teachers' handbook of suggestions for Religious Education*

Cohen A 1975 *Everyman's Talmud.* Schocken Books, New York

Cole W Owen and Sambhi Piara Singh 1978 *The Sikhs: their religious beliefs and practices.* Routledge & Kegan Paul

Cole W Owen 1978 (ed.) *World Faiths in Education.* Allen & Unwin

Community Relations Commission 1974 *Teacher Education for a Multi-cultural Society.* (with the Association of Teachers in Colleges and Departments of Education)

Community Relations Commission 1976 *World Religions: A handbook for teachers.* (2nd edn, W. Owen Cole ed.)

Coward Harold 1985 *Pluralism: Challenge to World Religions.* Orbis Books, Maryknoll

Cragg Kenneth 1958 *Sandals at the Mosque.*

Cragg Kenneth 1964 *The Dome and the Rock.*

Cragg Kenneth 1977 *The Christian and Other Religion*

Cragg Kenneth 1984 *Muhammad and the Christian.* Darton, Longman and Todd

Cragg Kenneth 1986 *The Call of the Minaret.* 2nd edn revised and enlarged, Collins

Cragg Kenneth 1986 *The Christ and the Faiths: Theology in Cross-reference.* SPCK see also under Husain Muhammad K

Davidman Joy 1965 *Smoke on the Mountain.* Hodder & Stoughton

Davis Enid 1981 *A Comprehensive Guide to Children's Literature with a Jewish Theme.* Schocken Books, New York

Dawidowicz Lucie S 1975 *The War Against the Jews 1933–1945.* Holt, Rinehart & Winston

Dawson Christopher 1937 *Enquiries into Religion and Culture.* Sheed & Ward, New York

Dawson Christopher 1948 *Religion and Culture.* Sheed & Ward

de Lange Nicholas 1987 *Judaism.* Oxford University Press

Derrick Christopher 1977 *Escape from Scepticism: liberal education as if truth mattered.* Sherwood Sugden & Co., Illinois

Droubie Riyadh el- and Hulmes Edward 1987 *The Religious Dimension: Islam.* 2nd revised edn. Longman

Drucker Malka 1981 *Rosh Hashanah and Yom Kippur: Sweet Beginnings*, Holiday House, New York

Drucker Malka 1982 *Sukkoth: A time to rejoice.* Holiday House, New York

Dubois Abbe J A and Beauchamp H K 1924 *Hindu Manners, Customs and Ceremonies.* 3rd edn, Clarendon, Oxford

Eban Abba 1978 *An Autobiography.* Weidenfeld and Nicolson

Eban Abba 1984 *Heritage: Civilization and the Jews.* Summit Books, New York

Eckstein Yechiel 1984 *What Christians should know about Jews and Judaism.* Word (Incorporated) Books, Texas

Eliot T S 1949 *Christianity and Culture. The Idea of a Christian Society*, and *Notes Towards the Definition of Culture.* Harcourt Brace and Co., New York

Embree Ainslie T (ed.) 1972 *The Hindu Tradition: readings in oriental thought.* Vintage Books, Random House, New York

Encyclopaedia Judaica 1972 Macmillan, Jerusalem (*Junior Judaica: Encyclopaedia Judaica for Youth*, editor-in-chief, Rabbi Dr. Raphael Posner, Keter Publishing House, Jerusalem 1982)

Encyclopaedia of Islam 1913–34 1st edn, E J Brill, Leiden, 4 vols

Encyclopaedia of Islam 1960–1987 2nd edn, E J Brill, Leiden, 5 completed volumes to date

Epstein Morris 1970 *All About Jewish Holidays and Customs.* revised edn, KTAV Publishing House

Esposito John L (ed.) 1983 *Voices of Resurgent Islam.* Oxford University Press

Flannery Austin see under Vatican Council II

Fleischner Eva (ed.) 1977 *Auschwitz: beginning of a new era.* KTAV
Publishing House
Gandhi Indira 1980 *Eternal India.* George Allen & Unwin
Gandhi M K 1949 *Hindu Dharma.* Navajivan Publishing House, Ahme-
dabad, 2nd edn
Gandhi M K 1962 *An Autobiography, or The Story of My Experiments
with Truth,* translated by M. Desai, Navajivan Publishing House,
Ahmedabad, second edition
Geertz Clifford 1973 *Islam Observed: religious development in Morocco
and Indonesia.* University of Chicago Press
Goldin Hyman E 1952 *A Treasury of Jewish Holidays.* Twayne
Publishers, New York
Goldin Judah 1957 *Mishna, Pirke Aboth, The Living Talmud: the
Wisdom of the Fathers, and its Classical Commentaries.* Selected and
translated, with an essay, University of Chicago
Goodhill Ruth M (selected and ed.) 1975 *The Wisdom of Heschel.*
Farrar, Straus & Giroux, New York
Goodman Saul L (ed. with an introduction) 1976 *The Faith of Secular
Jews.* New York
Grishaver Joel Lurie and Huppin Beth 1983 *Tzedakah, Gemilut, Chas-
adim and Ahavah: a manual for world repair.* Alternatives in
Religious Education Inc., 3945 South Oneida Street, Denver, Colo-
rado 80237, USA
Guillaume Alfred 1924 *The Traditions of Islam: an Introduction to the
Study of the Hadith Literature.* Oxford, Clarendon
Guillaume Alfred 1954 *Islam.* Penguin Books
Guillaume Alfred 1955 *The Life of Muhammad: a Translation of Ishaq's
Sirat Rasul Allah* (with Introduction and Notes). Oxford University
Press
Haddad Yvonne Y 1982 *Contemporary Islam and the Challenge of
History.* State University of New York Press
Hardy Alister C 1966 *The Divine Flame.* Collins
Hardy Alister C 1975 *The Biology of God. A Scientists Study of Man,
the Religious Animal.* Jonathan Cape
Hay David 1982 *Exploring Inner Space: scientists and religious experi-
ence.* Penguin Books
Heschel Abraham J 1966 *The Insecurity of Freedom: essays on human
existence.* Farrar, Straus & Giroux, New York
Hick John see under Askari Hasan
Hinnells John R (ed. with Sharpe Eric) 1972 *Hinduism.* Oriel Press
Hinnells John R (ed.) 1984 *The Penguin Dictionary of Religions.* Penguin
Books
Hinnells John R (ed.) 1985 *A Handbook of Living Religions.* Penguin
Books
Hiskett Mervyn 1973 *The Sword of Truth: the life and times of Shehu
Usuman dan Fodio.* Oxford University Press, New York
Hitti Philip K 1973 *History of the Arabs.* Macmillan (10th edn)
Hooker Roger 1973 *Uncharted Journey.* CMS
Hooker Roger 1979 *Voices of Varanasi.* CMS
Hooker Roger 1981 *A Christian Experience of Hinduism.* (Edward
Hulmes ed.) Farmington Occasional Papers, Oxford

Horder Donald and Smart Ninian (eds) 1975 *New Movements in Religious Education*. Temple Smith
Hourani Albert H 1962 *Arabic Thought in the Liberal Age 1798–1939*. Royal Institute of International Affairs, Oxford University Press
Hourani Albert H 1974 *Western Attitudes to Islam*. 10th Montefiore Memorial Lecture, University of Southampton
Howard Vanessa 1987 'A Report on Afro-Caribbean Christianity in Britain', *Community Relations Project Research Paper (NS) 4*. Department of Theology and Religious Studies, University of Leeds
Hull J M (ed.) 1982 *New Directions in Religious Education*. Falmer Press
Hulmes Edward 'Contemporary Muslim attitudes to the relationship between religious faith and education' in *Spectrum* vol. 10, no. 2, Jan. 1978, pp 29–30
Hulmes Edward 1978 'The problem of commitment' in *World Faiths in Education* W. Owen Cole (ed.) Allen & Unwin pp 26–37
Hulmes Edward 1979 *Commitment and Neutrality in Religious Education*. Cassell (Geoffrey Chapman)
Hulmes Edward 1985 'The irritant of agnosticism', in *The Princeton Bulletin*. New Series. vol. 6, no. 1 pp 14–24
Hulmes Edward 1986 with Brenda Watson *Openness and Commitment*. Farmington Occasional Papers, Oxford
Hulmes Edward 1987 (with Riyadh el-Droubie), *The Religious Dimension: Islam*. 2nd, revised edn Longman
Hulmes Edward 1988 'Developing a Critical Faculty in Religious Education', Farmington Occasional Papers, (Brenda Watson ed.), Oxford
Hulmes Edward 1988 'Christian Education in a Multi-culture Society', in book with the same title, edited by V. A. McLelland, Routledge
Hume Cardinal Basil G 1977 *Searching for God*. Hodder & Stoughton
Huppin Beth see Grishaver J L
Husain Muhammad K 1959 *City of Wrong: a Friday in Jerusalem*. Translated by Kenneth Cragg, Amsterdam
Husayn Taha 1932 *An Egyptian Childhood*. Translated by E H Paxton
Huxley Aldous 1958 *The Perennial Philosophy*. Fontana
Idowu E Bolaji 1966 *Olodumare: God in Yoruba Belief*. Longman
Idowu E Bolaji 1973 *African Traditional Religion: a definition*. SCM Press
Imasogie O 1986 *African Traditional Religion*. Oxford University Press
Iqbal Muhammad 1978 'First World Conference on Muslim Education, and its Possible Implications for British Muslims', in *Learning for Living*, vol. 17 no. 3 Spring, pp 123–125
Iqbal Muhammad 1980 *Call from the Minaret: a Muslim family in Britain*. Hodder & Stoughton, Union of Muslim Organisations Publications Committee
Iqbal Muhammad 1987 'Islamic Ethos on Education: A Muslim Response to the Swann Report' (paper presented at the Union of Muslim Organisations' National Conference on Islamic Education, June 1987), National Muslim Education Council of UK
Iqbal Muhammad (Sir) 1981 *The Reconstruction of Religious Thought in Islam*. Reprinted by Kitab Bhavan New Delhi
Jackson R M D 1985 'Hinduism in Britain: religious nurture and

religious education', in *British Journal of Religious Education* vol. 7, no. 2, Spring

Jackson R M D 1986 (and Eleanor Nesbitt) 'Sketches of Formal Hindu Nurture', in *World Religions in Education*. Journal of the Shap Working Party pp 25–29

Jaki Stanley L 1966 *The Relevance of Physics*. University of Chicago Press

Jaki Stanley L 1978 *The Road of Science and the Ways to God*. University of Chicago Press

Jakobovits Immanuel 1977 *The Timely and the Timeless: Jews, Judaism and society in a storm-tossed decade*. Vallentine-Mitchell

Jeffreys M V C 1966 *Personal Values in the Modern World*. Penguin Books

Journal of Ecumenical Studies 1984 vol. 23, no. 3, summer, is devoted to the subject of Jews and Judaism in Christian Education

Khan Mohammad Ayub 1967 *Friends not Masters: a political autobiography*. Oxford University Press

Khan Muhammad Zafrulla 1975 *Gardens of the Righteous: Riyad as-Salihin of Imam Nawawi*. Translated from the Arabic, Curzon Press

Khomeini Ayatollah Imam Ruhollah 1981 *Islam and Revolution: writings and declarations*. Translated by Hamid Algar, Berkeley

Khulusi Safa 1987 'Concept of Education in Islam' (paper presented at the Union of Muslim Organisations' National Conference on Islamic Education, June), National Muslim Educational Council of UK

Knitter Paul F 1985 *No Other Name? A Critical Survey of Christian Attitudes Towards the World Religions*. Orbis Books, Maryknoll

Knott K 1981 'Statistical analysis of South Asians in the UK by religion and ethnicity', *Community Relations Research Paper no. 8*. University of Leeds

Kook Abraham Isaac 1978 *The Lights of Penitence, and other Works*. Translated, with an Introduction, by Ben Z. Bokser, The Classics of Western Spirituality, Paulist Press, New York

Koran the, see under Qur°ān, al-

Kraft Charles H 1984 *Christianity in Culture*. Orbis Books, Maryknoll

Kritzeck James 1972 *Anthology of Islamic Literature*. Penguin Books

Law William 1978 *A Serious Call to a Devout and Holy Life* and *The Spirit of Love*. Paul G. Stanwood (ed.) The Classics of Western Spirituality, Paulist Press, New York

Lewis C S 1944 *The Abolition of Man: reflections on education with special reference to the teaching of English in the upper forms of schools*. University of Durham Riddell Memorial Lectures, 15th series, Oxford University Press

Livingstone Richard 1941 *The Future in Education*. Cambridge University Press

Livingstone Richard 1943 *Education for a World Adrift*. Cambridge University Press

Lowenthal D 1972 *West Indian Societies*. Oxford University Press

Lynch James 1986 *Multi-cultural Education: Principles and Practice*. Routledge & Kegan Paul

Mahadevan T M P 1956 *Outlines of Hinduism*. Chetana Limited, Bombay

Maquet Jacques 1981 *Civilizations of Black Africa*. Revised and translated by Joan Rayfield, Oxford University Press, New York

Mascaro Juan 1970 *The Bhagavad Gita*. Translated from the Sanskrit, with an introduction, Penguin Books

Maududi Sayyid Abul Ala 1944 *Towards Understanding Islam* Jamalpur

Maybaum Ignaz 1973 *Trialogue between Jew, Christian and Muslim*. The Littman Library of Jewish Civilization, Routledge & Kegan Paul

Mbiti John S 1969 *African Religions and Philosophy*. Heinemann

Mbiti John S 1970 *Concepts of God in Africa*. Heinemann

Mbiti John S 1975 *Introduction to African Religion*. Heinemann

Mbiti John S 1975 *The Prayers of African Religion*. SPCK (Orbis Books, Maryknoll, New York, 1976)

Mbiti John S 1978 *Prayer and Spirituality in African Religion*. Charles Strong Memorial Trust, Flinders University, South Australia

Mbiti John S 1986 *Bible and Theology in African Christianity*. Oxford University Press, Nairobi

McIntyre John 1978 *Multi-Culture and Multi-Faith Societies: some examinable assumptions*. Farmington Occasional Papers, Edward Hulmes (ed.), no. 3, Oxford

McLeod W H (ed. and translated) 1984 *Textual Sources for the Study of Sikhism* Manchester University Press

Meltzer Milton 1976 *Never to Forget: the Jews of the holocaust*. Harper and Row, New York

Metter Bert 1984 *Bar Mitzvah, Bat Mitzvah: How Jewish Boys and Girls Come of Age*. Clarion Books, Ticknor & Fields, New York

Miers Suzanne 1975 *Britain and the Ending of the Slave Trade* Longman

Millgram Abraham Ezra (ed. with introductory notes) 1985 *Concepts that distinguish Judaism*. B'nai B'rith, Washington, DC

Momen Moojan 1985 *An Introduction to Shiᶜi Islam: the history and doctrines of Twelver Shiᶜism*. Yale University Press

Murdoch G P 1968 'The Common Denominator of Cultures' in *Perspectives of Human Evolution*. S L Washburn and P C Jay (eds) Holt, Rinehart & Winston, New York

Nakamura Hajime 1971 *Ways of Thinking of Eastern Peoples: India, China, Tibet, Japan*. East-West Center Press, Honolulu, Hawai

Nasr Seyyed Hossein 1968 *Science and Civilization in Islam*. Harvard University Press
Islam and the Plight of Modern Man. Longman, 1975 'The western world and its challenges to Islam', in *The Islamic Quarterly* vol. 17, June 1973, pp 3–25

National Muslim Education Council of UK 1986 *Swann Committee's Report: a Muslim response*. Union of Muslim Organisations

Nehru Jawaharlal 1936 *An Autobiography*. John Lane, the Bodley Head

Neill Stephen 1970 *Christian Faith and Other Faiths: the Christian dialogue with other religions*. 2nd edn, Oxford University Press
Crises of Belief: the Christian dialogue with faith and no faith. Hodder & Stoughton, 1984

Nesbitt Eleanor see Jackson R M D

Newman Cardinal J H 1976 *The Idea of a University*. Republished with an introduction and notes by I T Ker, Clarendon Press, Oxford

Niebuhr Richard 1951 *Christ and Culture*. Oxford University Press

Nielsen Jørgen (ed.) 1983 *Muslim Children present their Faith*. Centre for the Study of Islam and Christian-Muslim Relations, Selly Oak Colleges, Birmingham. Research Papers *Muslims in Europe*, no. 19, Sept.

Noveck Simon (ed.) 1985 *Contemporary Jewish Thought*. B'nai B'rith Books, Washington, DC

Owens Joseph 1979 *Dread: the Rastafarians of Jamaica*. Heinemann

Padwick Constance 1969 *Muslim Devotions*. SPCK

Panikkar Raimundo 1978 *The Intra-Religious Dialogue*. Paulist Press, New York

Parrinder E G 1962 *African Traditional Religion*. SPCK

Parrinder E G 1967 *African Mythology*. Hamlyn

Parrinder E G 1987 *Encountering World Religions*. T & T Clark

Perrott Elizabeth 1982 *Effective Teaching: a practical guide to improving your teaching*. Longman

Pickthall M M see under *Qur'an al-*

Pilch Judah (ed.) 1968 *The Jewish Catastrophe in Europe*. The American Association for Jewish Education, New York

Post Laurens van der 1957 *Venture to the Interior*. Penguin Books

Post Laurens van der 1962 *The Lost World of the Kalahari*. Penguin Books

Post Laurens van der 1965 *The Heart of the Hunter*. Penguin Books

Qur'an al- (the Koran)
　The Holy Qur'-an. Text, translation, and Commentary. A Y ᶜAli, Lahore 1976
　　This version was originally published in 1934. Since then it has appeared in several editions, one of which (in 2 volumes) has the title *The Meaning of the Glorious Koran*. Cairo 1984. This is not to be confused with the version by Pickthall which is mentioned below
　The Koran. Translated by N J Dawood, Penguin Books, 1985
　The Meaning of the Glorious Koran. Translated by Marmeduke M Pickthall Mentor Books, New York, 1960
　The Koran. Translated by A J Arberry, Oxford University Press, 1985
　　This version was first published by OUP in 1964, with the title *The Koran Interpreted*

Rabinowicz Rachel Anne (ed.) 1982 *Passover Haggadah: the Feast of Freedom*. The Rabbinical Assembly, USA, 2nd edn

Radhakrishnan Sarvepalli 1953 (tr. with commentary) *The Principal Upanishads*. Allen & Unwin

Radhakrishnan Sarvepalli 1961 *The Hindu View of Life* (12th impression). Allen & Unwin

Rahman Fazlur 1966 *Islam*. Holt, Rinehart & Winston

Ramakrishna Sri 1903 *The Sayings of Sri Ramakrishna*. Compiled by Swami Abhedananda, the Vedanta Society, New York

Rawlinson H G 1965 *India: a short cultural history*. The Cresset Press, paperback edn

Robinson Edward 1977 *The Original Vision*. Religious Experience Research Unit (RERU), Oxford

Rose E J B 1969 *Colour and Citizenship*. Institute of Race Relations, Oxford University Press

Rosenthal Gilbert S 1978 *The Many Faces of Judaism: orthodox, conservative, re-constructionist, and reform*. Behrman House, New York

Rossel Seymour 1975 *When a Jew Seeks Wisdom: the Sayings of the Fathers*. Behrman House, New York

Rothermund Dietmar and Simon John 1986 *Education and the Integration of Ethnic Minorities*. Francis Pinter

Rummery Gerard 1975 *Catechesis and Religious Education in a Pluralist Society*. T Shand

Said Edward 1979 *Orientalism*. New York

Said Edward 1981 *Covering Islam*. New York

Sambhi Piara Singh see under Cole W Owen

Sanneh Lamin 1983 *West African Christianity: the religious impact*. Orbis Books, Maryknoll

Scott Rachel 1971 *A Wedding Man is Nicer than Cats, Miss: a teacher at work with immigrant children*. David and Charles, Newton Abbott

Sen K M 1961 *Hinduism: the World's Oldest Faith*. Penguin Books

Shap Working Party on World Religions in Education 1987 *Handbook for Teachers*

Shariᶜat ᶜAli 1979 *On the Sociology of Islam*. Translated by Hamid Algar, Berkeley

Shariᶜat ᶜAli 1981 *The Visage of Muhammad*. Translated A A Sachedin Teheran

Sharpe Eric J see under Hinnells J R

Shipler David K 1987 *Arab and Jew: Wounded Spirits in a Promised Land*. Bloomsbury

Shorter Aylward 1975 *Prayer in the Religious Traditions of Africa*. Oxford University Press, New York

Siddiqui Zeba (*et al.*) 1972 *The Parents' Manual, A guide for Muslim parents living in North America*. Muslim Students' Association of the United States and Canada, the Crescent Publications, Takoma Park, Maryland

Siegel Richard see under Strassfeld Michael

Sleeman W H 1973 *Rambles and Recollections of an Indian Official*. Republished from the original 1844 version, Oxford University Press, Karachi

Smart Ninian 1966 *A Dialogue of Religions*. Penguin Books

Smart Ninian 1971 *The Religious Experience of Mankind*. Fontana

Smart Ninian (ed. with Donald Horder) 1975 *New Movements in Religious Education*. Temple Smith

Smith Huston 1965 *The Religions of Man*. Harper & Row, New York Perennial Library

Sonyel Salahi Ramadan 1987 'Education of Muslim Children in British Schools' (paper presented at the Union of Muslim Organisations' National Conference on Islamic Education, June), National Muslim Education Council of UK

Soyinka Wole 1978 *Myth, Literature and the African World*. Cambridge University Press

Stone Maureen 1981 *The Education of the Black Child in Britain*. Fontana

Strassfeld Michael 1985 *The Jewish Holidays: a guide and commentary*. Harper Row, New York

Strassfeld Michael 1973 (with Siegel, Richard, and Strassfeld, Sharon), *The First Jewish Catalog*. Jewish Publication Society of America, Philadelphia

Strassfeld Michael 1976 (with Strassfeld, Sharon), *The Second Jewish Catalog*. Jewish Publication Society of America, Philadelphia

Strassfeld Michael (with Strassfeld, Sharon) 1980 *The Third Jewish Catalog*. Jewish Publication Society of America, Philadelphia

Sundkler B G M 1961 *Bantu Prophets of South Africa*. 2nd edn

Sutcliffe John M (ed.) 1984 *A Dictionary of Religious Education*. SCM Press

Swann Report 1985 *'Education for All': a Summary of the Swann Report on the Education of Ethnic Minority Children*. The Runnymede Trust

Tagore Rabindranath 1931 *The Religion of Man*

Taylor John V 1972 *The Go-Between God: The Holy Spirit and the Christian Mission*. SCM

Tibawi A L 1972 *Islamic Education. Its Traditions and Modernization into the Arab National Systems*. Luzac

Tillich Paul 1959 *Theology of Culture*, Robert C. Kimball (ed.) Oxford University Press, New York

Tritton A S 1968 *Islam*. Hutchinson University Library

Turner H W *Bibliography of New Religious Movements in Primal Societies*. G K Hall, Boston, Mass., vol. 1, *Black Africa*. 1977

Turner H W 1980 *Religious Innovation in Africa*. G K Hall, Boston, Mass.

Union of Muslim Organizations of United Kingdom and Eire *Islamic Education and Single Sex Schools*. 1975 *Guidelines and Syllabus on Islamic Education* 1976

Unterman Alan 1981 *Jews: their Religious beliefs and Practices*. Routledge & Kegan Paul

Upanishads, see under Radhakrishnan Sarvepalli and Zaehner R C

Vatican Council II 1975 *The Conciliar and Post Conciliar Documents*. General editor, Austin Flannery, Dominican Publications, Dublin

Verma G K and Bagley C (eds) 1975 *Race and Education across Cultures*. Heinemann

Verma G K and Bagley C (eds) 1975 *Race, Education, and Identity* Macmillan

Vermes Geza 1973 *Jesus the Jew*. Collins

Waddy Charis 1976 *The Muslim Mind*. Longman

Waddy Charis 1980 *Women in Muslim History*. New York

Warren M A C 1976 *I believe in the Great Commission*. Hodder & Stoughton

Washington Joseph R 1964 *Black Religion: the Negro and Christianity in the United States*. Beacon Press, Boston, Mass

Watson Brenda *Openness and Commitment*. Farmington Occasional Papers, Oxford, 1986

Watson Brenda 1987 *Education and Belief*. Basil Blackwell, Oxford

Watt W Montgomery 1953 *The Faith and Practice of al Ghazali*. Allen & Unwin

Watt W Montgomery 1961 *Muhammad, Prophet and Statesman*. Edinburgh University Press

Watt W Montgomery 1963 *Muslim Intellectual: a Study of al-Ghazali*. Edinburgh University Press

Waugh Evelyn 1985 *Remote People: A report from Ethiopia and British*

Africa, 1930–31. Penguin Travel Library

Weil Simone 1965 *Waiting on God*. Translated by Emma Craufurd, Fontana

Whitehead A N 1942 *Adventures of Ideas*. Penguin Books

Wiesel Elie 1971 *One Generation After*. Weidenfeld & Nicolson

Wood Heather 1980 *Third Class Ticket*. Routledge & Kegan Paul

Zaehner R C 1958 *At Sundry Times: an Essay in the Comparison of Religions*. Faber & Faber

Zaehner R C 1962 *Hinduism*. Oxford University Press

Zaehner R C 1966 *Hindu Scriptures*. ed. and translated, Everyman's Library, Dent

Zaehner R C 1980 *The City Within the Heart*. Unwin Paperbacks

INDEX

Abraham, 59, 61, 76 fn14
advocacy, 153
affirmation, 133–5
African educational insights
   see education
African Traditional Religion,
   102–3, 106–14, 118 fn3, 119
   fn10
ahiṁsā, 125, 141
aims and objectives in education
   see under education
alienation, 7, 91
Allāh, 33–4, 39, 42, 43, 44, 48,
   49 fn9
America
   United States of, 9, 25–6 fn5
apartheid
   separate development, 2, 125
Arabic, 37
Arjuna, 142 fn8
ashram, 134
āśrama-dharma, 139
āśramas, 139–41
assessment of students, 6
assimilation of ethnic minorities,
   2, 23, 116
Ātman, 127–8
authority, 51–2 fn29, 55
autonomy, 72–3, 97–100, 124
Azhar al-, 41

Baeck, Leo, 76 fn11
'Beautiful Names of God, the' (in
   Islam), 51 fn24
Bhagavad Gītā, 126, 142 fn8
bhakti, 132
Bible
   Christian, 71–2, 88, 91–4
   Jewish, 56, 60–1, 70–2
Biblicism, 94
black Zionism, 121 fn30

Blyden, Edward Wilmot, 103,
   118–19 fn6, 121 fn30
Brahman, 127–8
Brahman-Ātman, 127–8, 136
Buber, Martin, 101 fn38
Buddha, the (Siddharta
   Gautama), 136
Buddhism, 123

caste system, 135–7
catechesis, 84–5
celebration, 55, 67–70
charismatic movements, 116
Chesterton, G. K., 82
choice of personal beliefs, 55, 98,
   149–50, 158
chosen people, 55
Christ, 86–7, 88, 90
Christian education
   see education
colonialism, 104–5, 116, 123
commandments
   see Decalogue; mitzvoth
commitment
   definition of, 50 fn20, 156, 159
   education of, 147–60
community, 22, 32, 55, 106, 114
confessional education
   see education
contemporaneity, 108
contingency, 81
continuity and development in
   education, 8, 153
continuous assessment, 6
Covenant, 55, 57, 58, 76 fn14
critical faculty
   development of, 60–1, 68, 96,
   98–100, 145, 150, 158
Crowther, Samuel Ajayi, 121
   fn29
crucifixion of Jesus, 87